IMAGES
of America

THE PHILADELPHIA FLOWER SHOW

On the Cover: Three women in flower-festooned hats admire a bed of ranunculus at the 1950 Philadelphia Flower Show held at the Commercial Museum. (Courtesy Pennsylvania Horticultural Society, McLean Library.)

IMAGES
of America

THE PHILADELPHIA FLOWER SHOW

The Pennsylvania Horticultural Society
Edited by Janet Evans
Foreword by Drew Becher
Introduction by Sam Lemheney

ARCADIA
PUBLISHING

ISBN 978-1-4671-2099-9

Published by Arcadia Publishing
Charleston, South Carolina

Printed in the United States of America

Library of Congress Control Number: 2013945268

For all general information, please contact Arcadia Publishing:
Telephone 843-853-2070
Fax 843-853-0044
E-mail sales@arcadiapublishing.com
For customer service and orders:
Toll-Free 1-888-313-2665

Visit us on the Internet at www.arcadiapublishing.com

This book is dedicated to the hundreds of talented exhibitors, thousands of tireless volunteers, and millions of supportive visitors who have made the Philadelphia Flower Show an extraordinary experience that brings us together in appreciation for the natural world.

Contents

Foreword 6

Acknowledgments 7

Introduction 8

1. Early Shows 11
2. Commercial Museum 23
3. Civic Center 63
4. Pennsylvania Convention Center 95
5. Harvest Shows 115
6. The Greening of Philadelphia 121

About the Pennsylvania Horticultural Society 127

Foreword

For gardeners, growth is a sign of life. By that measure, the Pennsylvania Horticultural Society (PHS) Philadelphia Flower Show is very healthy and full of life. It has grown and changed dramatically and continues to grow in new ways. Its success is largely due to its roots in the first exhibition, held in 1829 by the Pennsylvania Horticultural Society, and to the passionate designers, exhibitors, and volunteers who have carefully nurtured the show through three centuries.

I love reading about the earliest exhibitions of PHS and the founders who showed off their beautiful fruits, vegetables, and flowers. Their motivation was more than pride, however. These were dedicated gardeners and botanists sharing knowledge and newly discovered plants with the American public.

In many ways, the mission of the Philadelphia Flower Show remains the same today. The 19th-century exhibition of a line of tables with homegrown plants and saplings has evolved into the $1 million structure called the PHS Hamilton Horticourt, which accommodates thousands of entries. This display, where novices can compete with leading horticulturists, is still the heart of the show.

The show has evolved in other ways, too. Exhibitors and judges come from around the world, and more than 4,000 volunteers participate in the event. The floral and landscape displays have grown more ambitious, with elaborate sets incorporating visual arts, digital technology, and lighting effects. Innovative displays created by high schools, universities, and environmental agencies now address the challenges of urban living and climate change.

As the Philadelphia Flower Show has flourished, its impact has spread throughout the area. An independent study found that the show has an astonishing $61 million economic impact on the region's businesses. It is recognized as a signature event for Philadelphia and is known as "America's Flower Show."

In many ways, the show lives on after the last day as PHS brings the ideas and inspirations of the Philadelphia Flower Show to public landscapes and neighborhoods. The show is our major fundraiser and supports the PHS City Harvest program, which grows and donates food for families in need; the Plant One Million tree-planting campaign; Philadelphia LandCare, which rejuvenates communities by greening vacant lots; and educational and gardening programs throughout the region.

The founders of the Pennsylvania Horticultural Society would be very proud of what has grown from the seeds they planted in 1829.

—Drew Becher, PHS President

ACKNOWLEDGMENTS

Grateful thanks to the hardworking, talented project team at PHS: Alan Jaffe, Jane Carroll, Anne Vallery, Priscilla Becroft, and Megan Hogan.

Many thanks to current and past PHS staff who answered questions or assisted in other vital ways: Linda Davis, Elsa Efran, Elinor Goff, Betty Greene, Ed and Carol Lindemann, Stephanie Meraklis, Lisa Miller, Flossie Narducci, Jane Pepper, Barbara Peterson, Pete Prown, Eva Ray, Jude Robison, Patricia Schrieber, Sharat Somashekara, Lisa Stephano, Ellen Wheeler, and Jaime Zucker.

Thanks to library volunteers Liz Carter, Stephanie Griffith, and Liz Nork.

Many thanks to those who provided images—Ramona Harrison Gibbs and Susan Fraser, director, Mertz Library, New York Botanical Garden—and to those who patiently answered questions and provided information: Tom Baione; Harold Boeschenstein, director, Department of Library Services, American Museum of Natural History; Peter F. Blume, director, David Owsley Museum of Art, Ball State University; John Faubion, Lawrence Tenney Stevens Trust; Sally Malenka, The John and Chara Haas Conservator of Decorative Arts and Sculpture, Philadelphia Museum of Art; Elizabeth McLean, historian; Jeff Richmond-Moll, archives coordinator, Pennsylvania Academy of the Fine Arts; Suzi Teghtmeyer, librarian, Michigan State University Libraries; Carolyn Adams, Chestnut Hill Historical Society; Fran Watkins, Lindley Library, Royal Horticultural Society; Perry Desmond, Downingtown Area Historical Society; Judith Warnement, director, Botany Libraries, Harvard University; Shelia Connor; Jenny Rose Carey, director, Amber Arboretum, Temple University; and Donna Cockenberg.

Unless otherwise noted, all images appear courtesy of the Pennsylvania Horticultural Society, McLean Library.

Introduction

Back in 2005, after years serving as manager of the gardens and special floral events at Epcot in Florida, I returned to my stomping grounds in southeastern Pennsylvania to take the only job that could be more fun than working for the Walt Disney Company—the job of designing the Philadelphia Flower Show, the largest horticultural event in the United States.

In recent years, the Philadelphia Flower Show has transported visitors to Ireland, the Italian countryside, Parisian parks, the jazzy landscapes of New Orleans, and the gardens of Great Britain. The hundreds of exhibitors in the show have included participants from every continent. Each year, 250,000 guests come from around the United States—and far beyond—to experience the Flower Show.

Of course, the show started more modestly back in 1829, with just a few dozen members of the Pennsylvania Horticultural Society (PHS) exhibiting in the Masonic Hall on Chestnut Street. But even then, there was representation from around the world: the plants.

That first year, the American public was introduced to an exotic plant from Mexico—the poinsettia, now a staple of holiday decor. Subsequent shows unveiled discoveries from every corner of the world: peonies from China, chrysanthemums from Japan, the rubber tree from India, the coffee tree from the Middle East, and sugar cane from the West Indies.

For a few years, shows were held in both the spring and the fall. However, forcing plants to bloom for the spring exhibition was expensive and not always successful in the early 19th century, and the spring shows ceased for several decades. Plants could be naturally grown for the fall show, and participants also competed for prizes by making preserves and pickles.

By popular decree, the spring shows resumed in 1872. By then, PHS had built its own Horticultural Hall and held shows there. The shows were held at that location until 1917, when the priorities of World War I led to the suspension of the exhibitions.

In the mid-1920s, under a new president and excellent manager, James Boyd, PHS developed a stronger financial base and close relationships with garden clubs and collaborated with a group of florists, nurserymen, and growers called the Incorporators. Together, they organized the official Philadelphia Flower Show, which was first held at the Commercial Museum from March 17 through March 20, 1925. The Incorporators founded the Philadelphia Flower Show, Inc., in 1927, and attendance reached 83,000 by 1929—an impressive figure for that period. PHS produced the show's amateur exhibits (now known as the competitive classes).

The Philadelphia region's affluent and avid gardeners were the stars of the shows in the late 1920s and 1930s. Joseph Widener exhibited his magnificent acacia collection. Fitz Eugene Dixon brought beautiful orchid exhibits. John T. Dorrance and Clarence Geist showed roses and geraniums.

The shows were suspended again during World War II and resumed in 1947. Beginning in the 1940s, PHS also resumed smaller fall exhibitions called Harvest Shows to celebrate the homegrown bounty of local gardeners.

In the 1960s, show attendance declined—from 82,000 in 1962 to 66,000 in 1964—and financial losses mounted under the management of Philadelphia Flower Show, Inc. The operator considered suspending the Philadelphia Flower Show for a period while the city constructed a new civic center.

A new leader at PHS, Ernesta Ballard, believed a hiatus could destroy the show and a great tradition, so, in 1965, PHS staged the Philadelphia Flower Show in the 23rd Street Armory. The show broke even. For the next two years, PHS staged the shows in the basement of the new Philadelphia Civic Center and turned a profit each time. In 1968, PHS completely took over operation of the Flower Show in the civic center's main hall. During this era, Ballard initiated the show's vital fundraiser, the Preview Dinner (now called the Preview Party), and built the solid foundation for the Flower Show's growth.

Another 20th-century driving force behind the show was J. Liddon Pennock Jr., a former director of Philadelphia Flower Show, Inc., who was elected president of PHS in the mid-1950s. The scion of a renowned family of florists, Pennock was known as "Mr. Flower Show" and the show's "Principal Perennial Advisor."

In 1981, Jane Pepper took on the executive role at PHS, bringing a keen sense of finance and marketing to the Philadelphia Flower Show and further developing the organization's urban greening programs. Under Pepper's guidance, the show blossomed into the leading horticultural event in the nation and began receiving international attention and participation.

In the 1980s, Ed Lindemann began his 25-year tenure as the creative director of the Philadelphia Flower Show. During his time as show designer, Lindemann brought a theatrical touch, dreamed up fantastic themes, and guided a troupe of superb floral and landscape exhibitors.

As its popularity increased through the 1990s, the Philadelphia Flower Show expanded to a six-acre space in the Philadelphia Civic Center. In 1996, it moved to the new Pennsylvania Convention Center, where the show covers 33 indoor acres, including 10 acres of space encompassing more than 50 major exhibits, educational displays, and a marketplace of 180 shops.

In the 21st century, Drew Becher, who became PHS president in 2010, is bringing a new energy and vision to the Philadelphia Flower Show. In recent years, I have worked with Drew on the introduction of digital projections and lighting effects that enhance the natural beauty of the exhibits and add an exciting dimension to the show experience. We have added a Designer's Studio, where professionals and amateurs demonstrate the creative process in live floral arranging competitions, and the Gardener's Studio, where guests can admire garden-building skills. The new do-it-yourself workshops provide opportunities to take home a piece of the Flower Show. PHS has returned to the roots of the early shows with a New Plants Showcase, which introduces amazing new plant varieties to visitors. In 2013, America's premier horticultural event changed its name once again, adding the designation of our proud organization to become the PHS Philadelphia Flower Show, which is the signature event of the Philadelphia region.

Other individuals have been pillars of the Philadelphia Flower Show for decades, including orchid grower and exhibitor Walt Off, whose father, George, began bringing his extraordinary flowers to the show in the 1930s, and Jack Blandy, of Stoney Bank Nurseries, who has recreated landscapes from around the world on the show floor. Designers like Jamie Rothstein, Michael Petrie, Bill Schaffer, Ron Mulray (of the American Institute of Floral Designers), Robertson's Flowers, and Burke Brothers Landscape Design/Build have raised horticultural design to an art form in their Flower Show exhibits.

The pages of this book shine a spotlight on many others, including thousands of volunteers who have devoted their talents and energies in so many ways—planning, organizing, construction, and welcoming visitors as they arrive. Our volunteers have been a vital component in helping to grow the Philadelphia Flower Show into what has been described as the "Olympics of horticulture," a competition that awards superb creations and inspires all of us to appreciate and beautify our world.

We hope you enjoy our story and that you will join us in writing the next chapters of the PHS Philadelphia Flower Show.

—Sam Lemheney, PHS Chief of Shows and Events

One

Early Shows

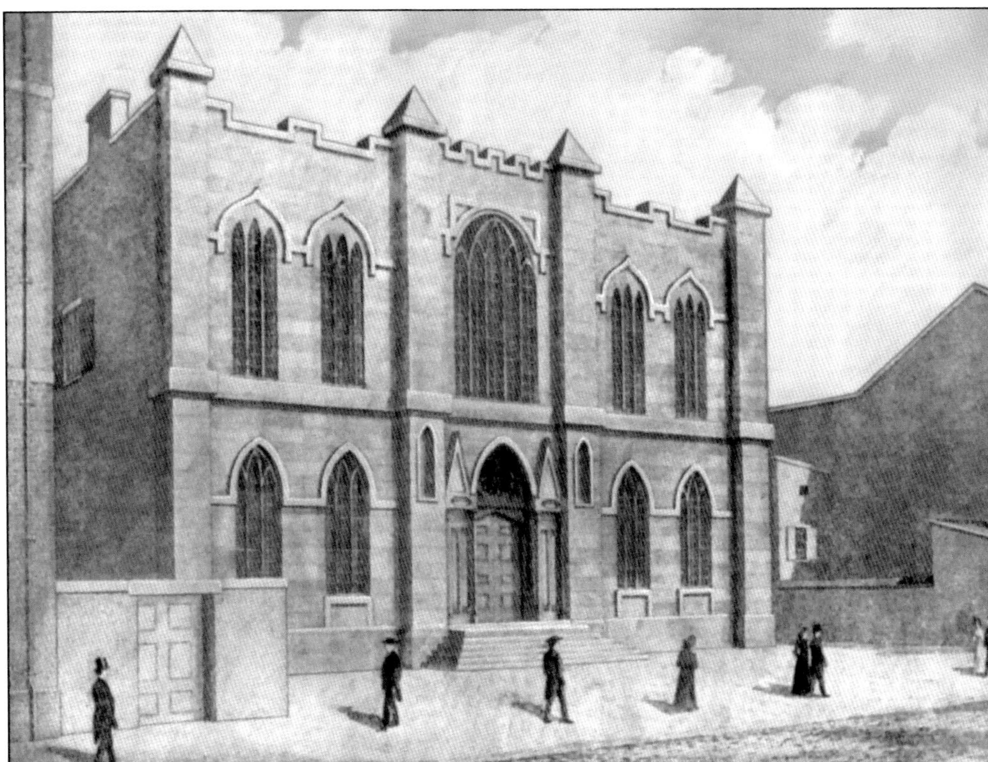

The Pennsylvania Horticultural Society (PHS) was founded in 1827 and incorporated in 1831 by a group of gentleman farmers, botanists, and nurserymen. Monthly meetings included exhibitions among members. PHS held the first public flower show in America in June 1829 in the Masonic Hall on Philadelphia's Chestnut Street. The one-day exhibition of fruits, flowers, and plants included the introduction of the poinsettia, recently imported from Mexico, to the public.

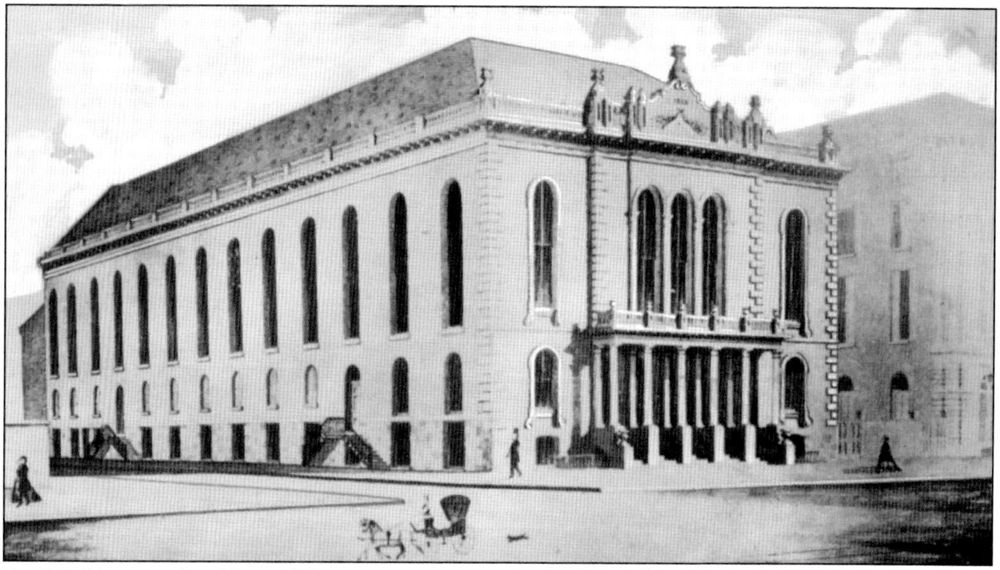

PHS held annual public exhibitions in venues throughout the city. The society built its first Horticultural Hall in 1867 near Broad and Locust Streets in Philadelphia. The most remarkable display in the first grand exhibition featured pears, grapes, plums, quinces, and pomegranates shipped from California—the first offerings from that state in a PHS show. The hall was destroyed by fire in 1881.

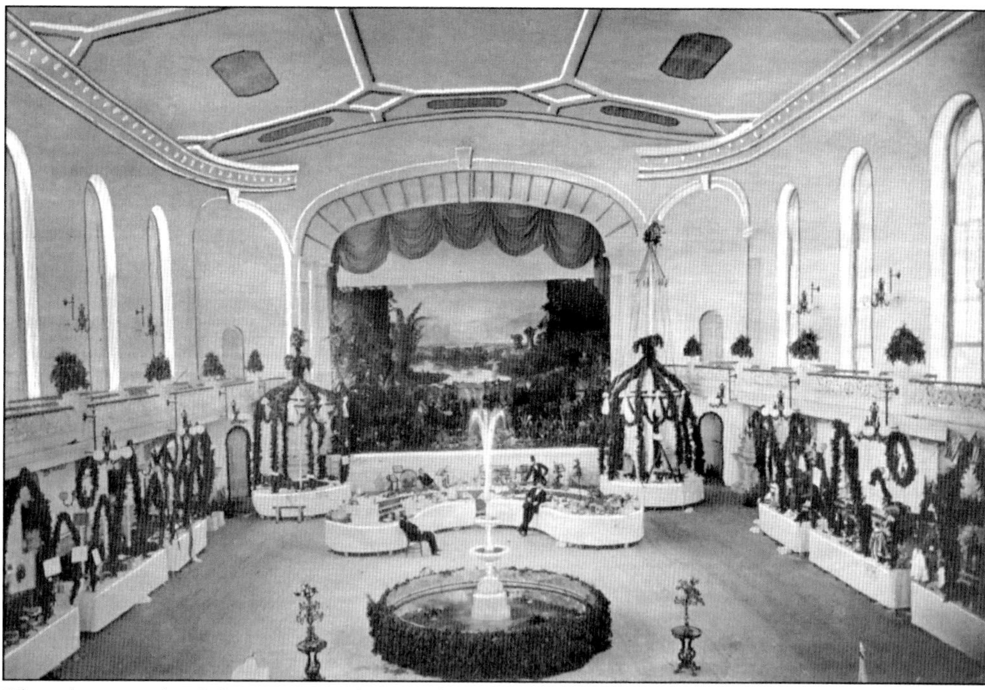

This photograph of the interior of PHS's first Horticultural Hall was taken sometime between 1867 and 1881. Commercial nurserymen and florists who often exhibited during this time included Henry A. Dreer, Pennock Brothers Florists, Thomas Meehan, Robert Buist, and Hugh Graham. Dahlias, roses, and gladiolus were often shown as well as more exotic plants such as dracaenas and marantas.

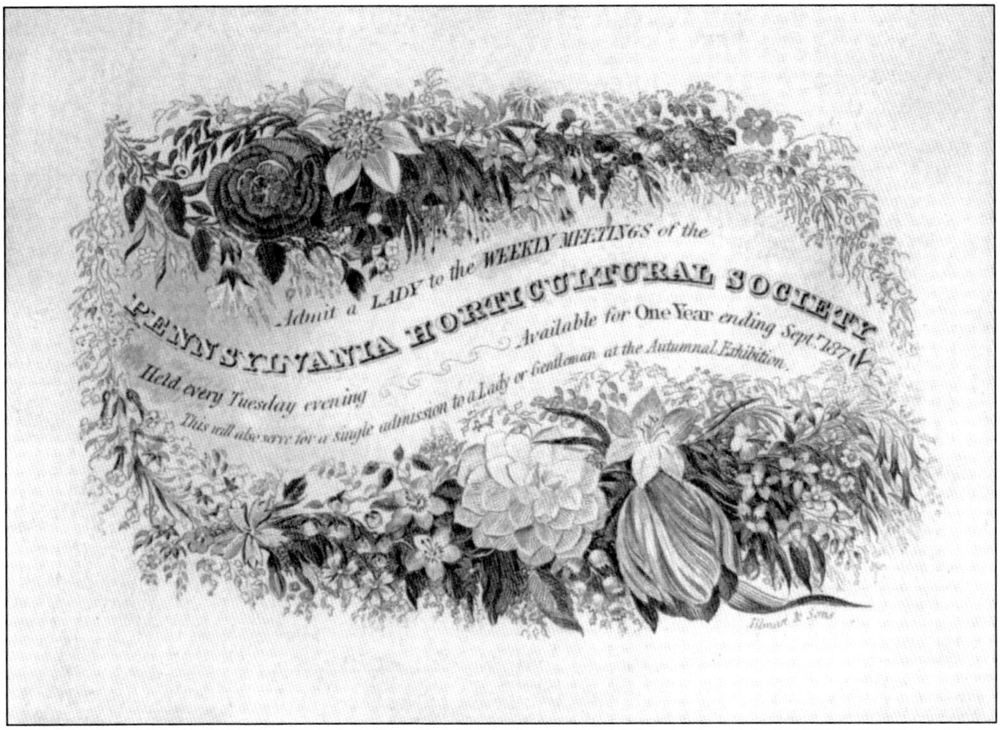

The text of this 1874 admission ticket reads: "Admit a LADY to the WEEKLY MEETINGS of the Pennsylvania Horticultural Society Held every Tuesday evening . . . This will also serve for a single admission to a Lady or Gentleman at the Autumnal Exhibition." Women were voted into membership in 1829, one and a half years after the society was founded.

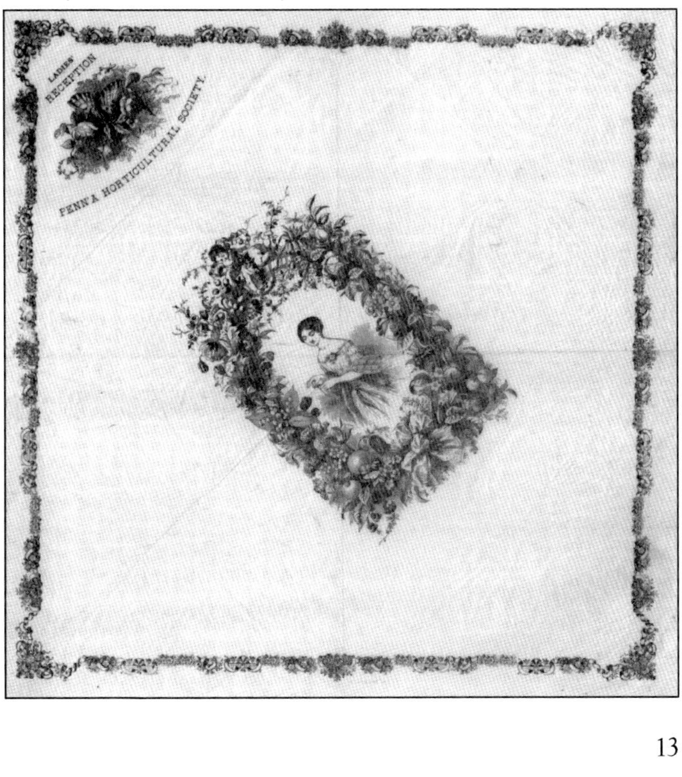

For many years, the Pennsylvania Horticultural Society's Ladies' Reception Committee organized annual events in June at Horticultural Hall. This Ladies' Reception souvenir may be from 1876, when all eyes were on Philadelphia as the host city of the nation's centennial, or it may have been from the 50th anniversary of the founding of the society, which was celebrated in 1877 with 1,250 attendees.

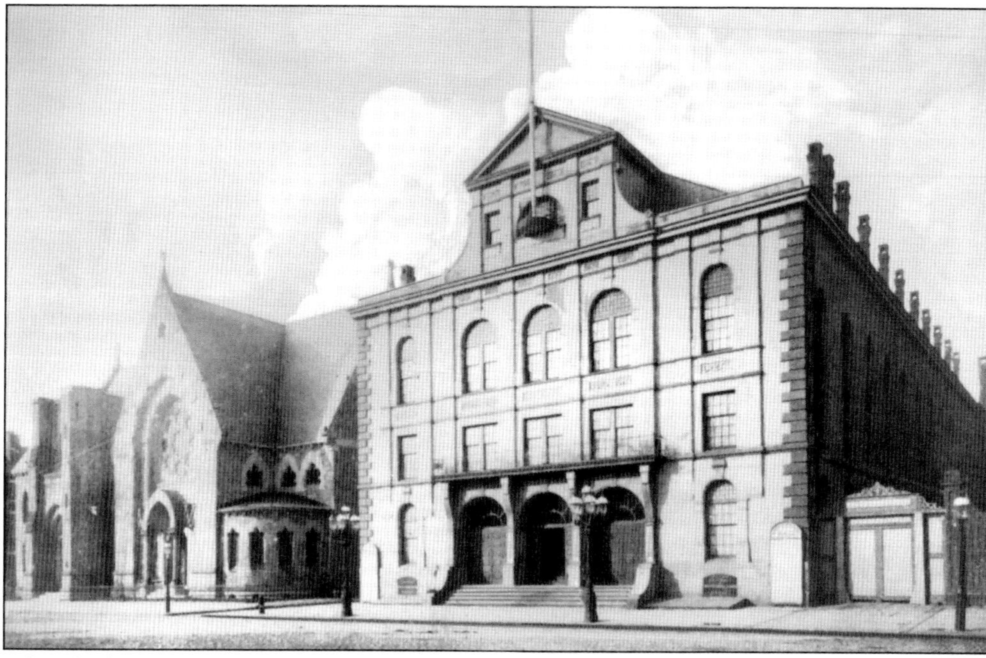

After the first Horticultural Hall was destroyed by fire in 1881, a second Horticultural Hall, built at the same location, was designed by prominent Philadelphia architect Addison Hutton and completed in 1882. In 1893, history repeated itself; during a candy fair, what began as a small fire quickly spread to the ceiling decorations hanging throughout the hall. Within a short time, the second hall was destroyed.

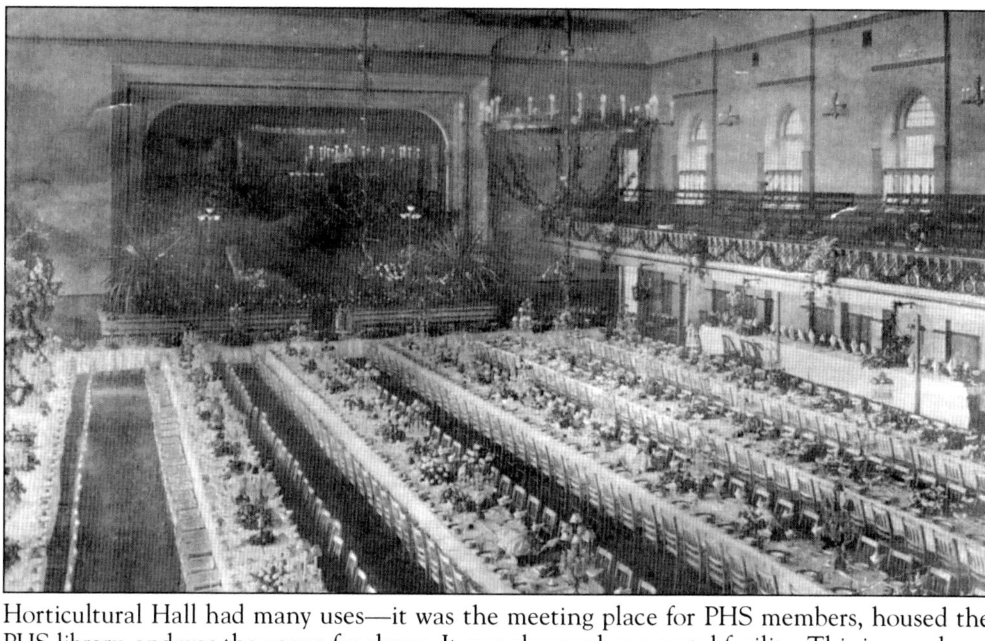

Horticultural Hall had many uses—it was the meeting place for PHS members, housed the PHS library, and was the venue for shows. It was also used as a rental facility. This image shows a banquet, seating 750, held in the late 1880s for the Master Builder's Exchange. The second Horticultural Hall was also home to the Florists' Club of Philadelphia, which had a bowling alley where matches were routinely held among florists.

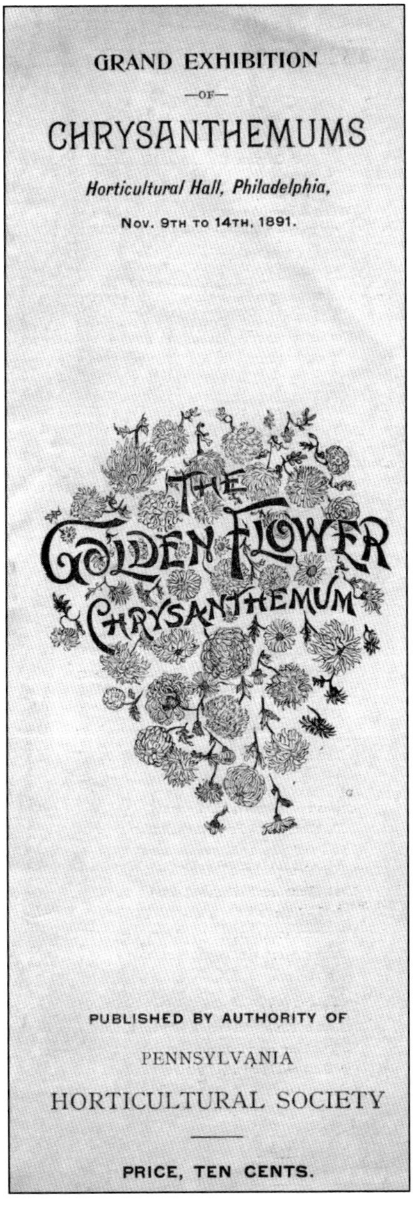

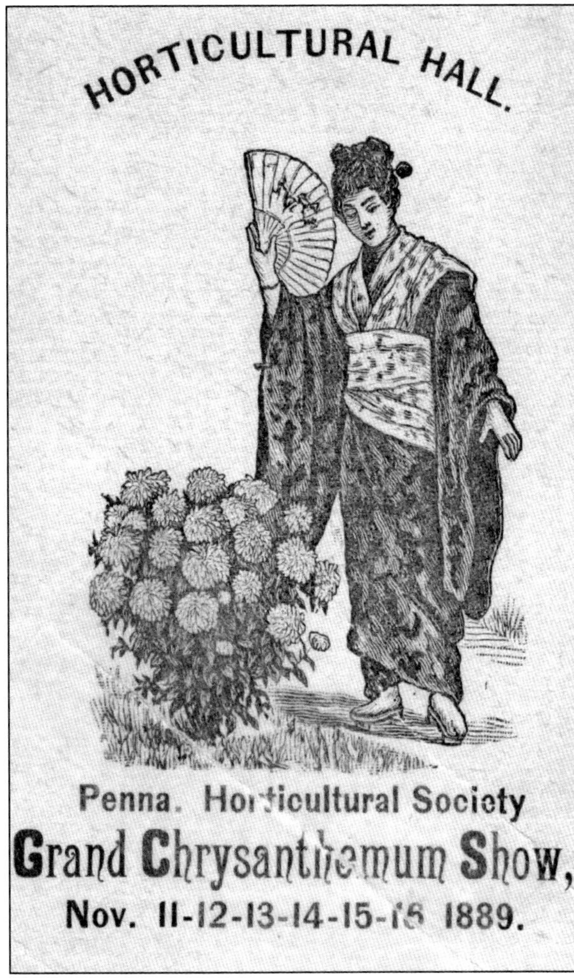

Chrysanthemum shows were immensely popular from the last quarter of the 19th century through the 1920s, with multiday shows held throughout the fall in major cities in the United States and Canada. The public was fascinated with the "wonderfully bizarre" Japanese forms introduced at this time. Exhibitors would graft different kinds and colors of chrysanthemums to one plant. Bigger flowers attracted attention; with the right coaxing, chrysanthemums could have flowers the size of dinner plates.

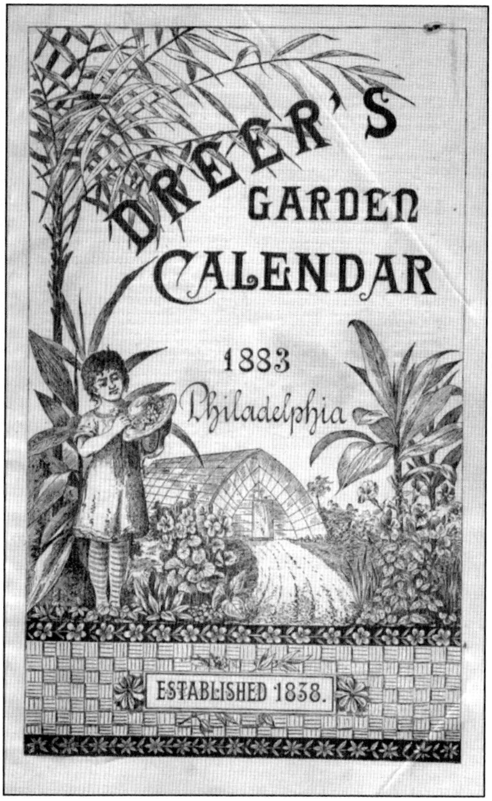

Henry Augustus Dreer started a seed business in 1838, offering bulbs, flower seeds, and vegetable seeds to an eager public. He served as treasurer of PHS from 1862 to 1873. His son William continued the business and was known for the premiums offered to competitors in flower shows of the 1900s. The H.A. Dreer Company exhibited at Philadelphia shows through the 1930s.

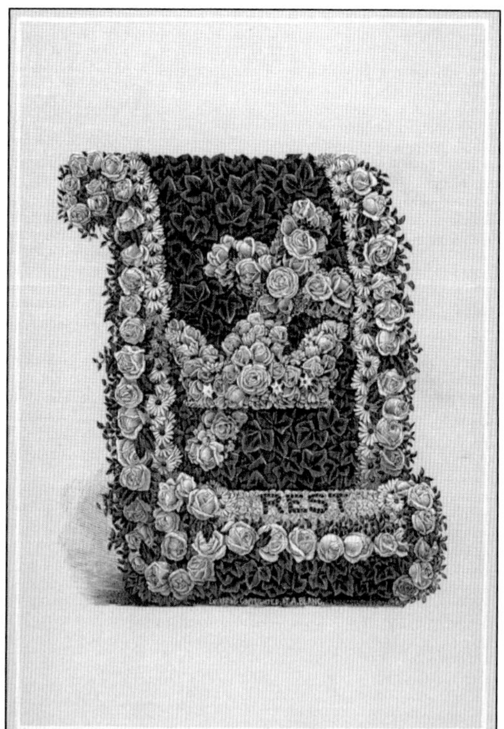

It was not uncommon for the floral competitions of the 1880s to include funeral designs. This illustration from J. Horace McFarland's 1888 book, *Floral Designs: a Handbook for Cut-Flower Workers and Florists*, featured a funeral design by longtime exhibitor Hugh Graham & Sons. This scroll, with cross and crown, is made of polished ivy leaves with Perle roses outlining the edge.

While the fall shows of the 1880s and 1890s continued to feature chrysanthemums, Albert Blanc was attracting attention with his displays of cactus (a novelty at the time). Blanc was a cactus collector turned dealer. Through his exhibits, such as the one shown in the foreground of the photograph below (from *The American Florist*), and his mail-order catalog, *Hints on Cacti*, he started a cactus craze in the 1890s in the United States. He was awarded a special premium of $50 for his display in the 1891 show. (Below, courtesy New York Botanical Garden, Mertz Library.)

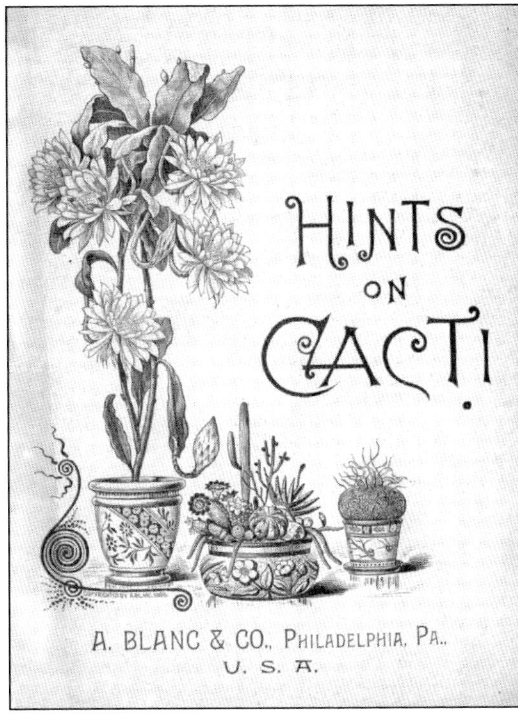

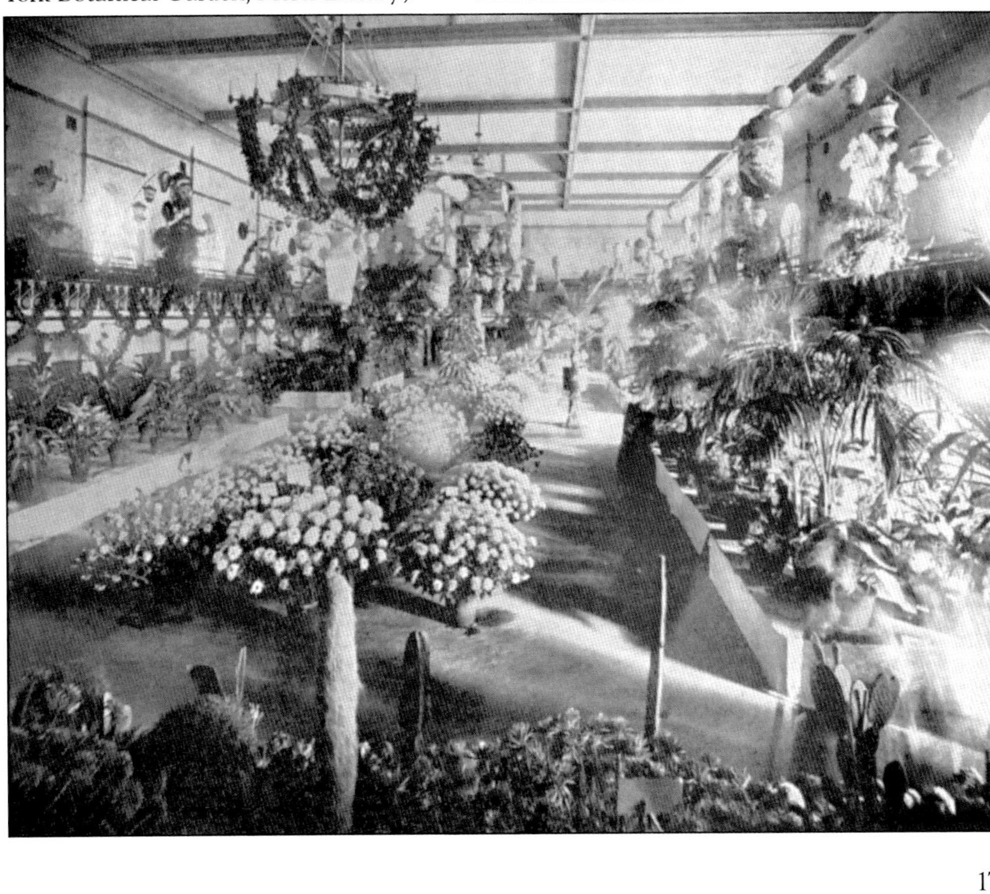

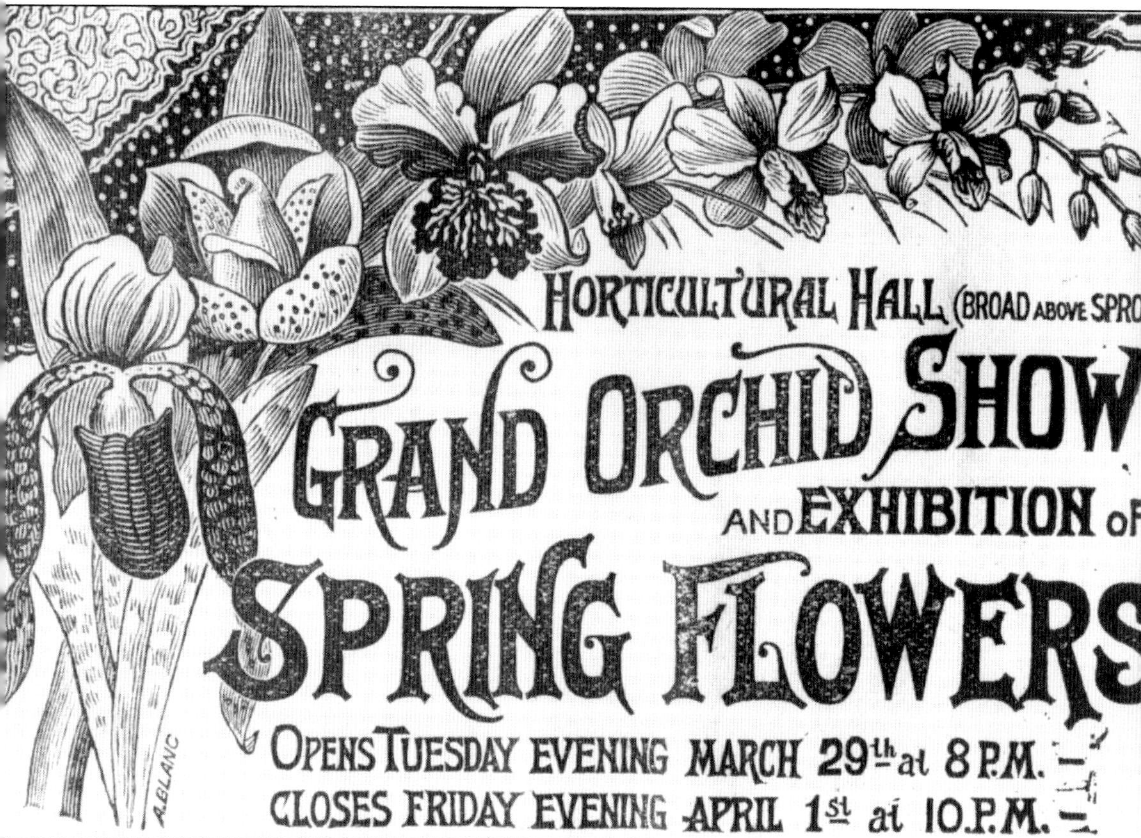

Beginning in 1890, the Florists' Club of Philadelphia handled the decorations for PHS's spring and fall shows, turning Horticultural Hall into "a veritable bower of grace and beauty," according to a review in *The American Florist*. Visitors showered much admiration on orchid displays from Pitcher & Manda of Short Hills, New Jersey, and Siebrecht & Wadley of New Rochelle, New York.

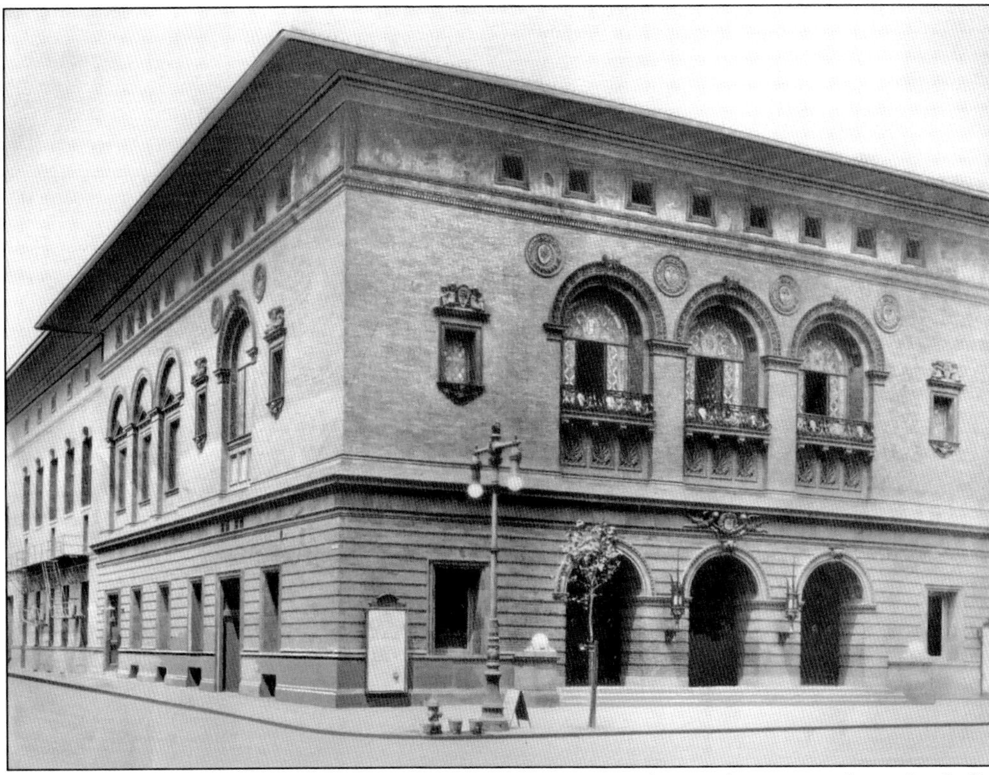

PHS's third Horticultural Hall opened in 1896 at the same Broad Street location as the earlier halls. Designed by Philadelphia architect Frank Miles Day, this hall was patterned after a Florentine Renaissance palace. Its interior was ornate, with a large foyer, stained-glass windows, and a grand staircase to the main hall brilliantly lit by electric light. An inability to make a profit on shows or hall rentals forced PHS to sell this building in 1917, and it was demolished that year.

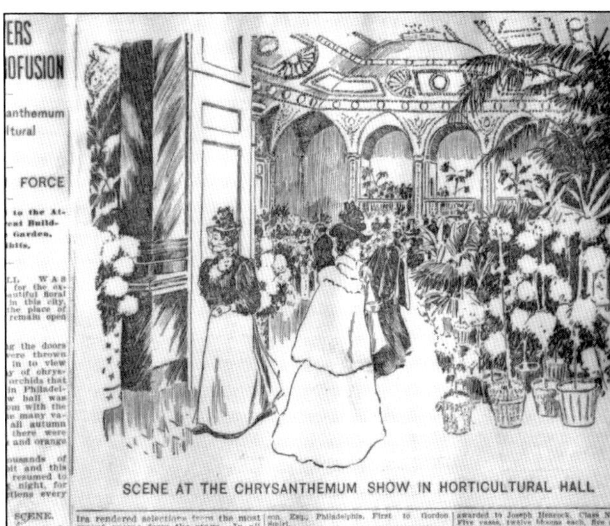

The 1896 Chrysanthemum Show and Exhibition of Flowers, Fruits, and Vegetables was a five-day event and the first major show held in PHS's new Horticultural Hall on Broad Street. The exhibition included chrysanthemums, orchids, foliage plants, palms, ferns, Japanese evergreens, ornamental grasses and bamboos, berry-bearing plants, crotons, dracaenas, carnations, caladiums, and roses. The premiums awarded totaled $1,491. This illustration showing the interior of the new hall appeared in the *Philadelphia Inquirer* on November 11, 1896.

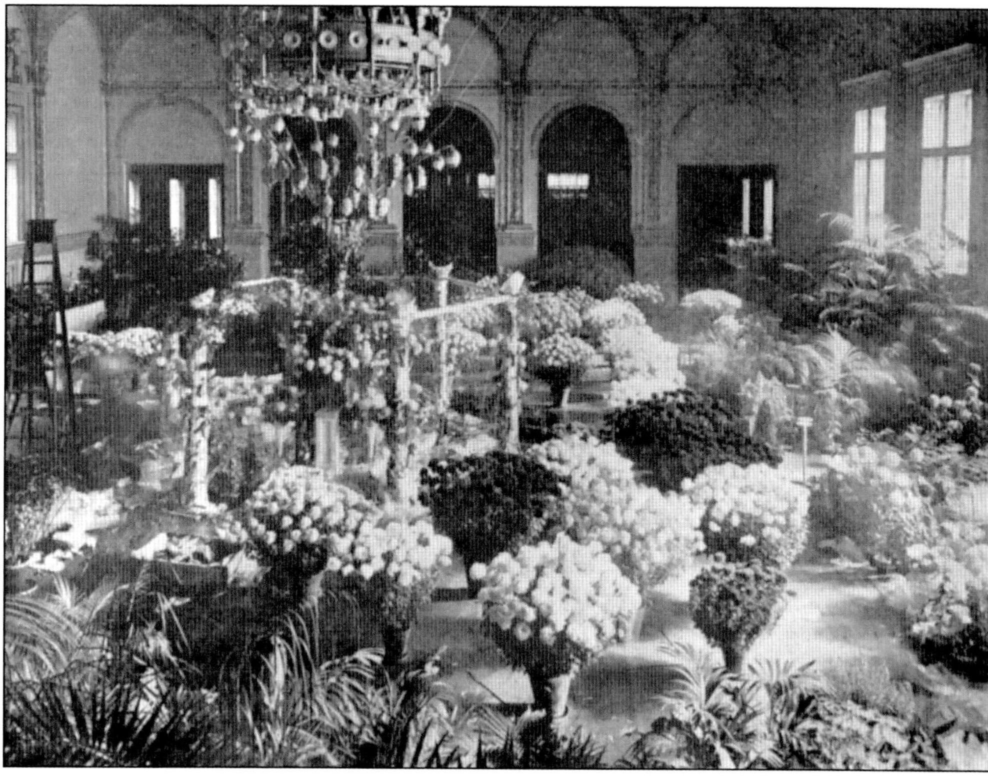

This photograph from *The American Florist* is from the 1903 autumn show and depicts William Graham Company's exhibit of a pagoda of white birchbark pillars canopied with asparagus and Chinese lanterns. The pillars were studded with chrysanthemums inserted in glass bulbs. (Courtesy New York Botanical Garden, Mertz Library.)

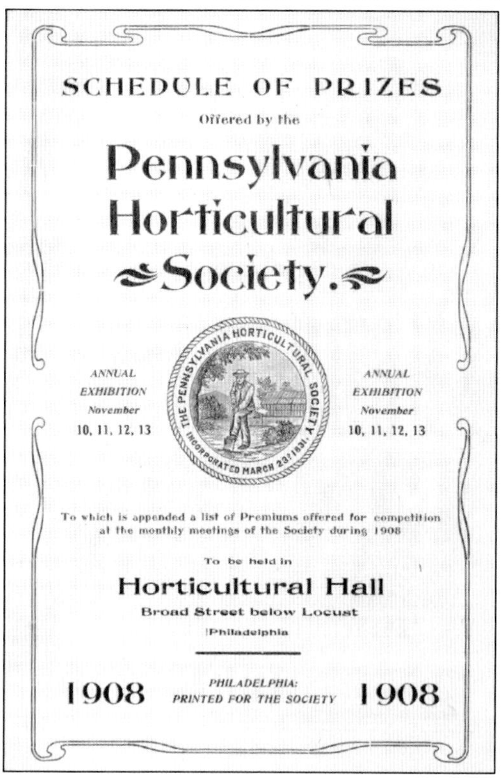

SCHEDULE OF PRIZES

Offered by the

Pennsylvania Horticultural Society.

ANNUAL EXHIBITION November 10, 11, 12, 13

ANNUAL EXHIBITION November 10, 11, 12, 13

To which is appended a list of Premiums offered for competition at the monthly meetings of the Society during 1908

To be held in

Horticultural Hall

Broad Street below Locust

Philadelphia

1908 PHILADELPHIA: PRINTED FOR THE SOCIETY 1908

Wealthy estate owners, called "private growers," and commercial growers, such as florists and seed and nursery businesses, offered prize money ("premiums") to winners. Private growers competed with other private growers; commercial growers did likewise. Premiums were awarded for a specific class, such as "cut flowers—chrysanthemums" or "group of foliage and flowering plants, arranged for effect." At the 1908 exhibition, premiums amounted to $1,152—the equivalent of roughly $30,000 in 2013.

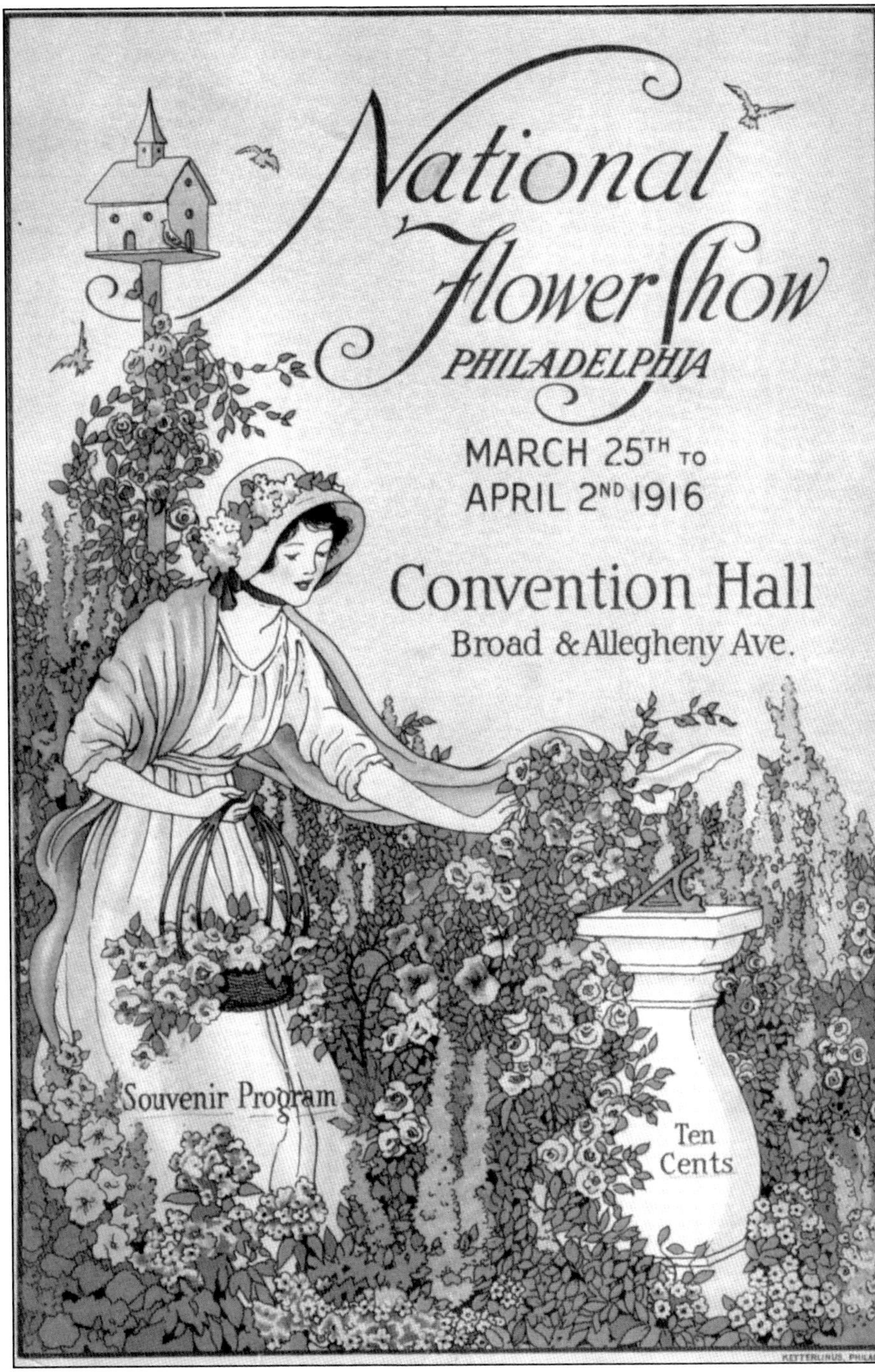

The National Flower Show was held in Philadelphia from March 25 through April 2, 1916, at the Convention Hall at Broad Street and Allegheny Avenue. This was a large show organized by the Society of American Florists in cooperation with PHS, the Florists' Club of Philadelphia, and several trade, professional, and educational groups. Its success convinced local organizers that the public was interested in large spring flower shows. Many participants in this show reunited in the mid-1920s to organize a spring event—the Philadelphia Flower Show.

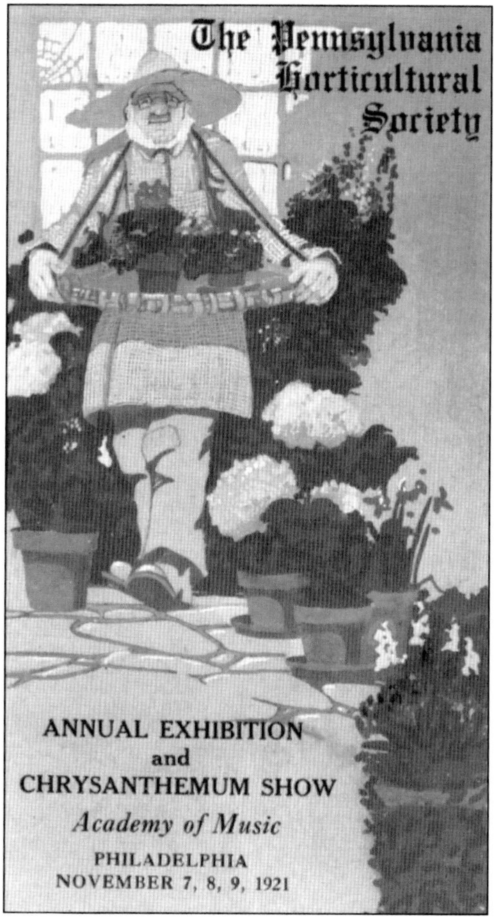

To promote PHS's 1921 show, held from November 7 to 9 at the Academy of Music, a pilot flew over Philadelphia's downtown and, according to newspaper accounts, "pelted pedestrians with roses, orchids, carnations and chrysanthemums," along with 50,000 flyers promoting the show. Debutantes served tea every afternoon of the three-day show, and music and dancing were scheduled for the afternoons and evenings.

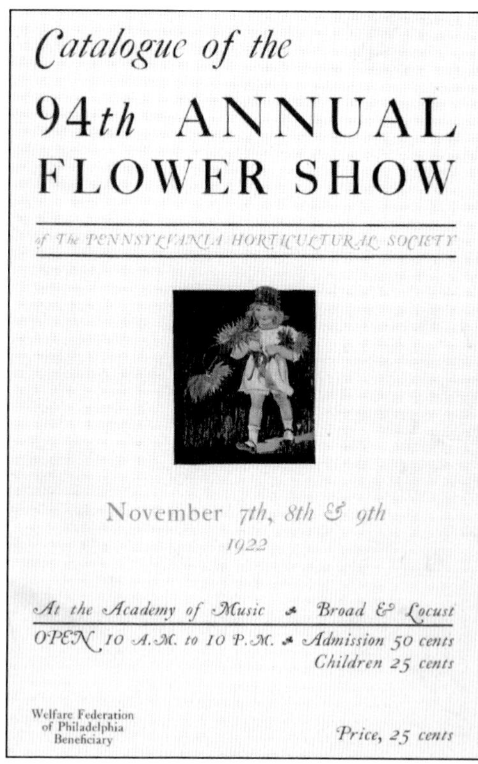
Catalogue of the

94*th* ANNUAL FLOWER SHOW

of The PENNSYLVANIA HORTICULTURAL SOCIETY

November *7th, 8th & 9th*

1922

At the Academy of Music ❧ *Broad & Locust*

OPEN 10 A.M. to 10 P.M. ❧ *Admission 50 cents*
Children 25 cents

Welfare Federation
of Philadelphia
Beneficiary

Price, 25 cents

When flower shows were held at the Academy of Music, a temporary wooden floor was placed on top of the seats in the main hall. The 1922 November show's main attractions were chrysanthemums, but the show also featured collections from estate greenhouses that included vegetables, orchids, roses, and sweet peas. For the first time, the public was asked to assist in judging by filling out ballots distributed at the door.

Two

COMMERCIAL MUSEUM

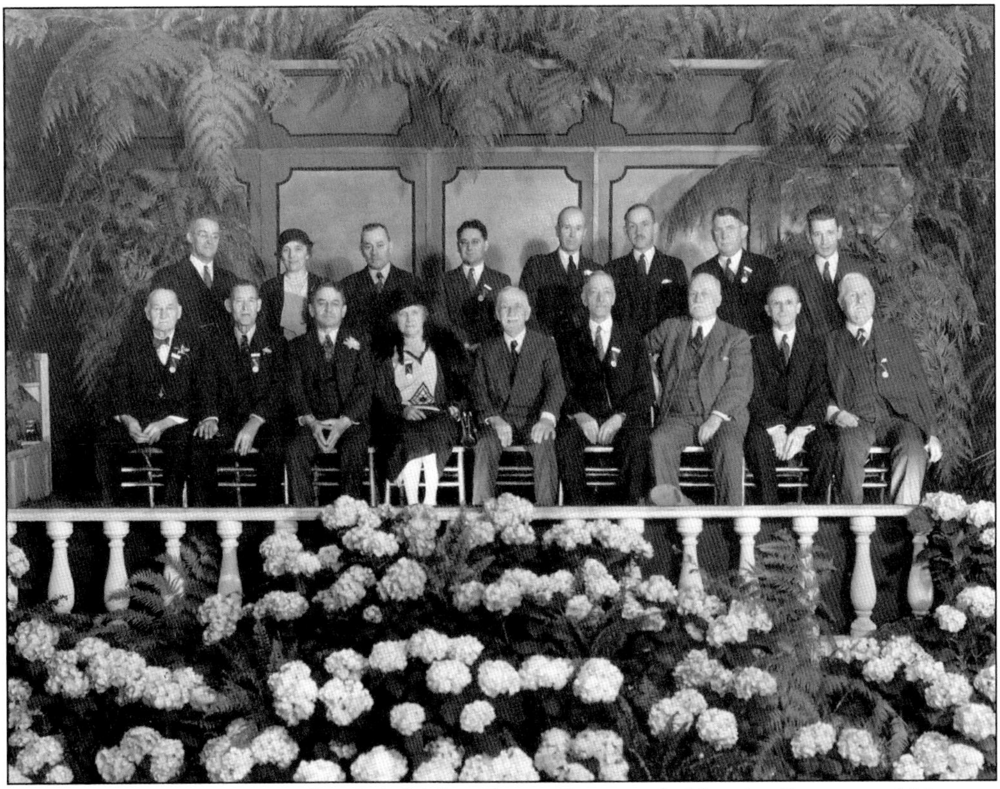

From the mid-1920s to 1964, the Philadelphia Flower Show was held at the Commercial Museum in west Philadelphia. To manage this show, a group of florists and growers created a separate entity called the Philadelphia Flower Show, Inc. The "Incorporators" handled the show design, operations, and commercial entries, while PHS organized the show's amateur and garden club classes, educational exhibits, and lectures.

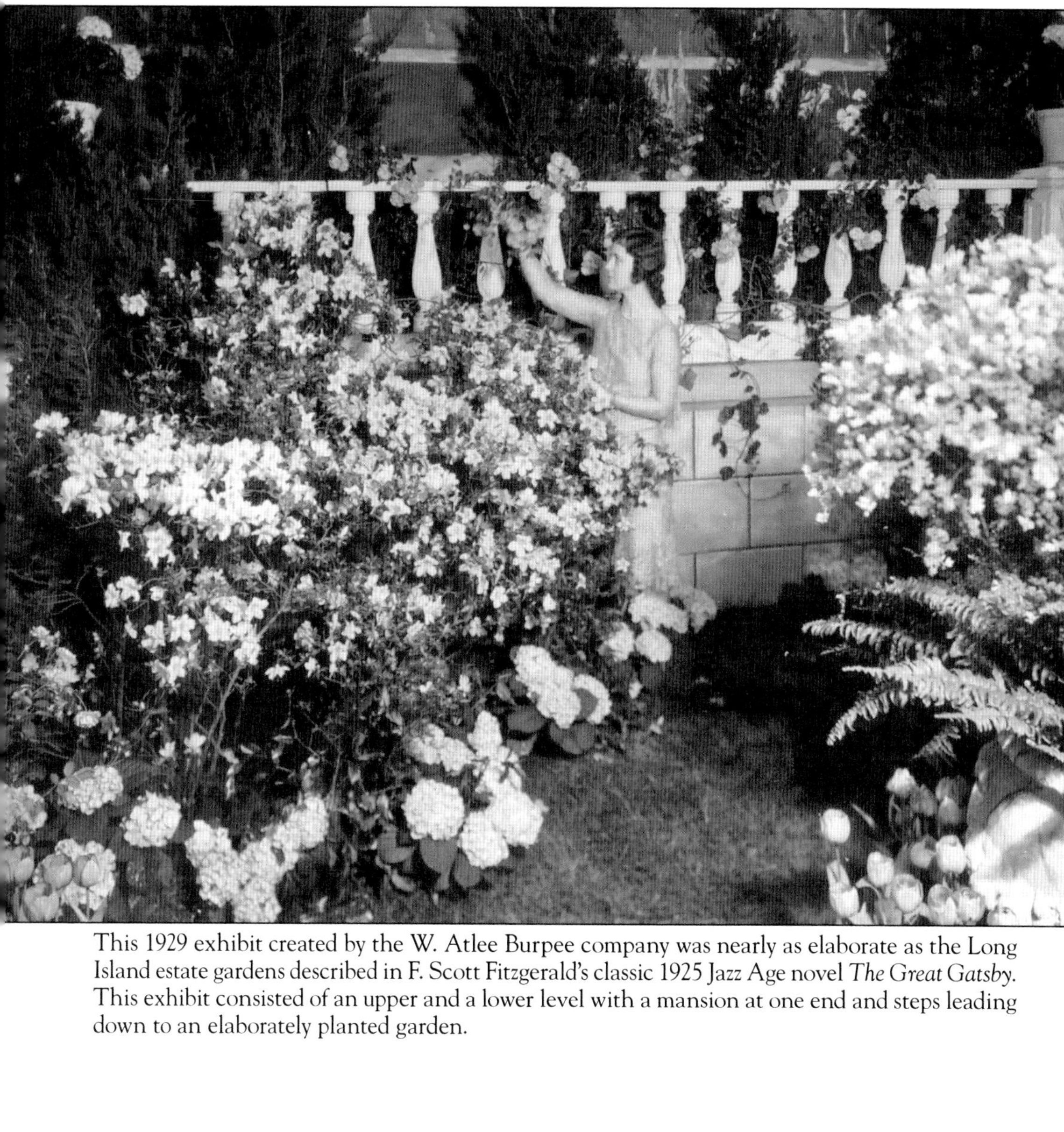

This 1929 exhibit created by the W. Atlee Burpee company was nearly as elaborate as the Long Island estate gardens described in F. Scott Fitzgerald's classic 1925 Jazz Age novel *The Great Gatsby*. This exhibit consisted of an upper and a lower level with a mansion at one end and steps leading down to an elaborately planted garden.

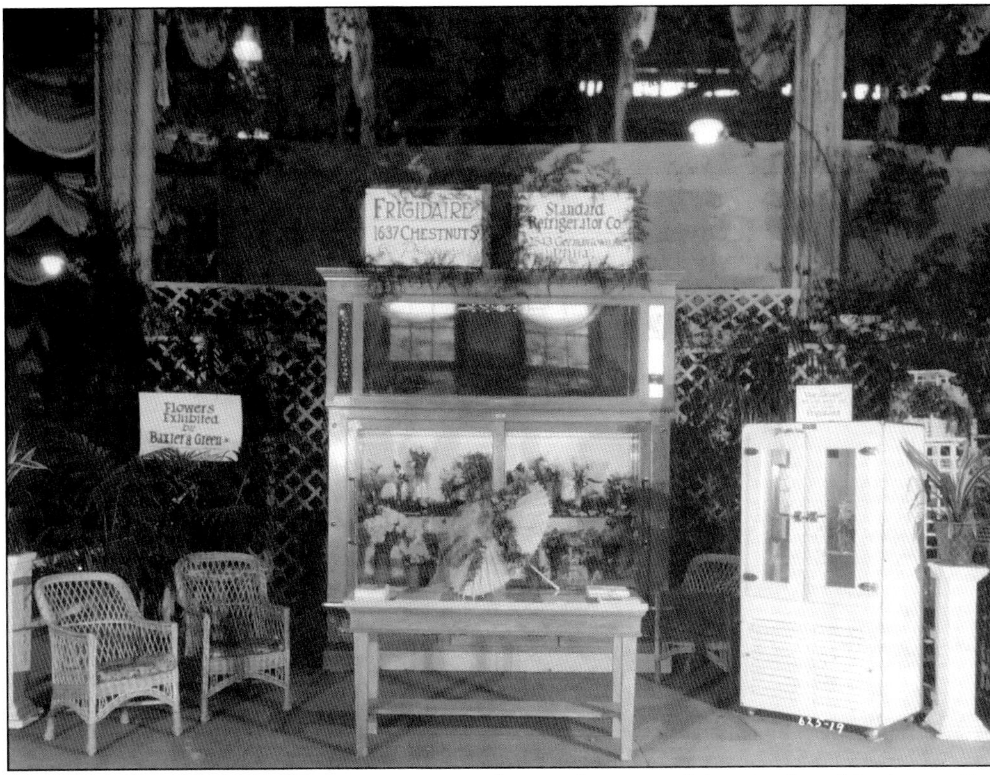

It took almost 20 years for florists to transition from ordering ice deliveries from "the iceman" to having refrigerators in their shops. Pennock Brothers Florists in Philadelphia was the first florist shop in the United States known to use refrigeration, beginning in 1907. This 1927 exhibit featured a Frigidaire model; the sign above the refrigerator at right reads, "Your Corsage will look better and last longer—Frigidaire."

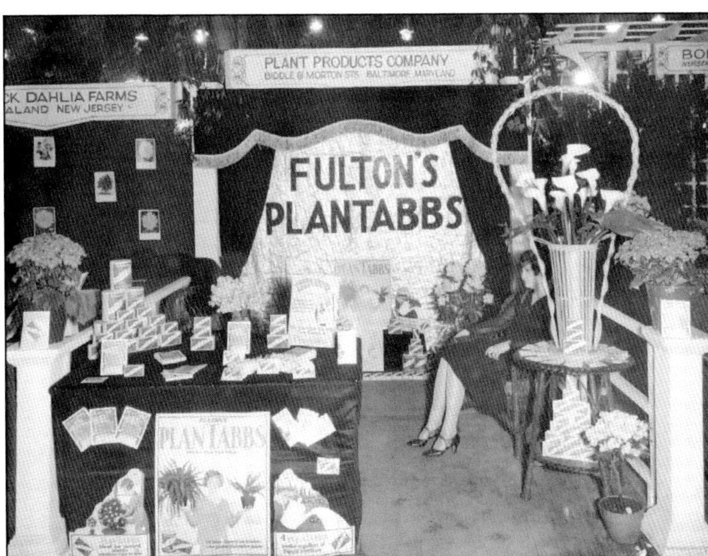

Fulton's Plantabbs, located on Biddle and Morton Streets in Baltimore, Maryland, sold odorless plant food tablets used for making liquid fertilizer. Plantabbs Products, founded in 1921 by avid gardener and pharmacist T.R. Fulton and his brother David H. Fulton, was among the first manufacturers of tablets for fertilizing houseplants; this exhibit appeared in the 1929 show.

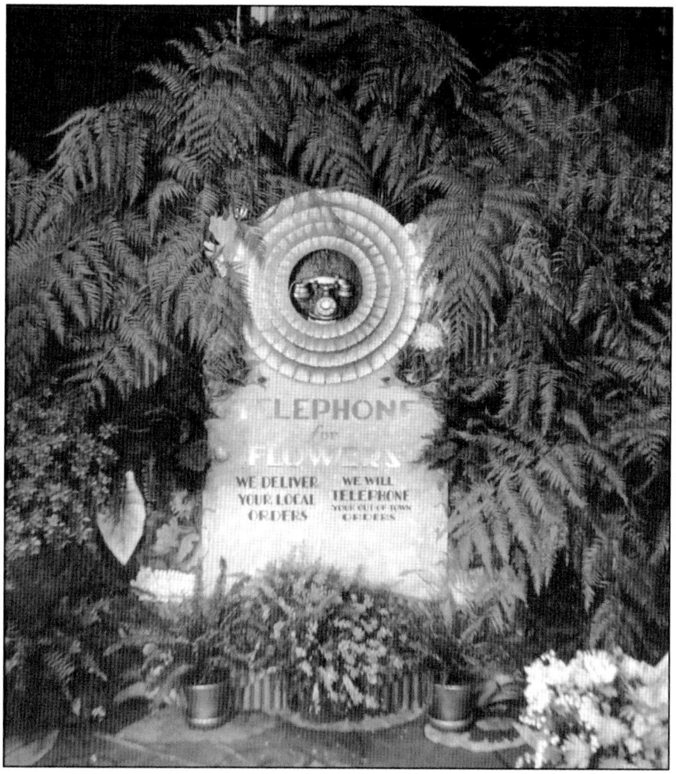

This 1,200-square-foot 1930 exhibit of the Philadelphia unit of FTD (Florists' Telegraph Delivery) featured an illuminated telephone and telegraphs from Western Union and Postal Telegraph companies as well as an operator (below) who placed orders for flowers wired from the exhibit. FTD, a flowers-by-wire association, was founded in 1910 and expanded through the 1920s. Florists used the telegraph and telephone to place orders for customers for deliveries in other cities. Florists had always had informal networks, but not only did FTD allow them to expand their markets, it also ensured that they would be paid for their transactions.

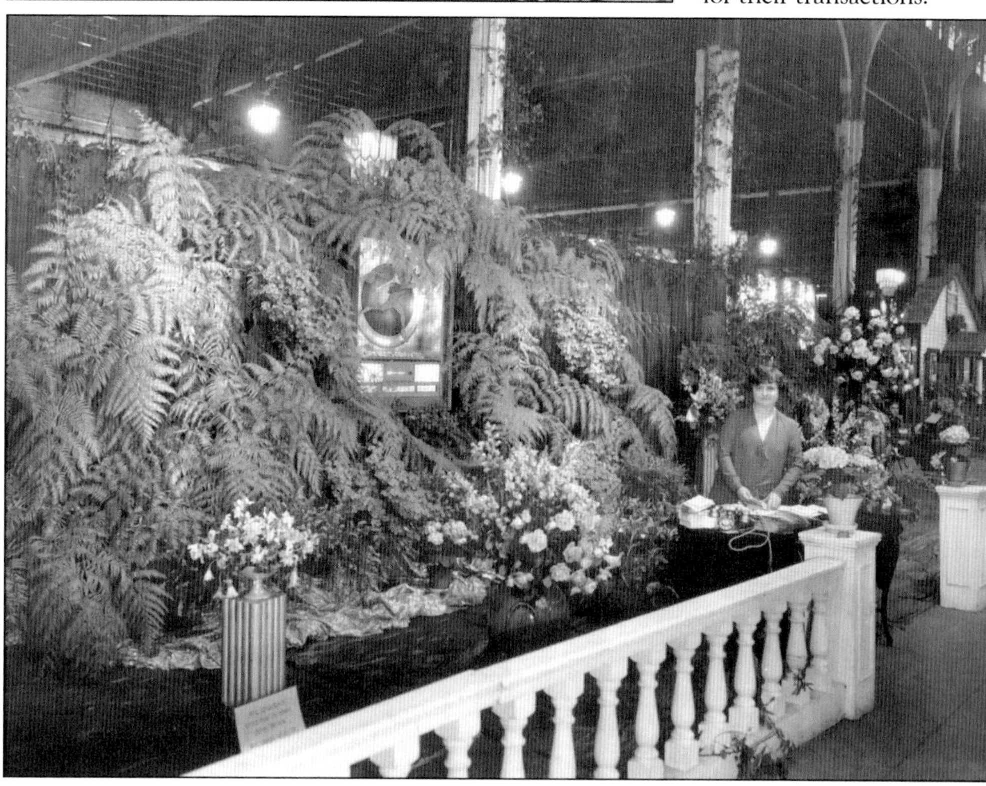

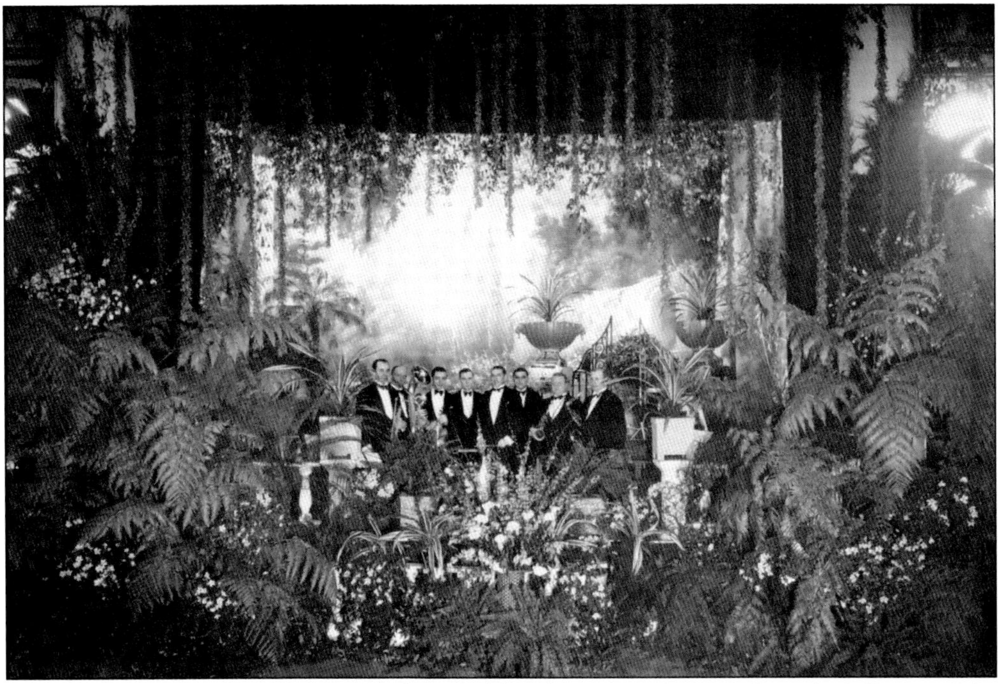

Live music was a regular feature of the shows held in the 1930s. The stage from the ballroom of the Bellevue-Stratford Hotel was transported to the Commercial Museum and served as both music stand and lecture platform during the show. It was decorated by the florist J.J. Habermehl's Sons.

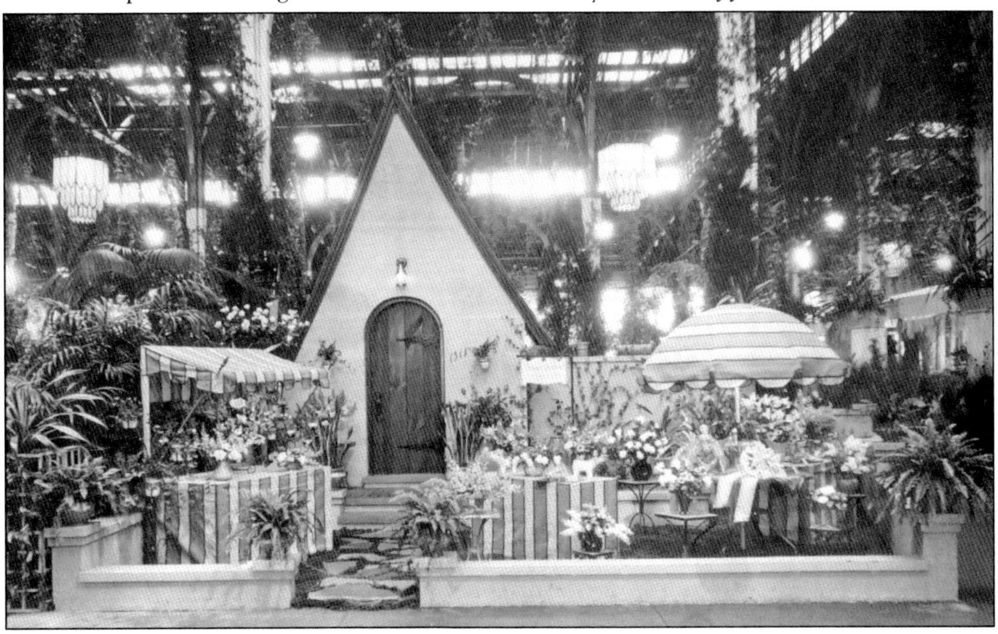

This 1930 exhibit by Pennock Brothers Florists attracted attention with its festively arranged vases, flower baskets, and bouquets set up for an afternoon lawn party. The small house, numbered 1514, was a nod to the florist's address—1514 Chestnut Street in Philadelphia. In the 1930s, owner J. Liddon Pennock Sr. and his son J. Liddon Jr. exhibited together. J. Liddon Pennock Jr. later exhibited under the name of his business, Meadowbrook Farm.

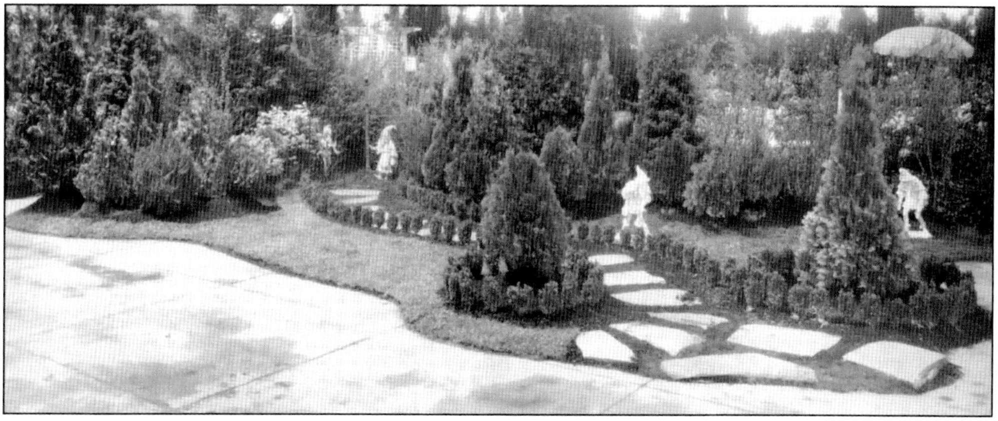

The origins of garden gnomes have been traced to Northern European folk traditions and beliefs in fairies, elves, and leprechauns. Nineteenth-century English tourists who travelled to Germany and became enchanted by the gnomes displayed in gardens there imported the figures to England. The gnomes' popularity spread to the United States, and they were featured in this Hengel Brothers exhibit from the 1930 show.

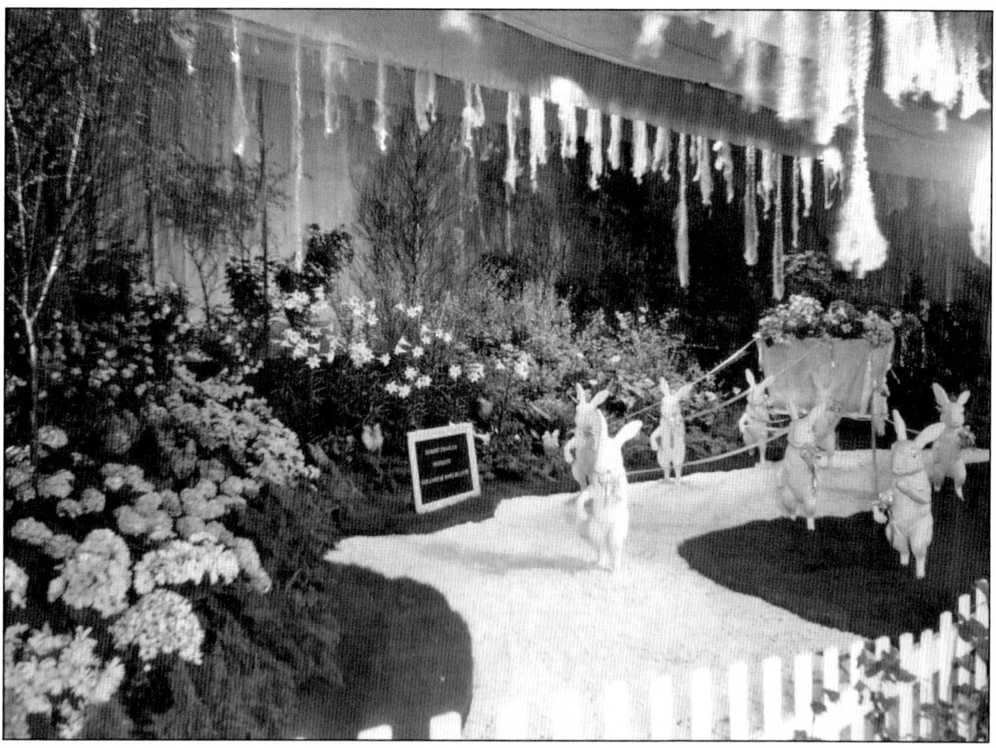

Robert Craig Company's Easter bunny display in the 1930 show was much admired by the public as well as by members of the florist trade. From the end of the 19th century through the 1950s, Easter was the busiest holiday of the year for florists. Spring flower shows were scheduled to be held about three weeks before Easter—the timing helped attract customers.

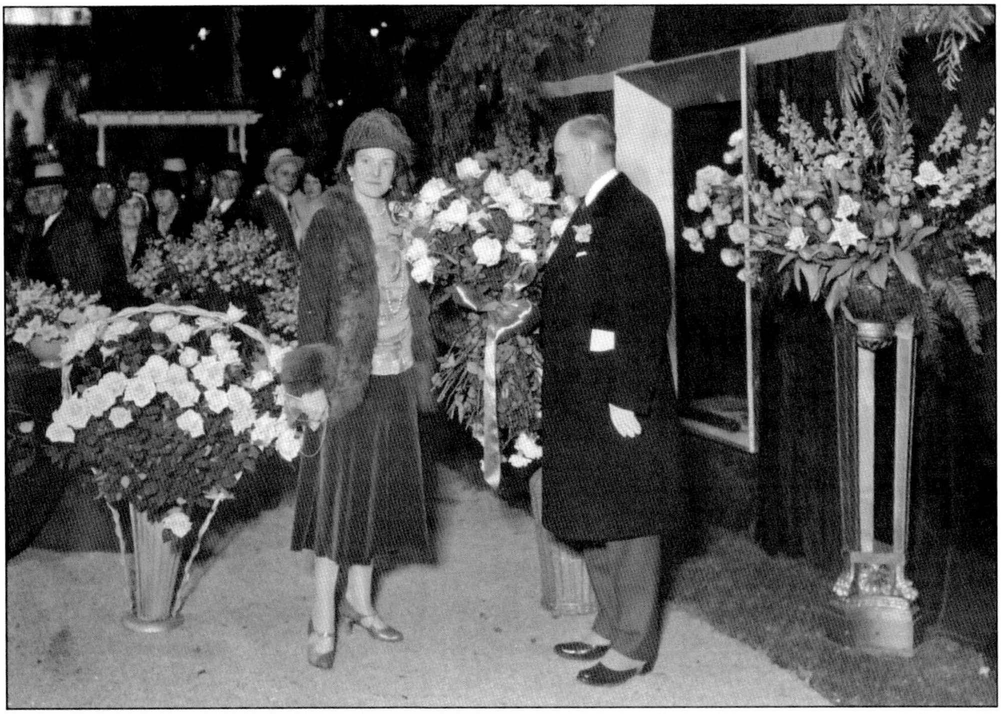

Cornelia Bryce Pinchot (left), wife of Pennsylvania governor Gifford Pinchot, opened the 1931 show along with Philadelphia mayor Harry Arista Mackey (right). Even in the depths of the Great Depression, the Philadelphia Flower Show was wildly popular, with attendance at over 115,000. At that time, the show opened at noon on Monday and closed on Saturday; Pennsylvania's "Blue Laws" prohibited commerce—including the Flower Show—on Sundays.

Louis Burk supplied Philadelphians with hot dogs and scrapple through his meatpacking business. He also built and operated the original Steel Pier in Atlantic City, New Jersey. Burk was known for his orchids and entered them in Philadelphia and New York flower shows. *New Yorker* writer E.B. White playfully sketched Burk's orchid obsession in a 1928 article. Burk exhibited at the Philadelphia Flower Show from the 1890s through the early 1930s; his 1931 exhibit is pictured here.

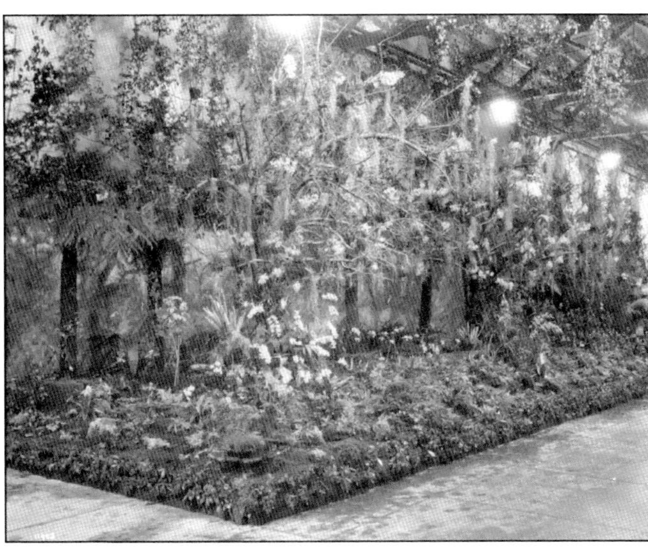

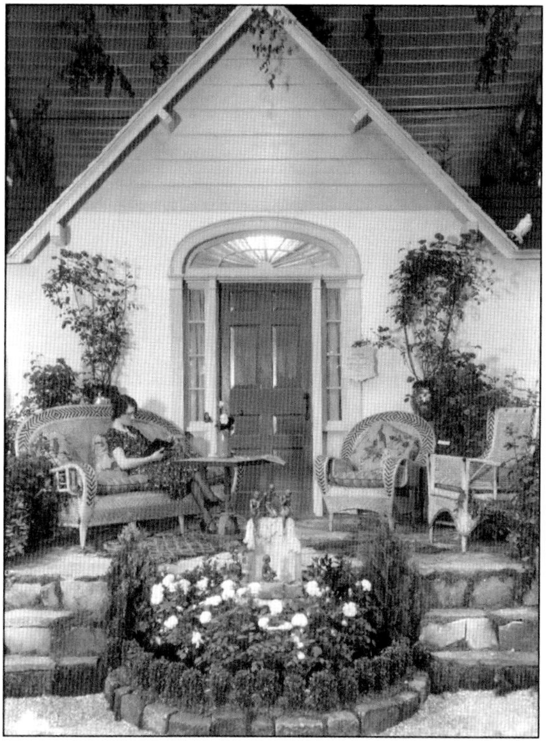

Conard-Pyle, which is still in business today, introduced many well-known roses to American gardens, including the "Peace" rose and the "Knock Out" family of roses. Many varieties of roses were used in this charming 1,200-square-foot exhibit in 1931. The flagstone patio in front of the arched doorway features garden furniture supplied by Karcher & Rehn Company of Philadelphia, a prominent furniture dealer of the day.

This 1931 exhibit was created by Hosea Waterer, a seedsman and bulb importer with a business at 714 Chestnut Street in Philadelphia. A reviewer for *Horticulture* magazine admired this bulb display, calling it an example of an "everyman's garden—one within the reach of thousands of families." Show visitors wanted to see more than just the "millionaire's flowers" from greenhouses of the wealthy; they also yearned to create their own backyard Edens.

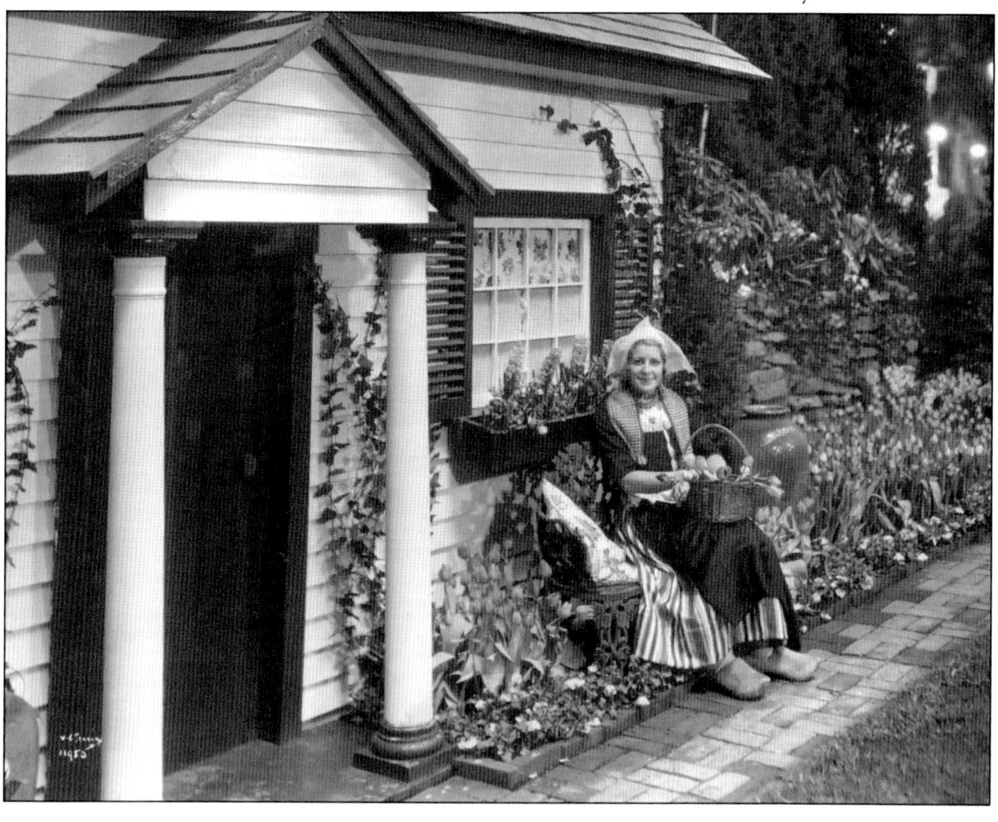

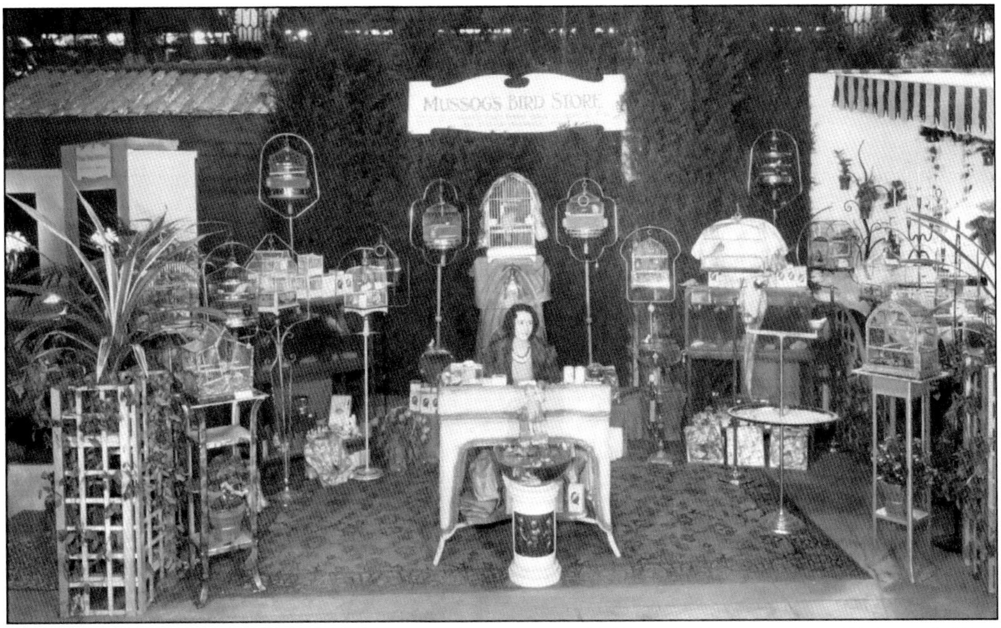

Emil Mussog founded his Philadelphia pet business in 1916 with the opening of Mussog's Bird Store, carriers of the highly popular canaries, imported "fancy birds," and goldfish. Since pet shops were a specialty business at this time, it was not uncommon for florists to also sell birds and fish. As a vendor at the 1932 show, Mussog would have found a receptive audience. Cages of the 1930s were predominantly made of brass and bamboo.

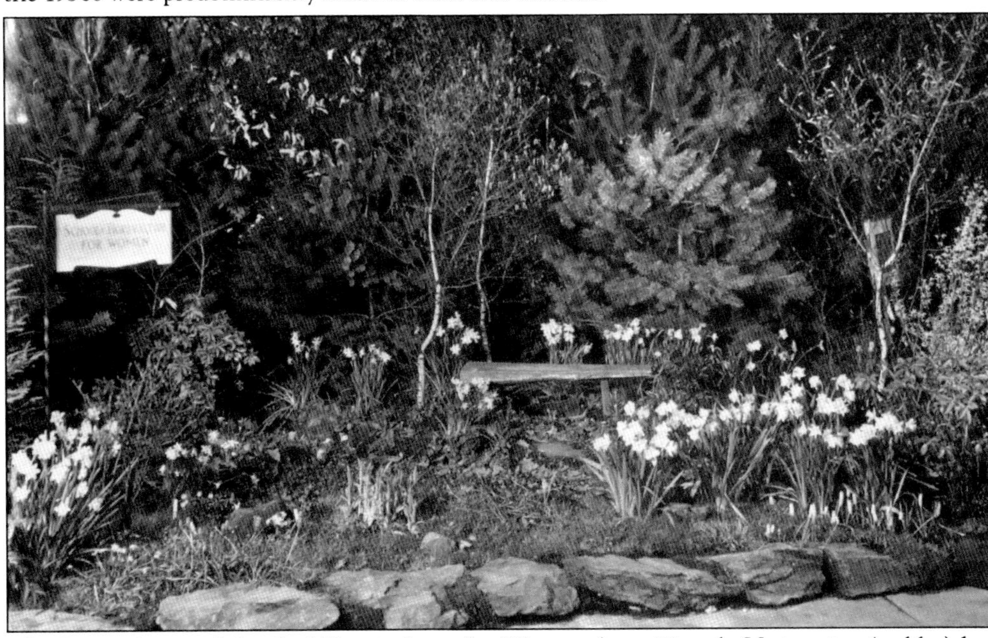

The Pennsylvania School of Horticulture for Women (now Temple University Ambler) has regularly exhibited from the show's days in the Commercial Museum up through the shows of today. Other academic exhibitors have included Delaware Valley College, the University of Delaware, William Saul High School, Abraham Lincoln High School, and the Williamson Free School of Mechanical Trades.

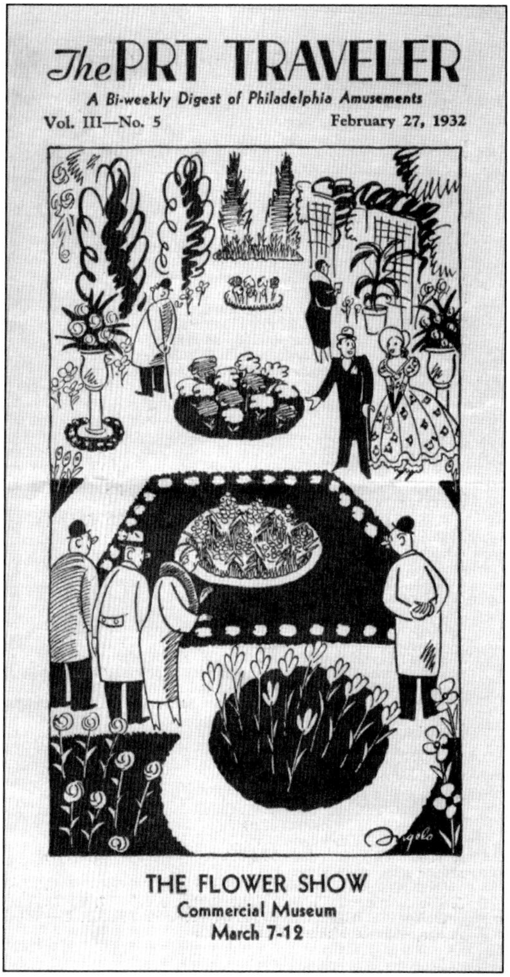

Conveniently sized for pocket or purse, *The PRT Traveler* was a biweekly news leaflet produced by the Philadelphia Rapid Transit Company (a predecessor of today's mass transit system, SEPTA) and placed in transit vehicles and stations throughout the city. The 1935 *PRT Traveler* (pictured below) included tips on how to get to the Philadelphia Flower Show. Visitors had a choice of taking the Market-Frankford EL, one of several bus and trolley routes, or a "Yellow or Quaker Cab (in which five can ride as cheaply as one)." Transporting visitors to the show was and continues to be a priority for SEPTA.

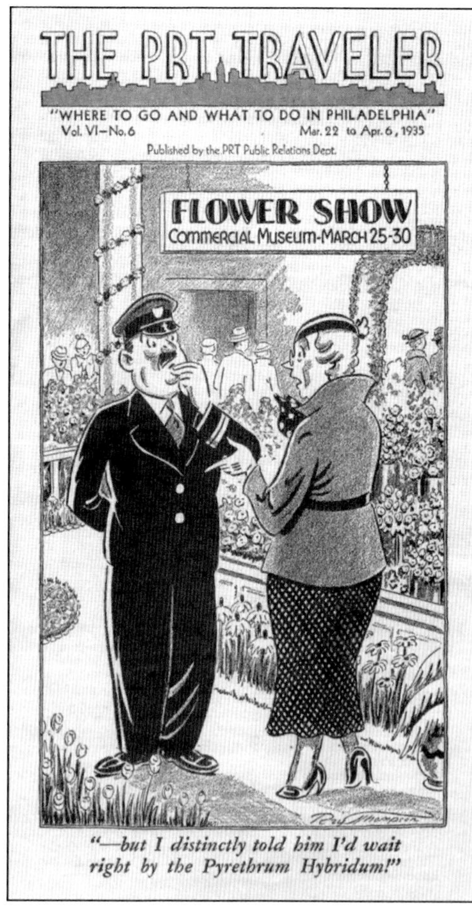

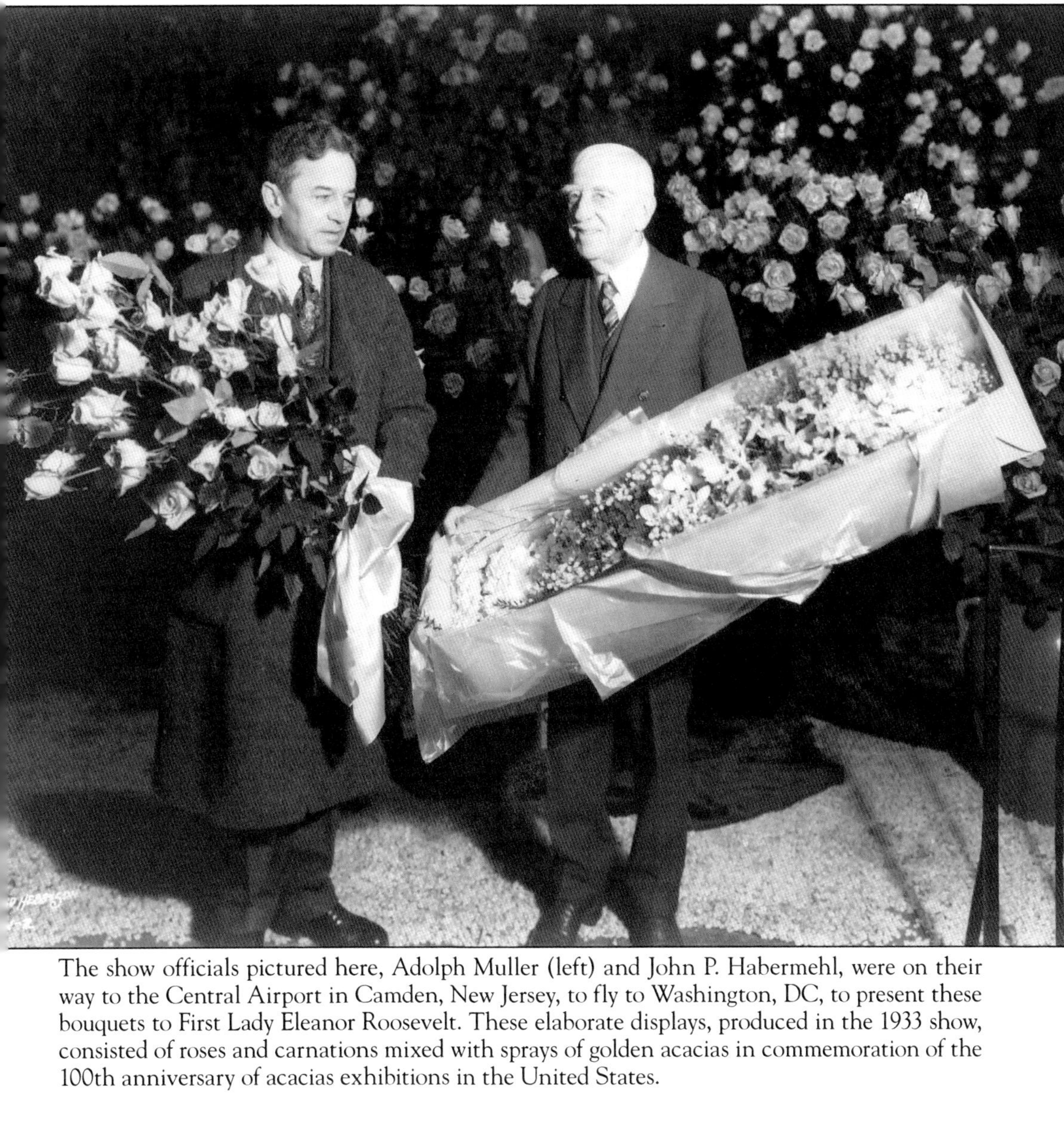

The show officials pictured here, Adolph Muller (left) and John P. Habermehl, were on their way to the Central Airport in Camden, New Jersey, to fly to Washington, DC, to present these bouquets to First Lady Eleanor Roosevelt. These elaborate displays, produced in the 1933 show, consisted of roses and carnations mixed with sprays of golden acacias in commemoration of the 100th anniversary of acacias exhibitions in the United States.

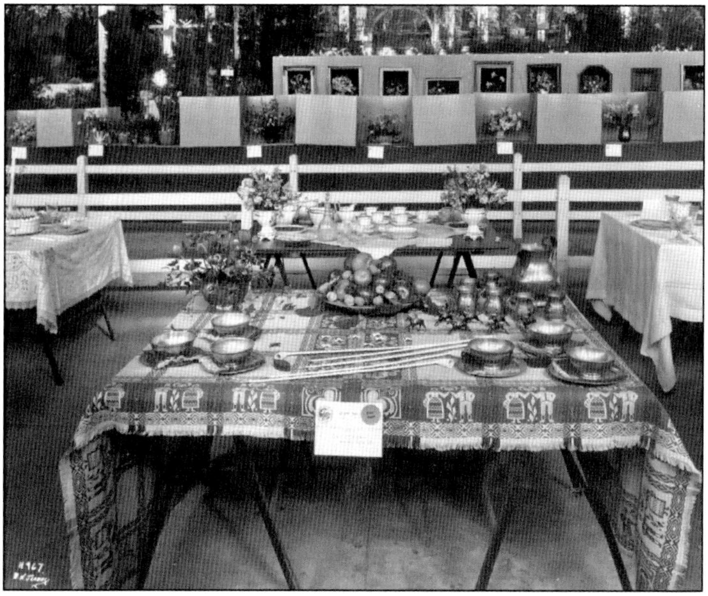

In the 1920s, the competitive and artistic classes were known as the "Women's Classes" or "Women's Club" entries. Starting in 1929, PHS was responsible for organizing this section of the show and created and distributed an exhibitor's schedule completely separate from the schedule for commercial growers. The 1931 entries shown here included table decorations, pressed flowers, and, niches.

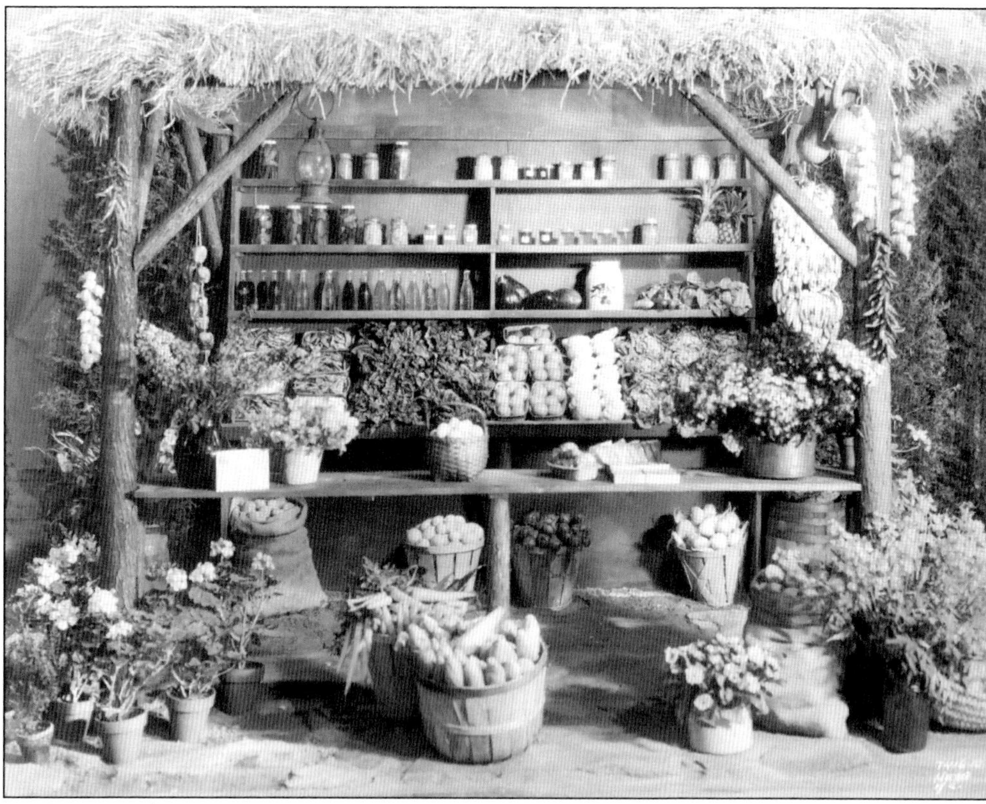

In the 1933 show, six garden clubs competed to create attractive "Wayside Markets"—or farmers' produce stands—in an effort to promote highway beautification. This entry was by The Gardeners garden club. Highway and roadside improvement efforts were a common theme in flower shows from the 1930s through the 1960s, and garden clubs were powerful advocates of beautification projects.

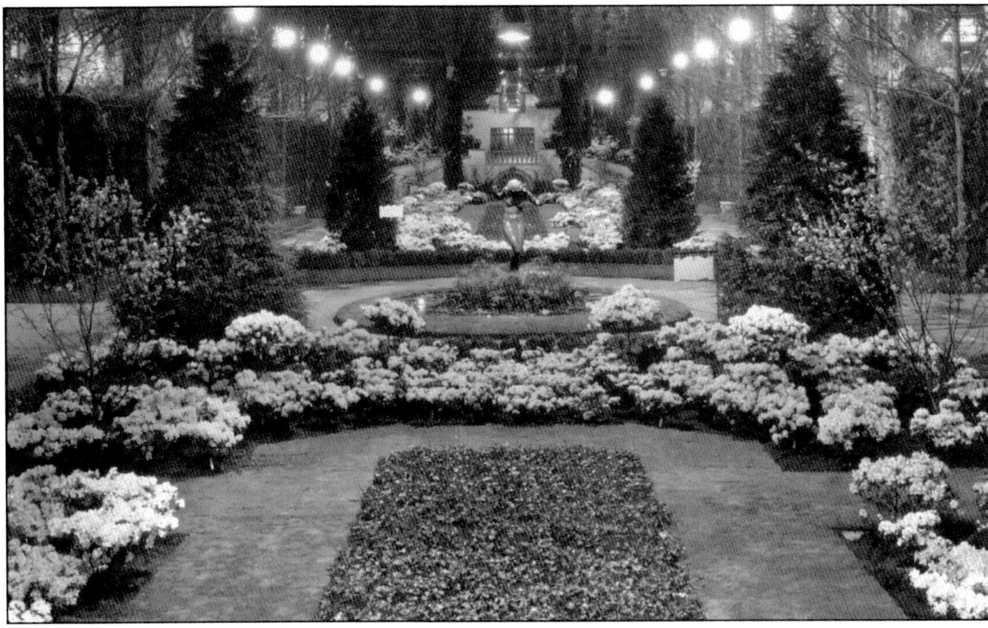

Philadelphia landscape architect Thomas Sears, designer of the 1934 show, was the first designer to use a "central feature," or main exhibit. This feature consisted of a long, linear azalea garden, staged by Bobbink & Atkins, on the main aisle that terminated at a summerhouse. Twin stairways flanked the outside of the house, and visitors were invited to climb the stairs to enjoy the view.

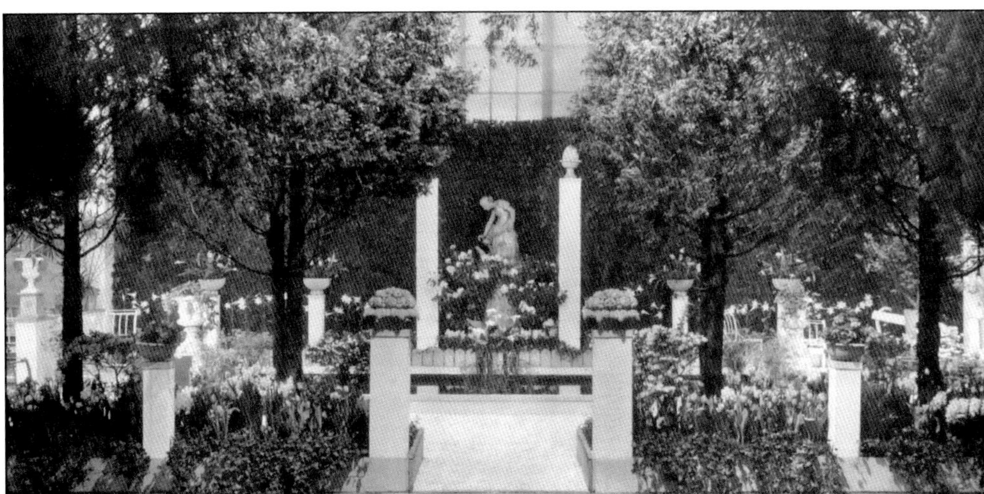

The 1934 PHS exhibit featured an elegant formal garden with a pool and terrace. It was designed and executed by Philadelphia architect Charles Willing. Known for his skills in landscape design, Willing specialized in designing country estates for Philadelphia's elite. He also had his own line of garden ornaments.

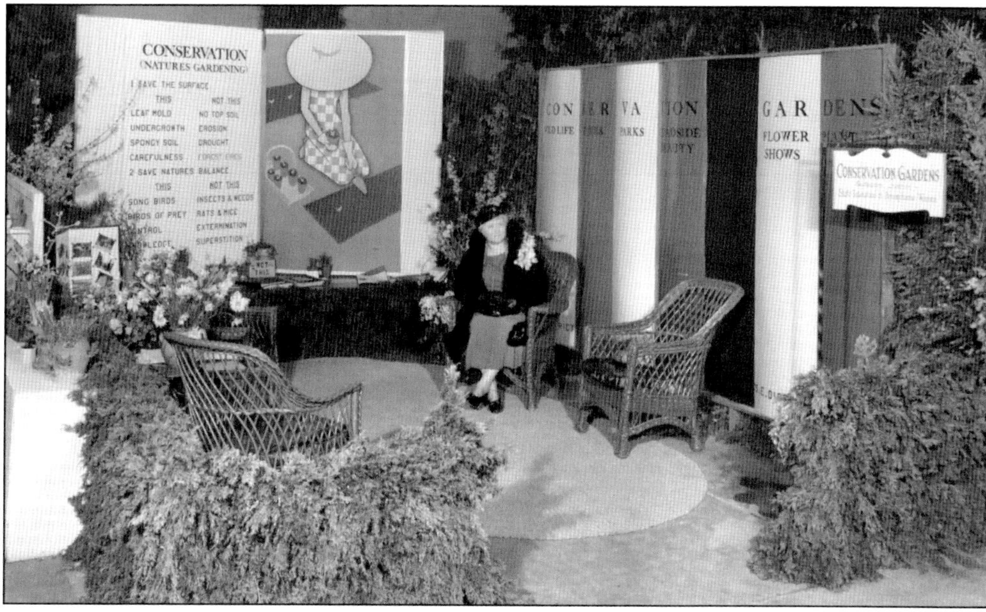

The State Federation of Pennsylvania Women, founded during the Progressive Era in 1895, had a long-standing position as advocates for the preservation of Pennsylvania's forests, wildlife, and parks. This 1935 educational exhibit, titled "Gardener's Open Book," described conservation projects in the areas of wildlife, trees, parks, and roadside beauty through the medium of huge books, which were opened for visitors.

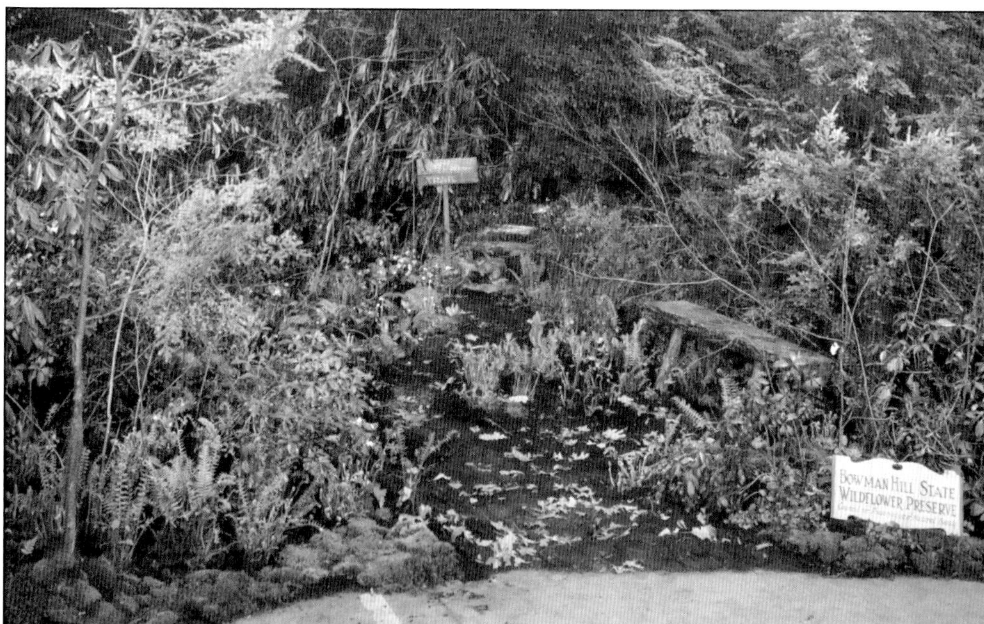

In the 1930s, Bowman's Hill Wildflower Preserve, located in Washington Crossing Park in Bucks County, Pennsylvania, was just getting established. This 1935 exhibit was created by botanist Edgar T. Wherry and Margaret Zantzinger, chair of the Council for the Preservation of Natural Beauty in Pennsylvania. This important wildflower preserve is now home to 800 of the 2,000 plant species native to Pennsylvania.

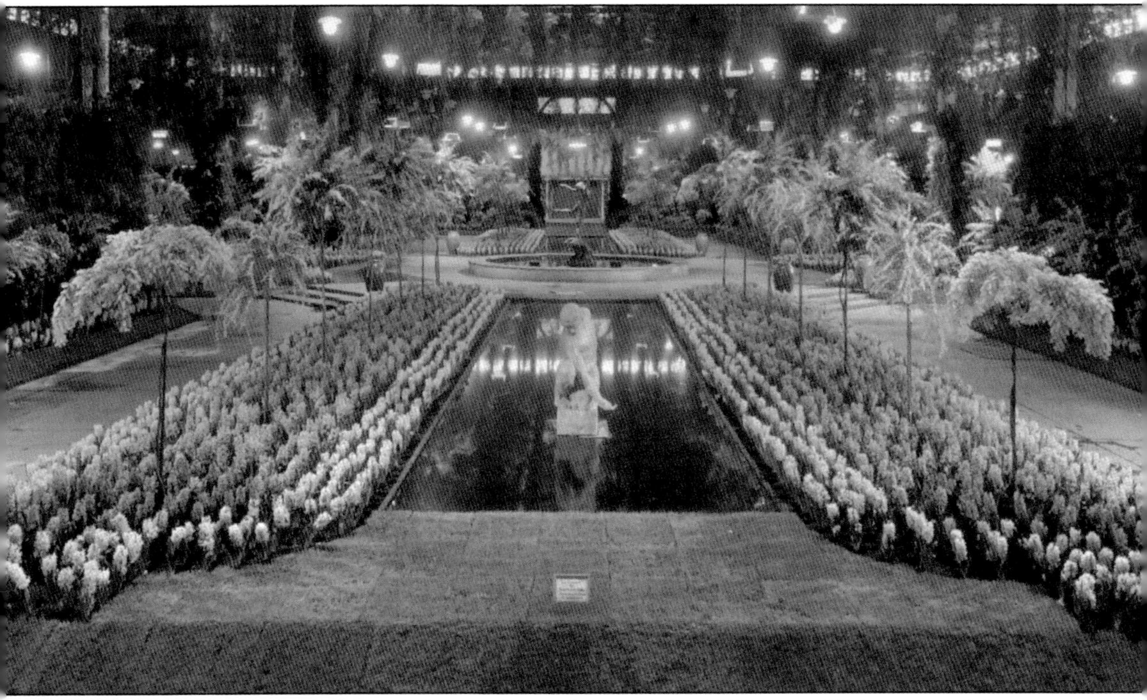

Philadelphia landscape architect Thomas Sears designed the 1935 show. With a central feature of acacias in golden bloom with 20,000 blue hyacinths below them, the show was described in the April 1, 1935, issue of *Horticulture* as the "most distinguished show ever held in Philadelphia." The Joseph E. Widener acacia collection (shown here) was reputed to be the largest in the world. He exhibited them for years—as many as 300 at a time, comprising 25 varieties. In 1941, Widener gave the acacias to the National Gallery of Art at the same time he gave that museum his famous art collection. Head gardener Arthur Hauenstein, who had worked for the Widener family for 40 years, was said to have wept as the trucks of acacias rolled down the driveway.

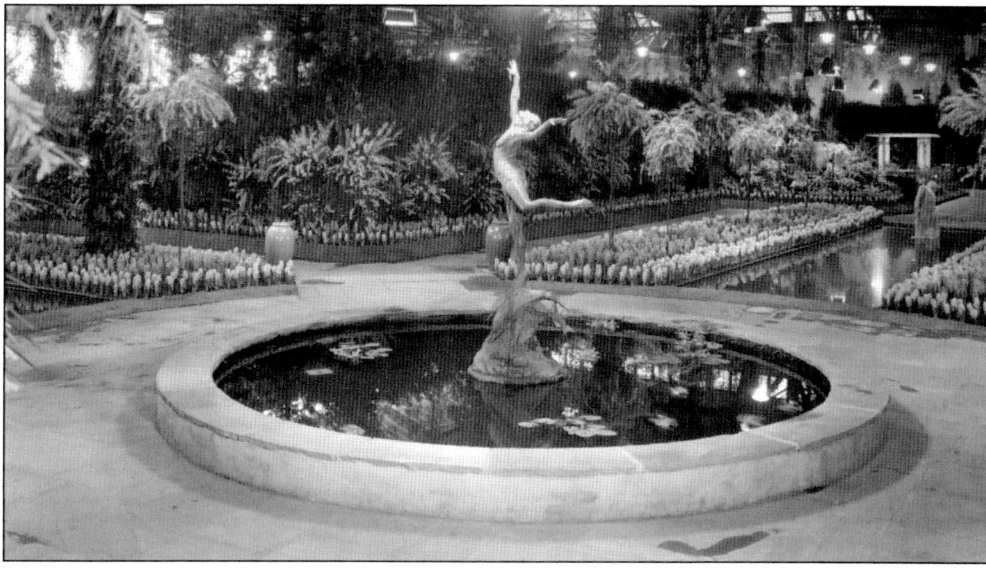

Beatrice Fenton's *Nereid* fountain was the centerpiece of the main exhibit of the 1935 show. Fenton was a well-known Philadelphia sculptor who specialized in figures, often of children and animals. Fenton's *Nereid* reappeared in the 1977 show with her *Seaweed Girl* sculpture before they were moved to their current home at the Horticulture Center in Fairmount Park.

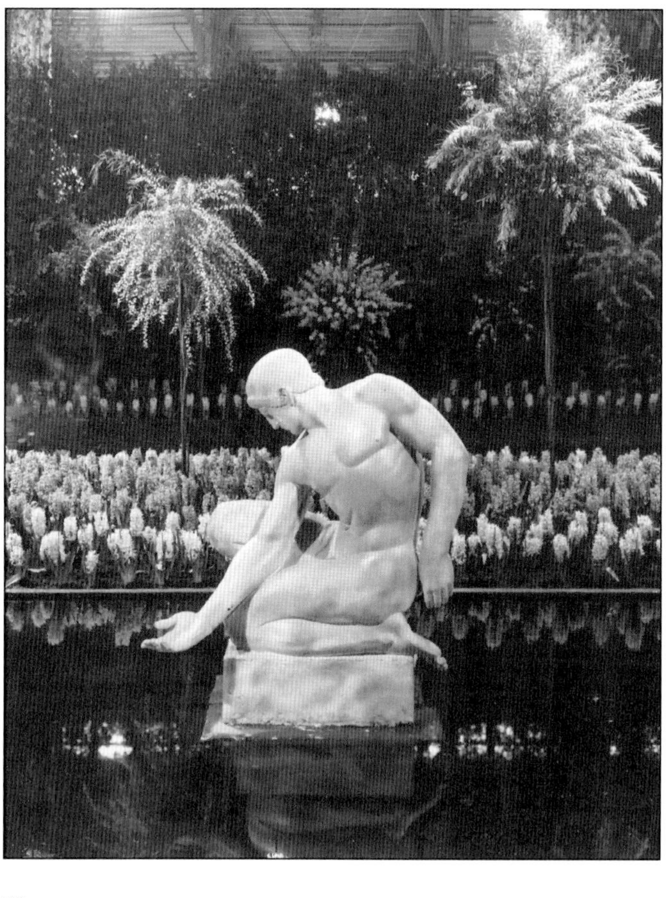

The 1935 show included several stunning garden sculptures, including *La Source* by Harrison Gibbs. Gibbs graduated from the Pennsylvania Academy of the Fine Arts and exhibited his works there as well as at the Philadelphia Museum of Art, the American Academy in Rome, and the 1939 New York World's Fair. Gibbs was killed in 1944 in World War II. (Courtesy Ramona Harrison Gibbs.)

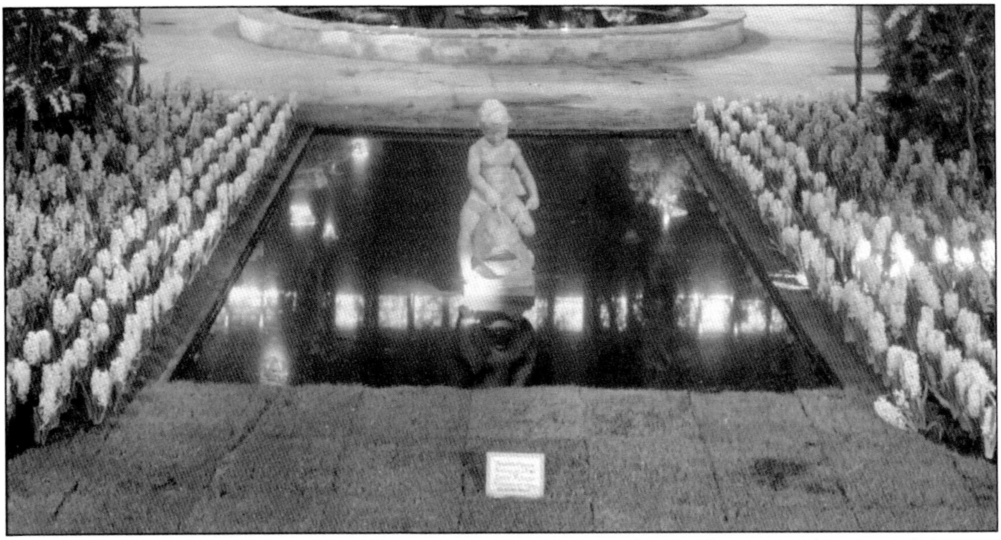

Fountain Figure Riding on a Fish, by Louis Milione, was another sculpture in the central feature of the 1935 show. Born in Padua, Italy, Milione studied sculpture at the Pennsylvania Academy of the Fine Arts and exhibited regularly there. In addition to teaching at Philadelphia's School of Industrial Art (now the University of the Arts), he completed several architectural sculpture commissions in Philadelphia and elsewhere.

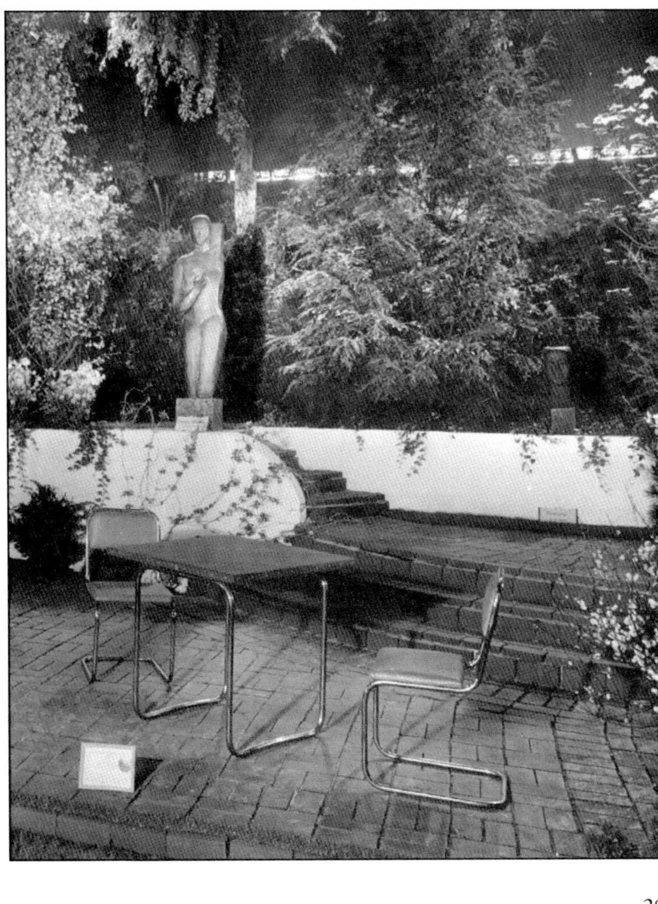

This 1936 exhibit featured sculptor Ossip Zadkine's *Pomone* set in a garden terrace. A Russian artist who spent most of his life in Paris, Zadkine was best known for his cubist-inspired sculptures. He was awarded the grand prize for sculpture at the 1950 Venice Biennale, and many of his works can be seen today at the Zadkine Museum in Paris.

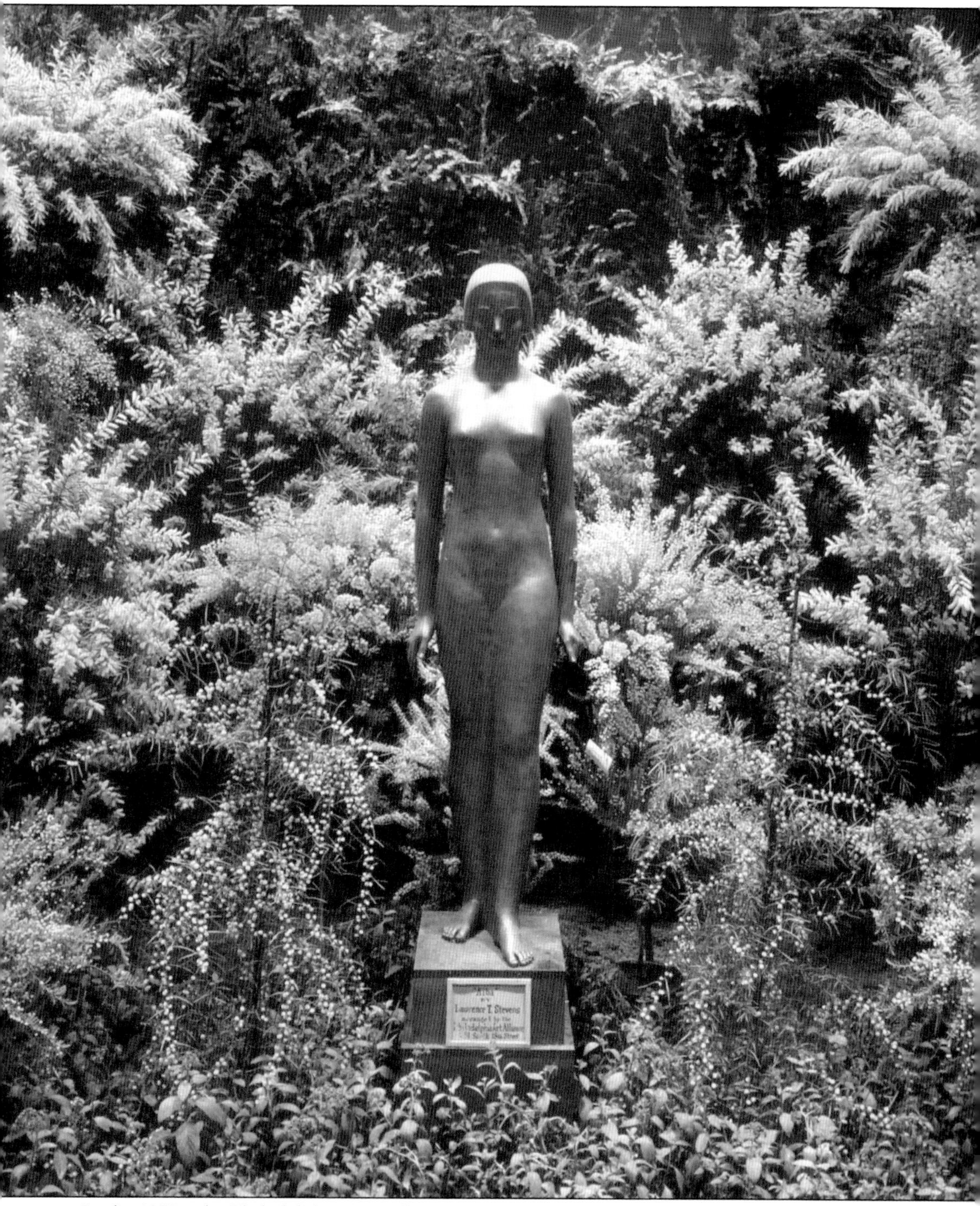

In the 1930s, the Philadelphia Art Alliance organized sculpture shows at the Philadelphia Flower Show. In 1936, *Alba*, a 64-inch-tall bronze work by Lawrence Tenney Stevens, was staged in the Widener acacia collection. Stevens is best known for his work in the American West, including his architectural sculpture at the Centennial Fairgrounds for the 1936 Texas Centennial Exposition in Dallas.

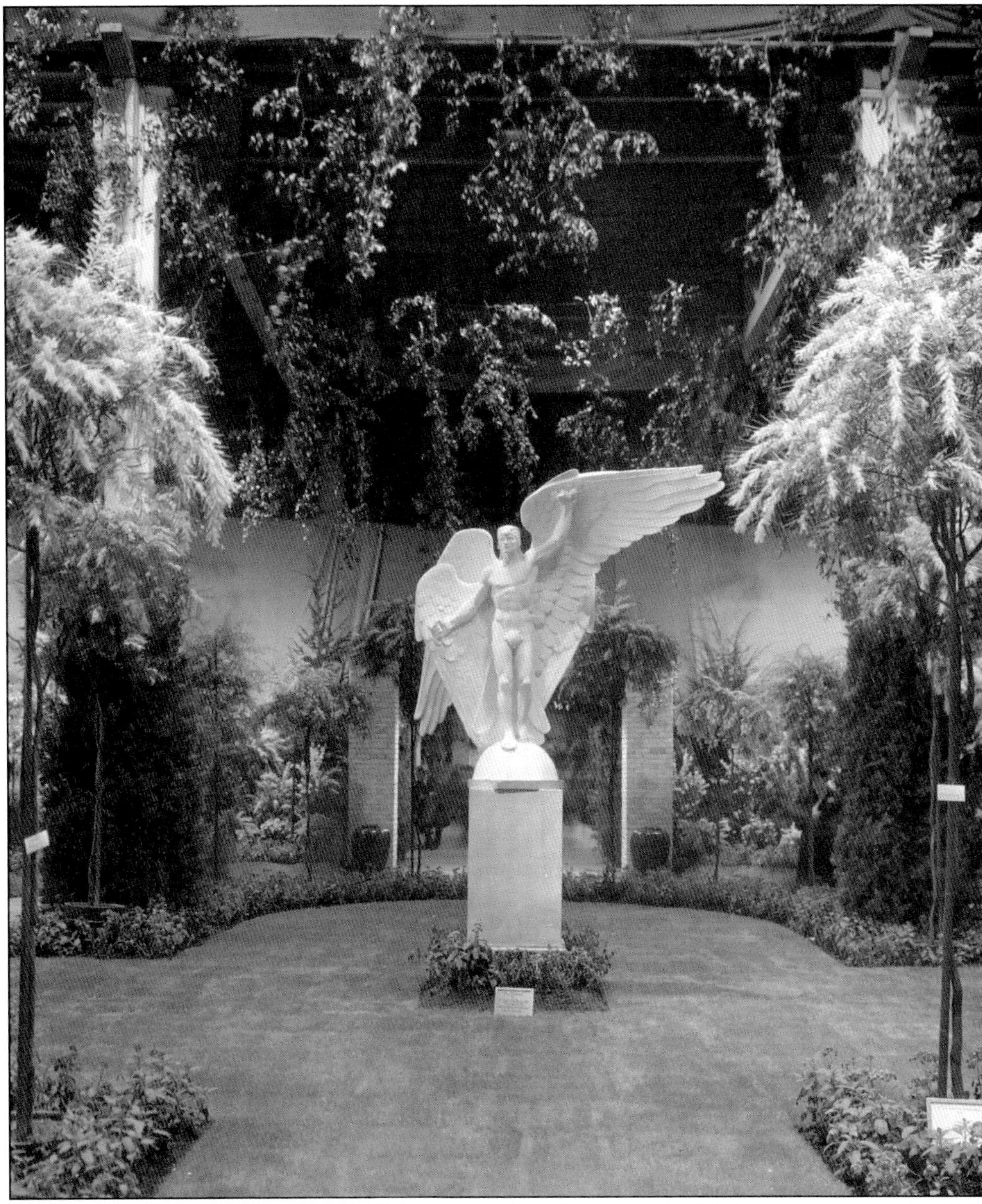

Robert Tait McKenzie's work, *The Falcon*, was placed among the Widener acacias at the 1936 show. McKenzie was a Canadian sculptor, doctor, teacher, and athlete. He taught at the University of Pennsylvania and was a strong proponent of physical education. His most well-known public artwork, *The Boy Scout*, was installed near Philadelphia's Benjamin Franklin Parkway.

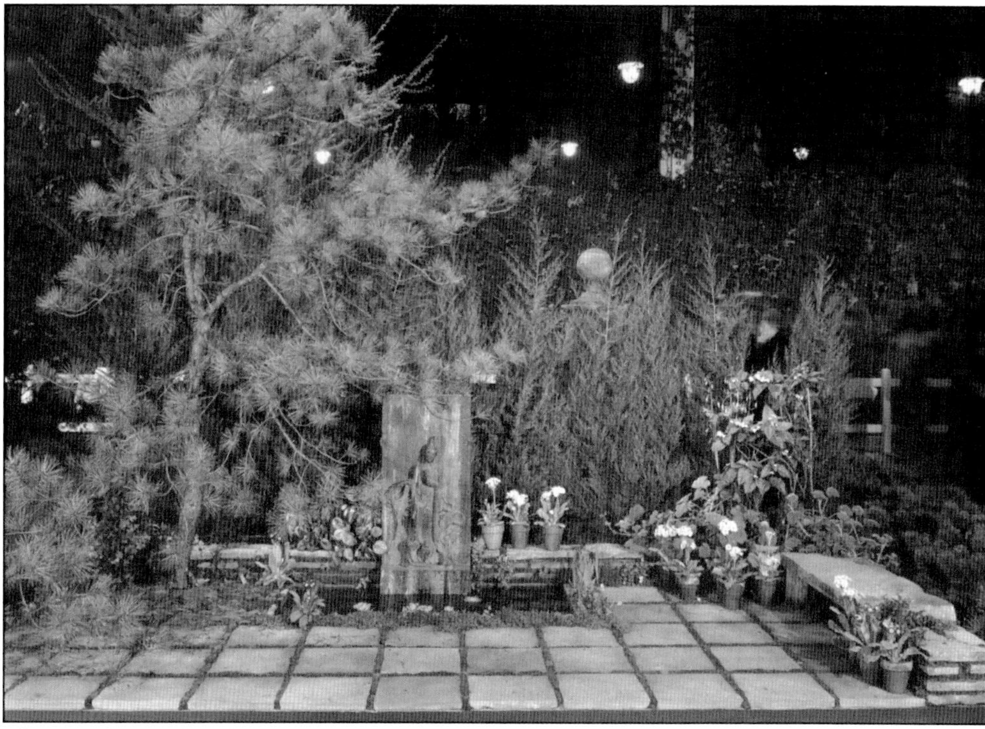

The Weeders garden club captured first prize in the 1936 garden class. This simple and charming entry with a small pool, a tall pine tree, and potted primulas was complemented by a stone figure, *Kaan Yin*, a Buddhist goddess of compassion and kindness.

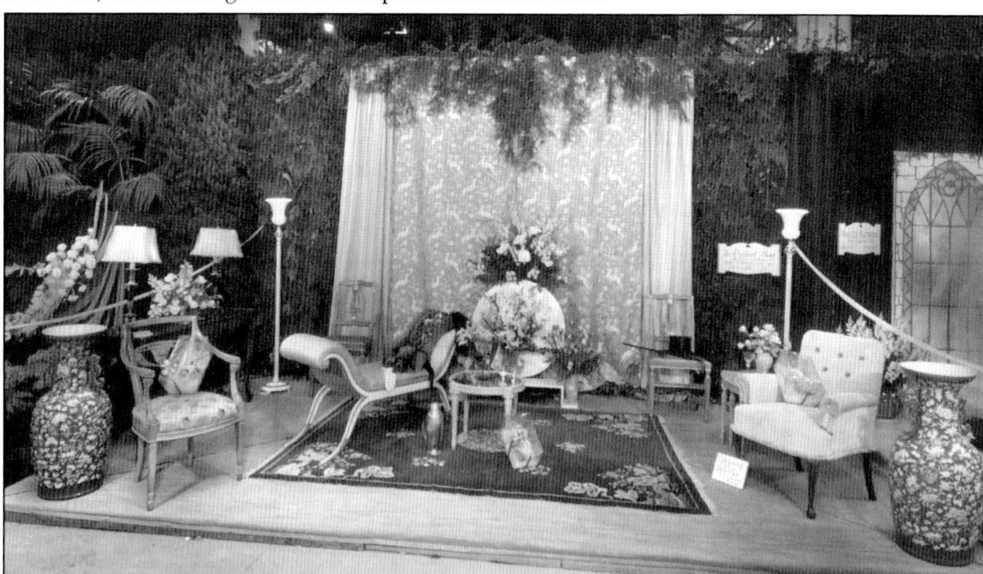

Young florists were invited to exhibit in the 1938 show. This eye-catching display featured the talents of Miss "Steve" Stephenson, owner of The Orchid Shop at 1633 Chancellor Street in Philadelphia, which was in business well into the 1950s. Stephenson staged her arrangements in a sitting room with furnishings courtesy of Sanford H. Kean, an interior decorator from the Warwick Hotel.

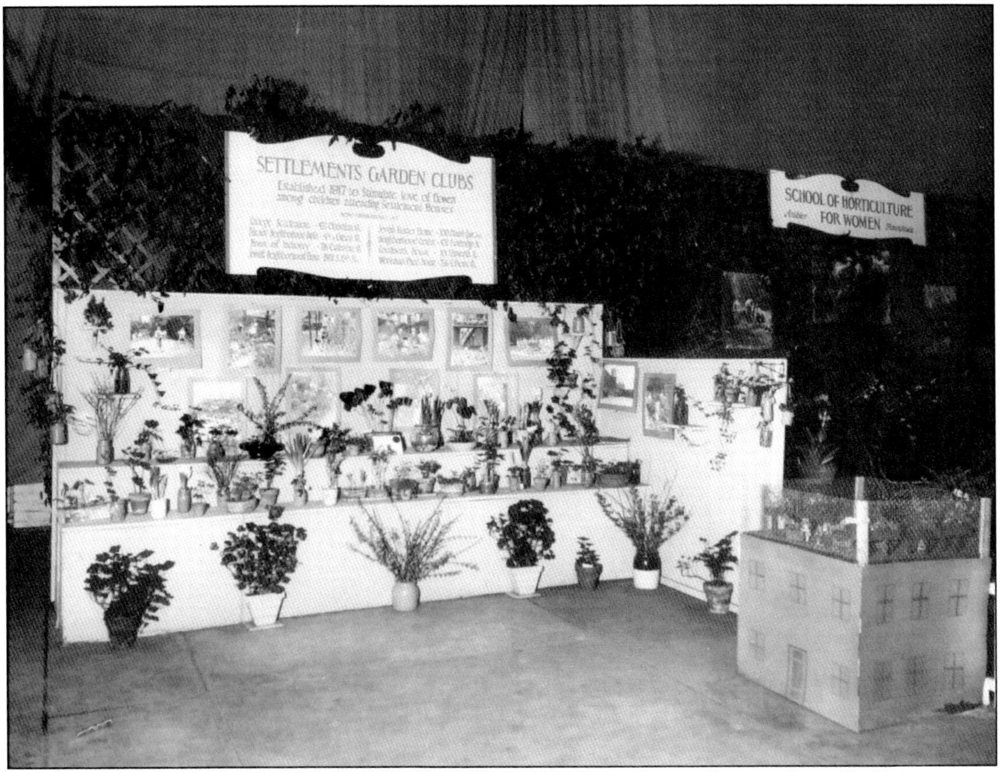

The Settlements Garden Clubs often exhibited in the shows of the 1920s and 1930s. These clubs were formed in 1917 "to stimulate love of flowers among children attending settlement houses." Settlement houses were located in poor urban neighborhoods and offered services to new immigrants. The settlement houses provided social, cultural, and educational programs for young mothers and children. These exhibits were created entirely by children.

The F.A. Bartlett Tree Expert Company regularly exhibited in shows from the 1930s through the 1950s as well as in recent years. Bartlett Tree Experts has always stressed the importance of educating the public about proper tree care, as shown in this 1939 exhibit. Bartlett has generously sponsored past PHS exhibits and regularly holds tree care seminars at the Philadelphia Flower Show.

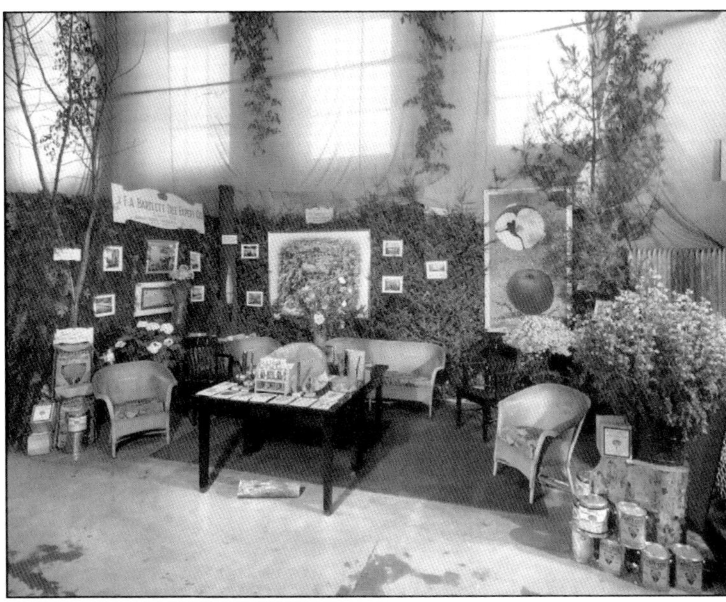

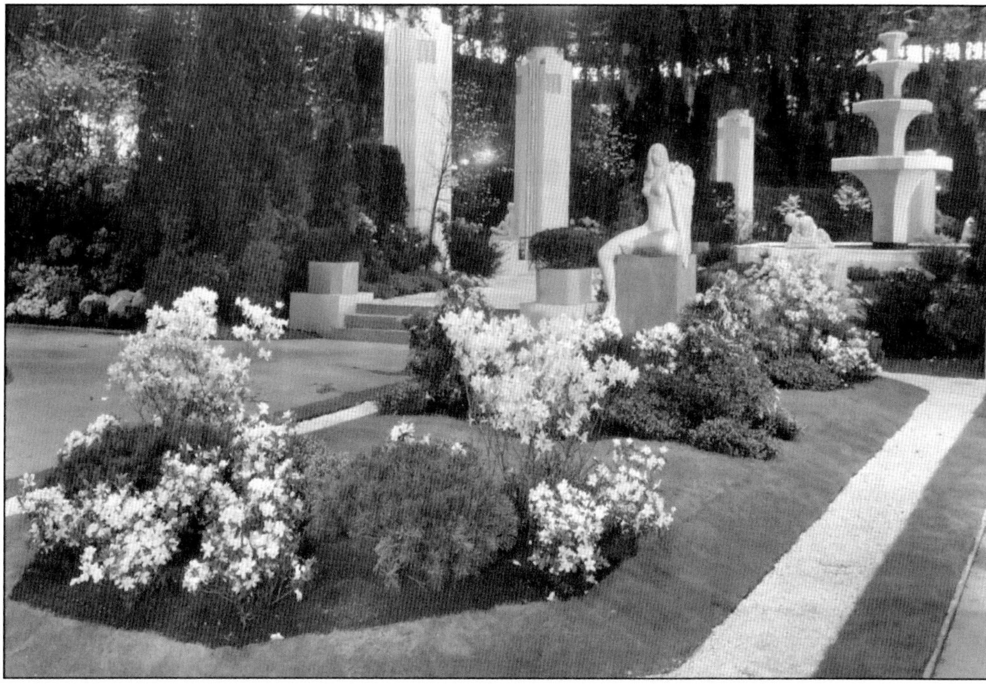

The theme of the 1939 show was "The World of Tomorrow"—a nod to the New York World's Fair. The modern central feature was designed by Walter Van Den Hengel, who also designed the Glendinning Rock Garden in Fairmount Park. Van Den Hengel was a talented artist who studied painting at the Pennsylvania Academy of the Fine Arts.

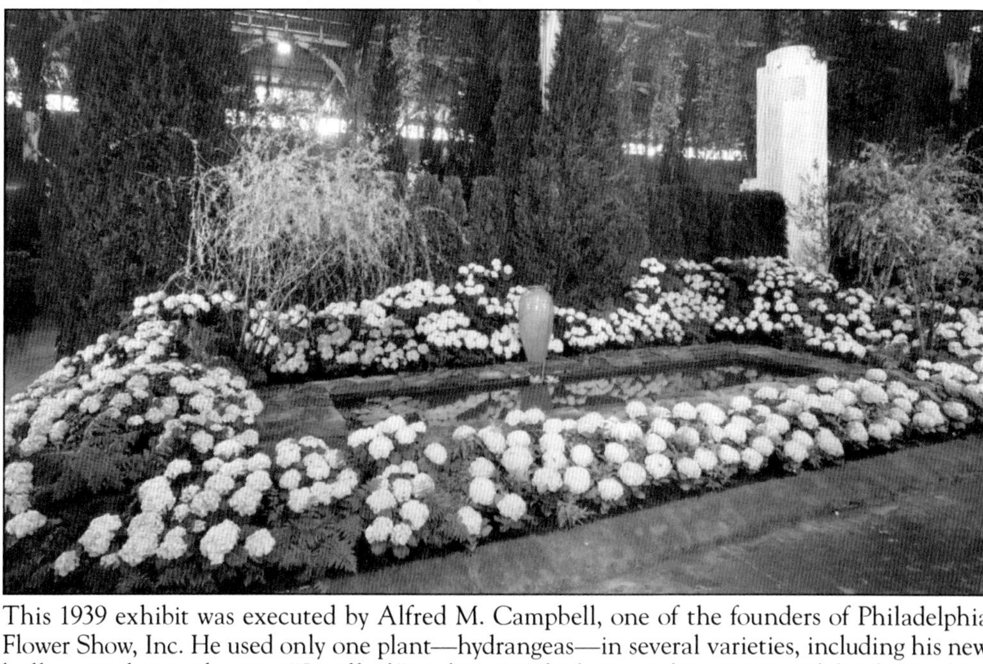

This 1939 exhibit was executed by Alfred M. Campbell, one of the founders of Philadelphia Flower Show, Inc. He used only one plant—hydrangeas—in several varieties, including his new brilliant pink introduction, "Strafford," and a mix of other popular varieties of the day, such as "Madame Emile Mouilliére," "Europa," "Deutschland," and "Merveille." Each year, show visitors eagerly awaited the Campbell hydrangea displays.

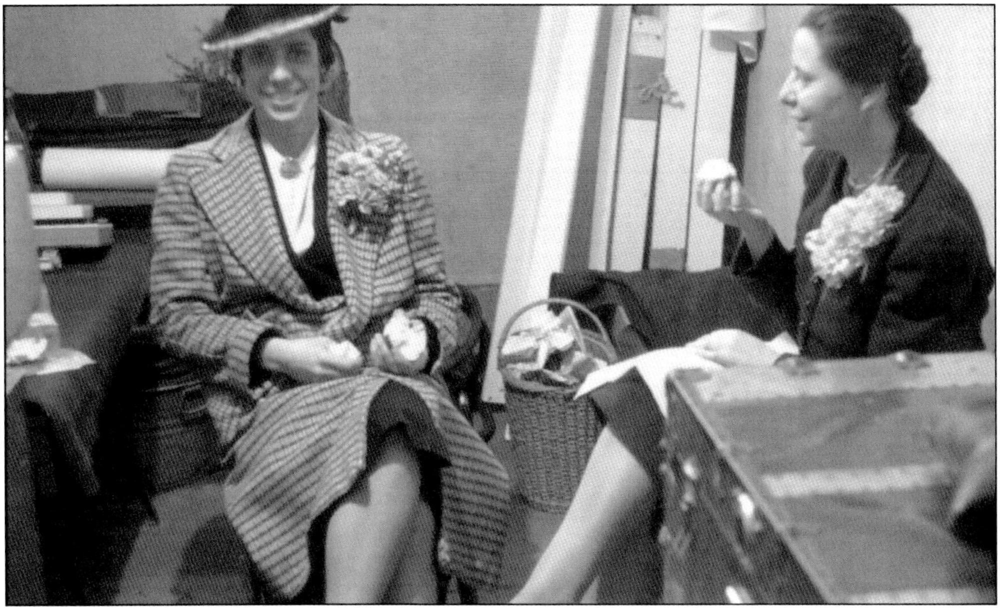

Here, Anne Wertsner Wood (left) and Maria Samuel take a break at the 1941 show. Wood, a graduate of the Pennsylvania School of Horticulture for Women (now Temple University Ambler), joined the PHS staff in 1937. She staged the Philadelphia Flower Show, as well as the Victory Garden shows, during the World War II years, and she wrote *The Flower-Show Guide*, a definitive book on producing shows.

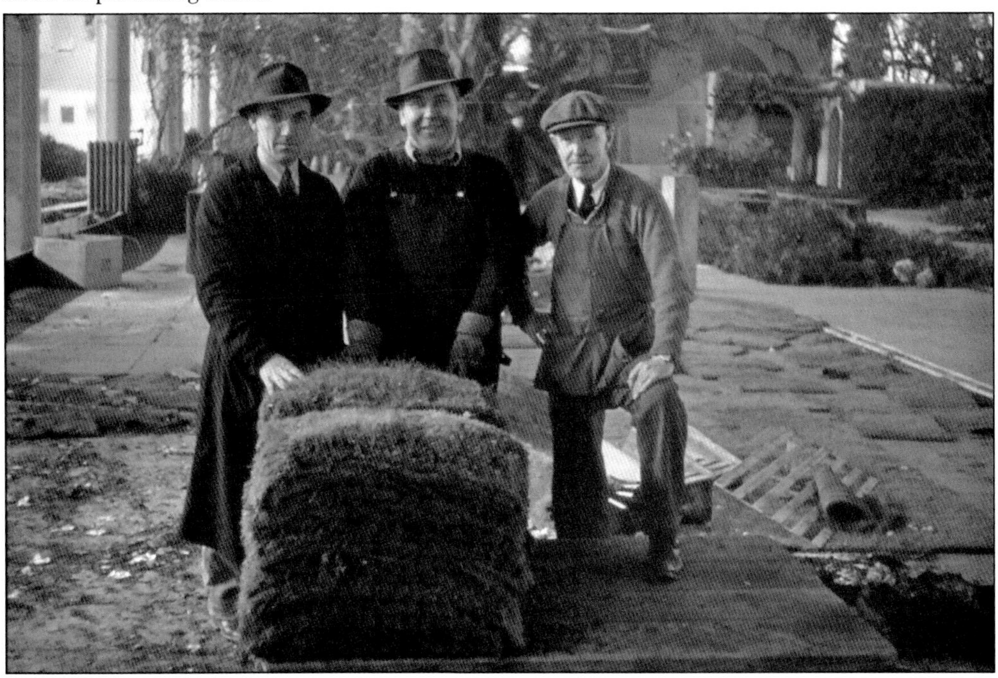

J.J. Habermehl Florists handled all of the decorations for shows held in the Commercial Museum. This crew from the 1941 show put up drapery, hung smilax and decorations from the ceiling, installed evergreen screens as back walls for the exhibits, and put down sod tiles. No show could run efficiently without "Habermehl's Men."

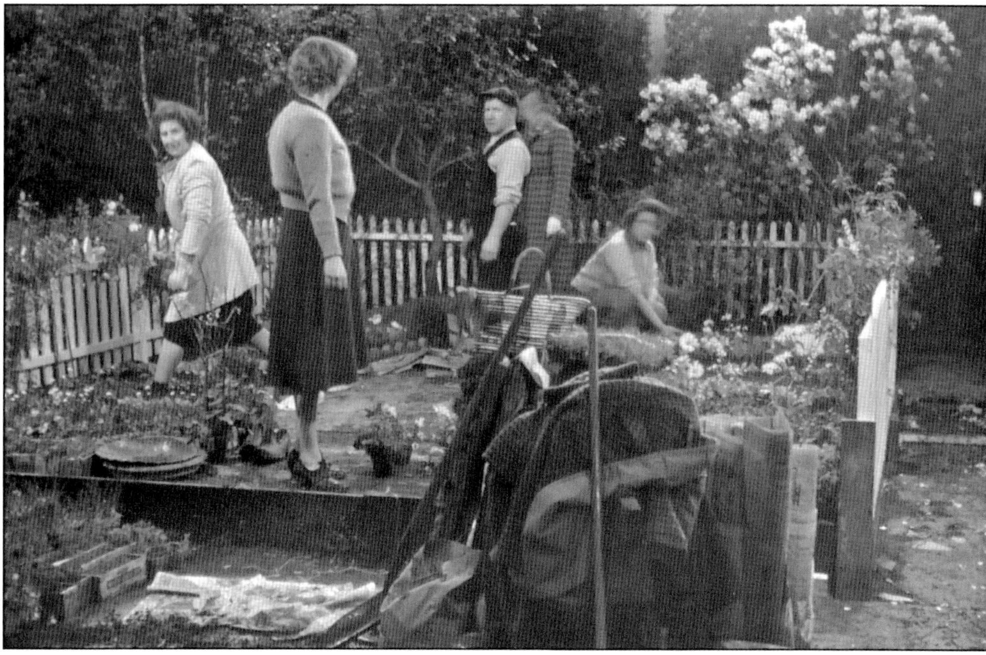

Garden clubs created cottage gardens of flowers and vegetable plots to represent wartime Victory Gardens at the 1941 show. Here, members of the Norristown Garden Club install their exhibit, which won first prize in this class. This exhibit's plants included blueberries, raspberries, flowers, radishes, peppers, and an edging of strawberries, all enclosed in a brown picket fence with a green gate.

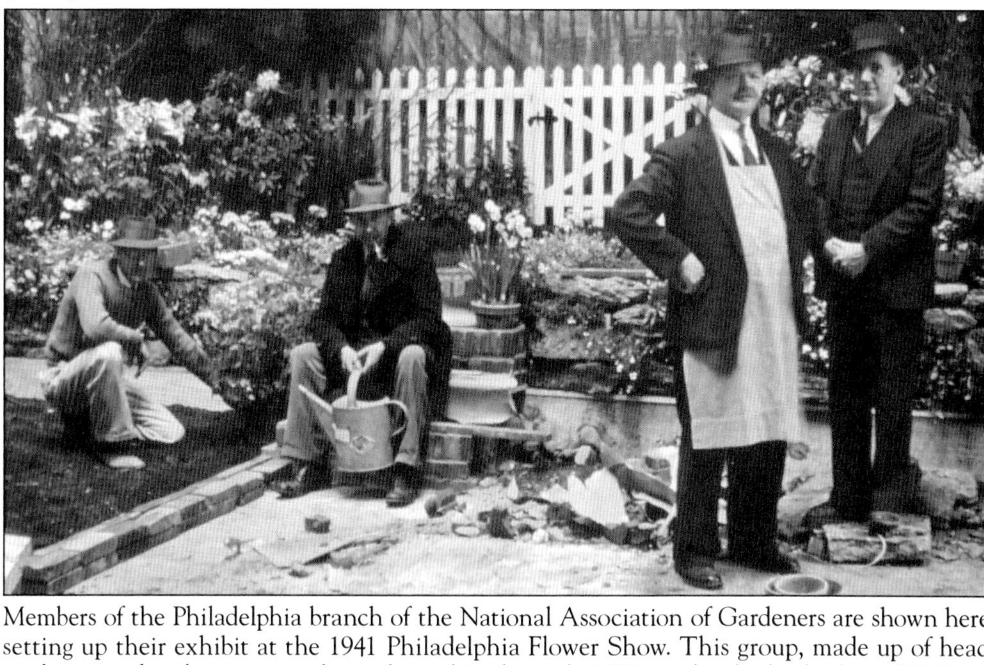

Members of the Philadelphia branch of the National Association of Gardeners are shown here setting up their exhibit at the 1941 Philadelphia Flower Show. This group, made up of head gardeners and park superintendents, formed in the early 1900s under the leadership of William Kleinheinz, superintendent of the Joseph E. Widener estate in Elkins Park, Pennsylvania, and, for many years, a key organizer of the Flower Show.

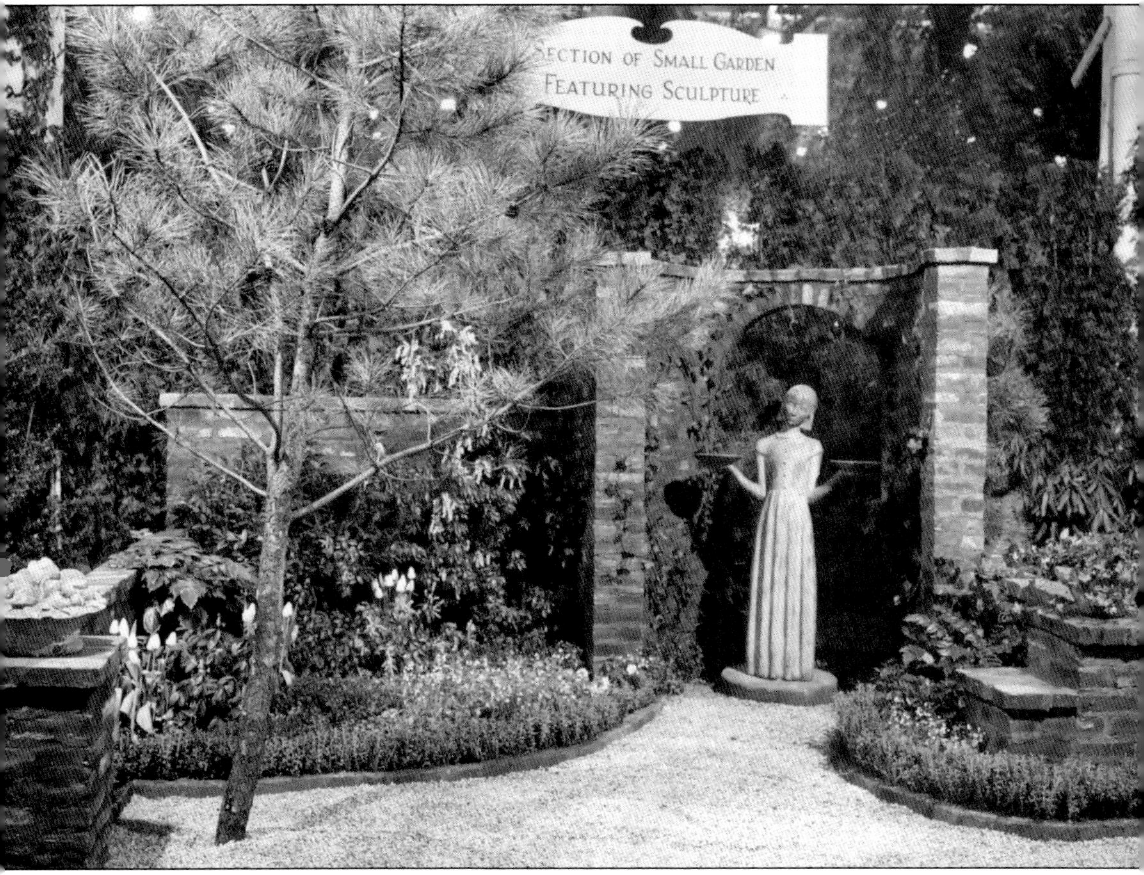

This sculpture, *Bird Girl*, was created in 1936 by Sylvia Shaw Judson, who made four bronze statues from one plaster cast. One sculpture appeared in this 1941 exhibit, and another was placed in Bonaventure Cemetery in Savannah, Georgia. The Savannah sculpture eventually appeared on the cover of John Berendt's 1994 bestselling book *Midnight in the Garden of Good and Evil.* Fans of the book flocked to Savannah to pay homage to *Bird Girl,* but 1941 show visitors admired her before she was "discovered."

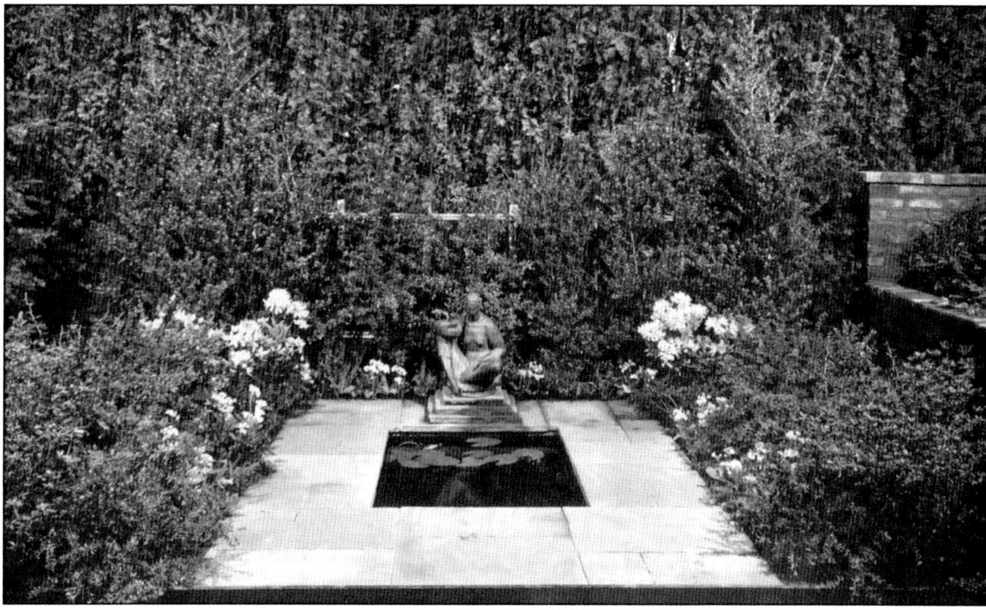

In the 1941 Philadelphia Flower Show, Ramon Bermudez's work *Seated Woman* was awarded second prize by a jury from the Pennsylvania Academy of the Fine Arts. The judges also commended the serene, restrained formality of the garden setting, executed by the Wissahickon Garden Club. Bermudez, born in the Philippines, spent much of his professional career in the exhibition department of New York's American Museum of Natural History.

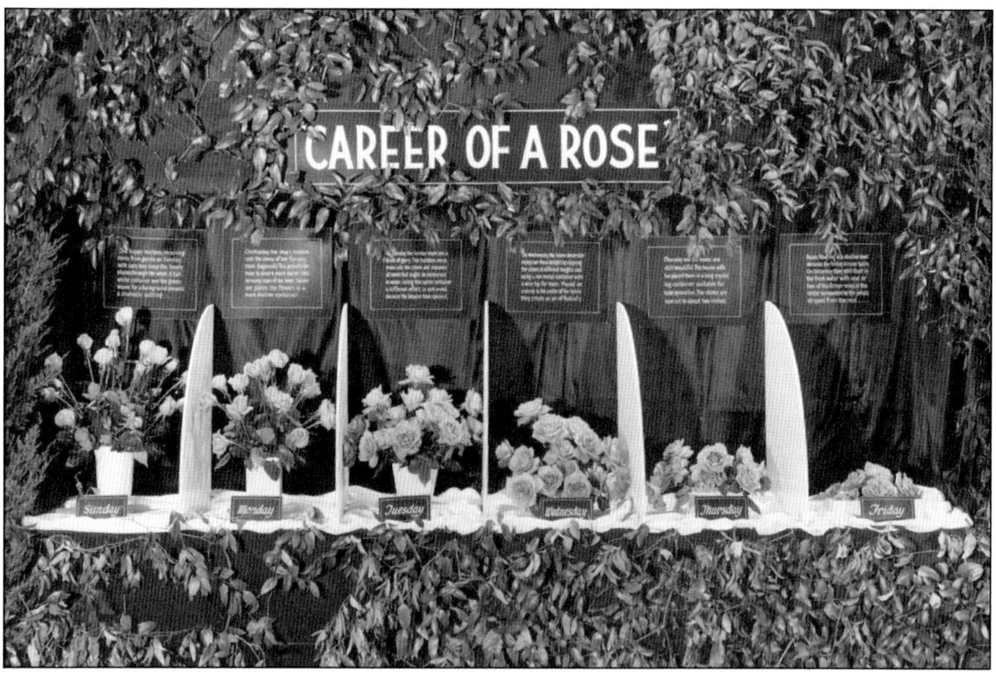

In this popular 1942 exhibit, signs and arrangements traced the life of a rose from Sunday, when the hostess received a bouquet of roses from her guests, through Friday and Saturday, when the remaining roses were floated in a shallow bowl to decorate the dinner table. The exhibitor was Roses, Inc., with arrangements created by Philadelphia's Pennock Brothers Florists.

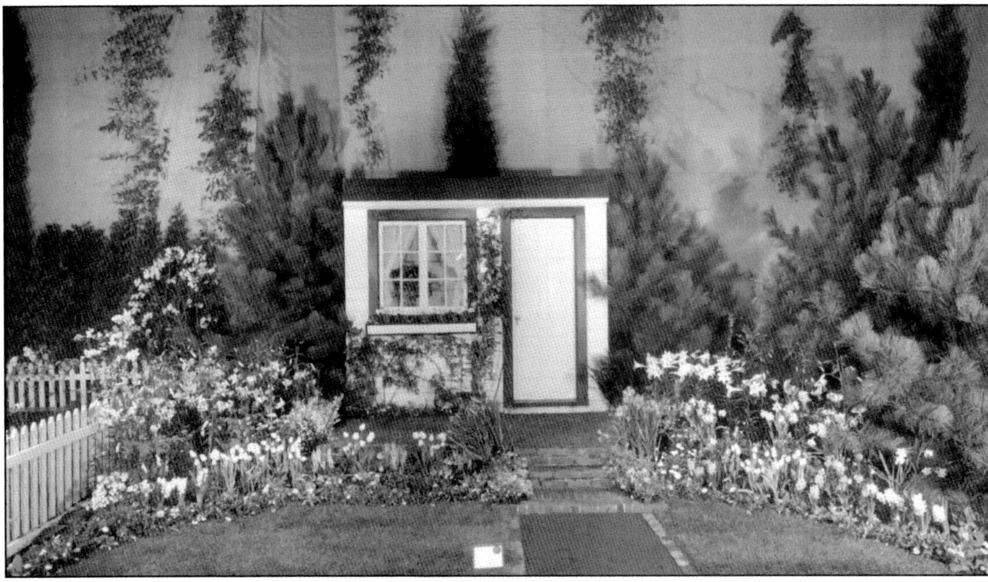

The bulbs featured in this 1942 exhibit were grown on American soil. During World War II, no bulbs were imported from Europe. This wartime trade embargo was also in effect for *Lilium longiflorum*, a mainstay in Easter floral arrangements; these lily bulbs came from Japan. In the war years, the Easter lily was replaced by domestically grown potted hydrangeas, azaleas, roses, and spring bulbs.

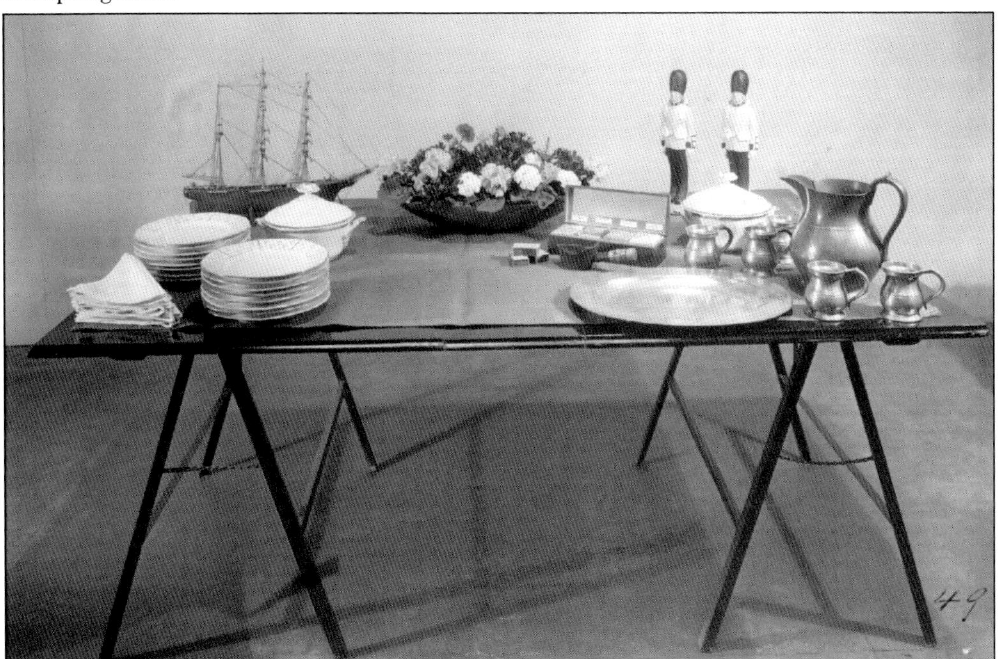

The theme of this 1942 table class was "Morale Contributes to Victory. Flowers Contribute to Morale." Exhibitors were asked to create a buffet supper table set for entertaining men in the service. This winning exhibit featured red and white geraniums flanked by toy soldiers and a model sailing vessel, along with dishes, a tray, pitchers, mugs, and (sign of the times) a cigarette box and a Chinese ashtray.

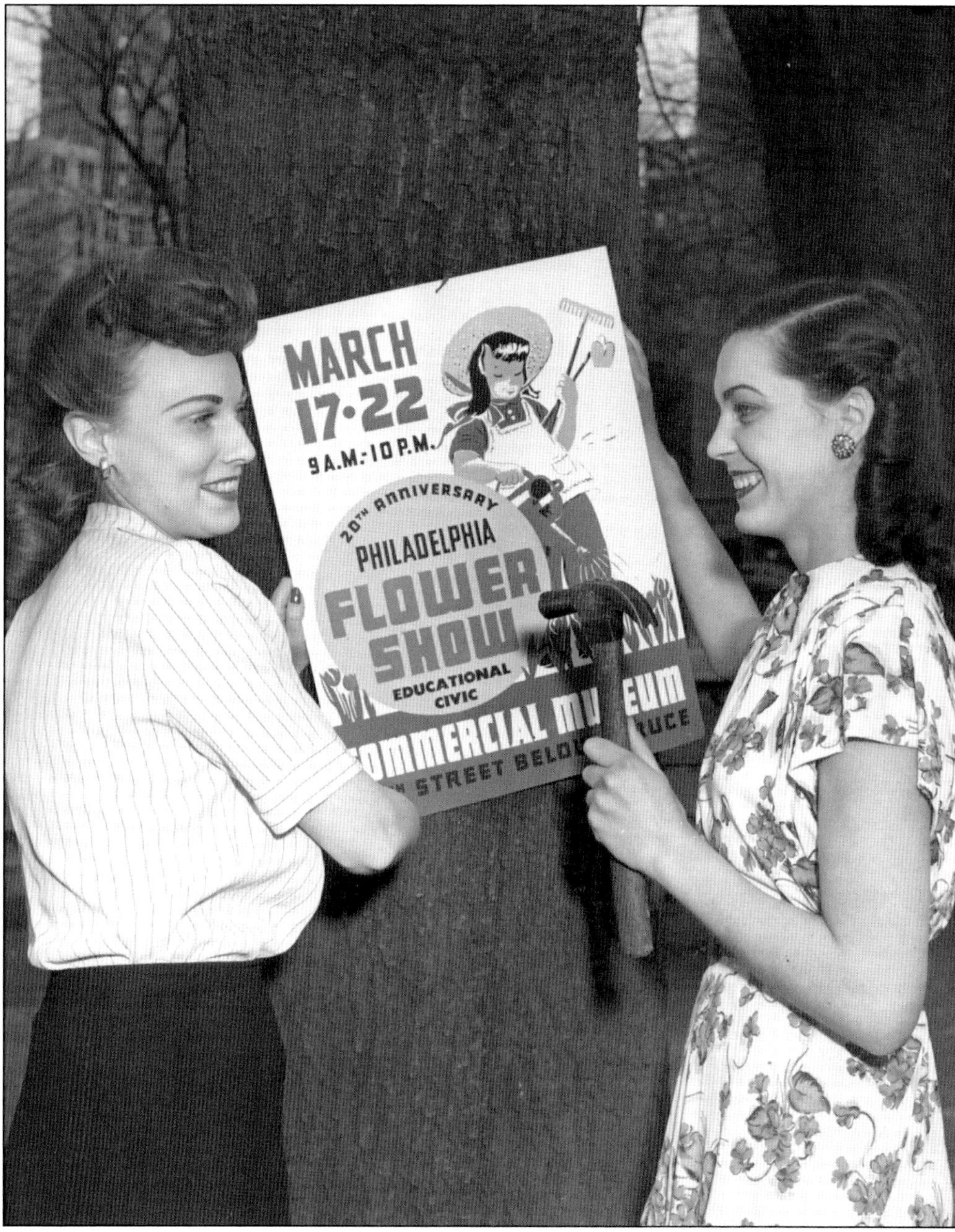

During the war years, flowers were luxuries. While flowers continued to be used for weddings, birthday celebrations, and funerals, the number and variety diminished, and the floral trades suffered. The Philadelphia Flower Show was not held from 1943 to 1946. By the time of this 1947 photograph, Philadelphians, starved for peace and beauty, were eager to once again attend the Flower Show.

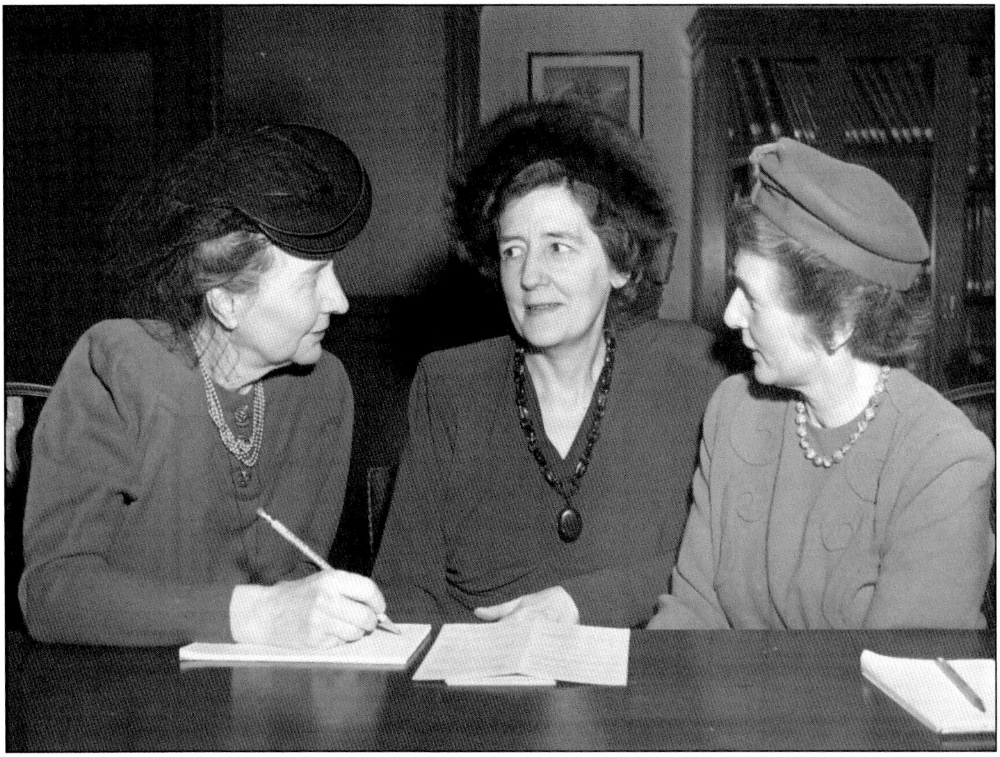

PHS's Philadelphia Flower Show committee members, referred to as the Women's Committee, met at PHS headquarters to plan the competitive classes of the 1947 show. Pictured here are, from left to right, Mrs. J. Gibson McIlvain, chair of exhibits; Mrs. Homer Reed, vice chair of the schedule committee; and Mrs. G. Ruhland Rebmann Jr., chair of the schedule committee.

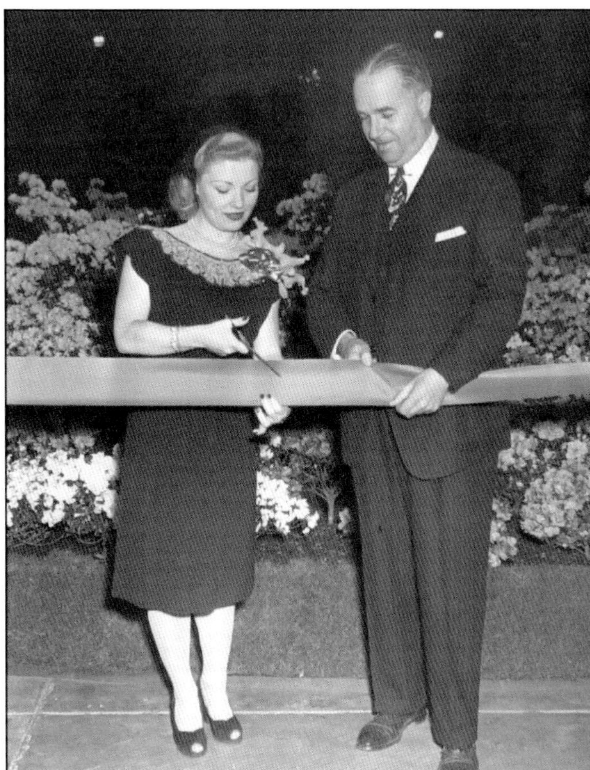

From the 1920s to the early 1960s, Flower Show official W. Atlee Burpee Jr. was the public face of the show, officiating at every ribbon-cutting ceremony; Burpee (right) is shown here opening the 1947 show with champion skater Eileen Seigh. Spring flower shows were perfect vehicles for seed businesses to promote their latest novelties to a winter-weary public.

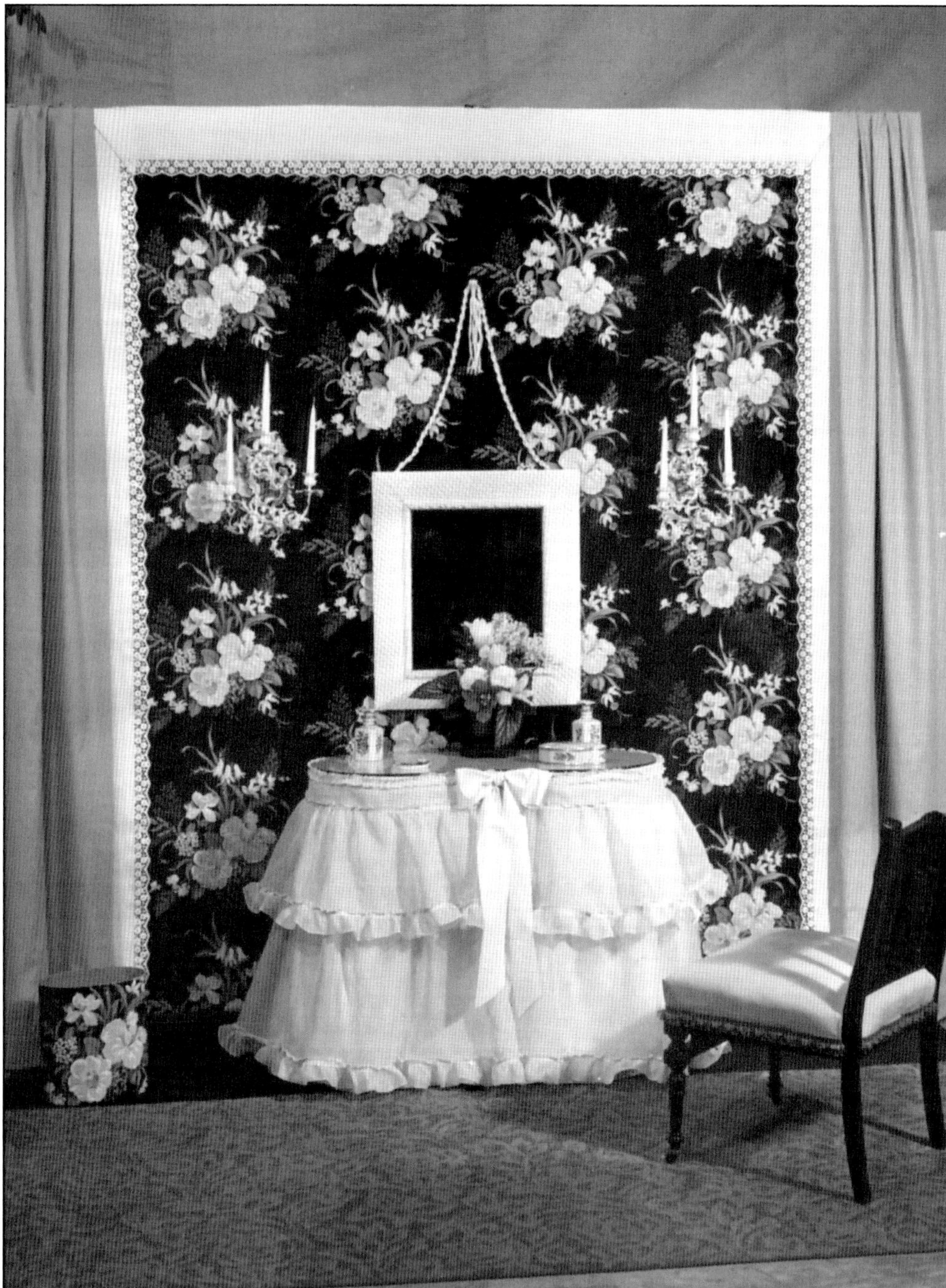

In an entry reflecting au courant decorating trends in 1947, competitors were asked to integrate plants, wallpaper, fabric, and furniture "stressing economy and ingenuity." The Valley Garden Club won a blue ribbon (first place) for this room entry. At that time, competitors were given one hour to stage their artistic class exhibits.

New Jersey governor Alfred E. Driscoll toured the 1948 show and examined the Blue Star Memorial Highway marker, a tribute to those who served in World War II. The Blue Star Memorial Program started in New Jersey and was adopted by the National Council of State Garden Clubs, which arranged to have markers placed throughout the highway system in the United States.

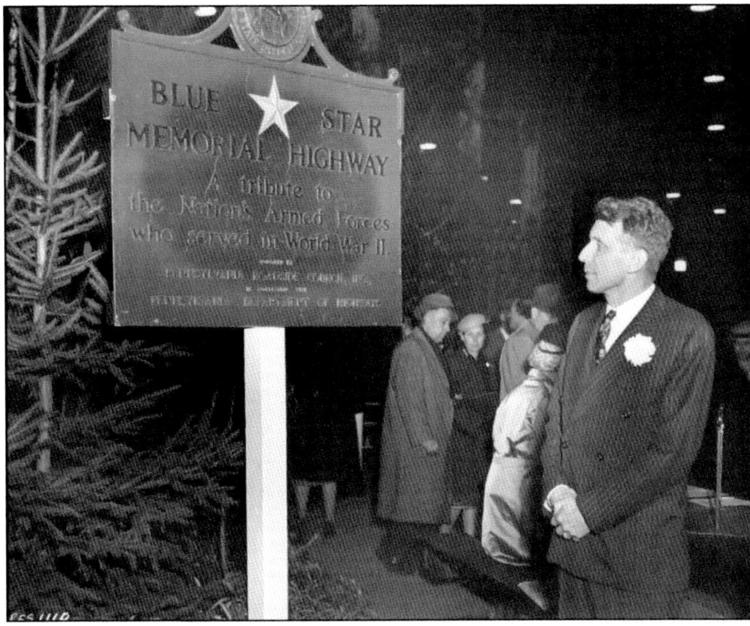

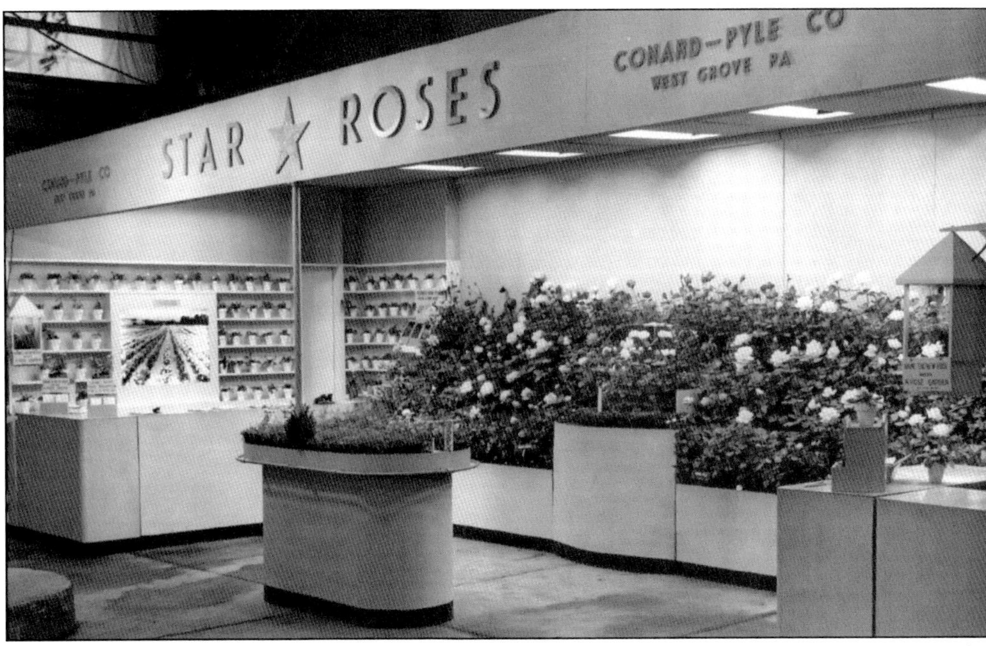

Conard-Pyle's 1949 Star Roses exhibit included the "Peace" rose. Just before Germany invaded France, the French rose grower Francis Meilland shipped budwood of a new and promising rose variety to Conard-Pyle in West Grove, Pennsylvania, for safekeeping. After growing it in successful trials, Conard-Pyle suggested the name "Peace." The rose became a huge success and helped to rekindle gardeners' yearnings to grow flowers.

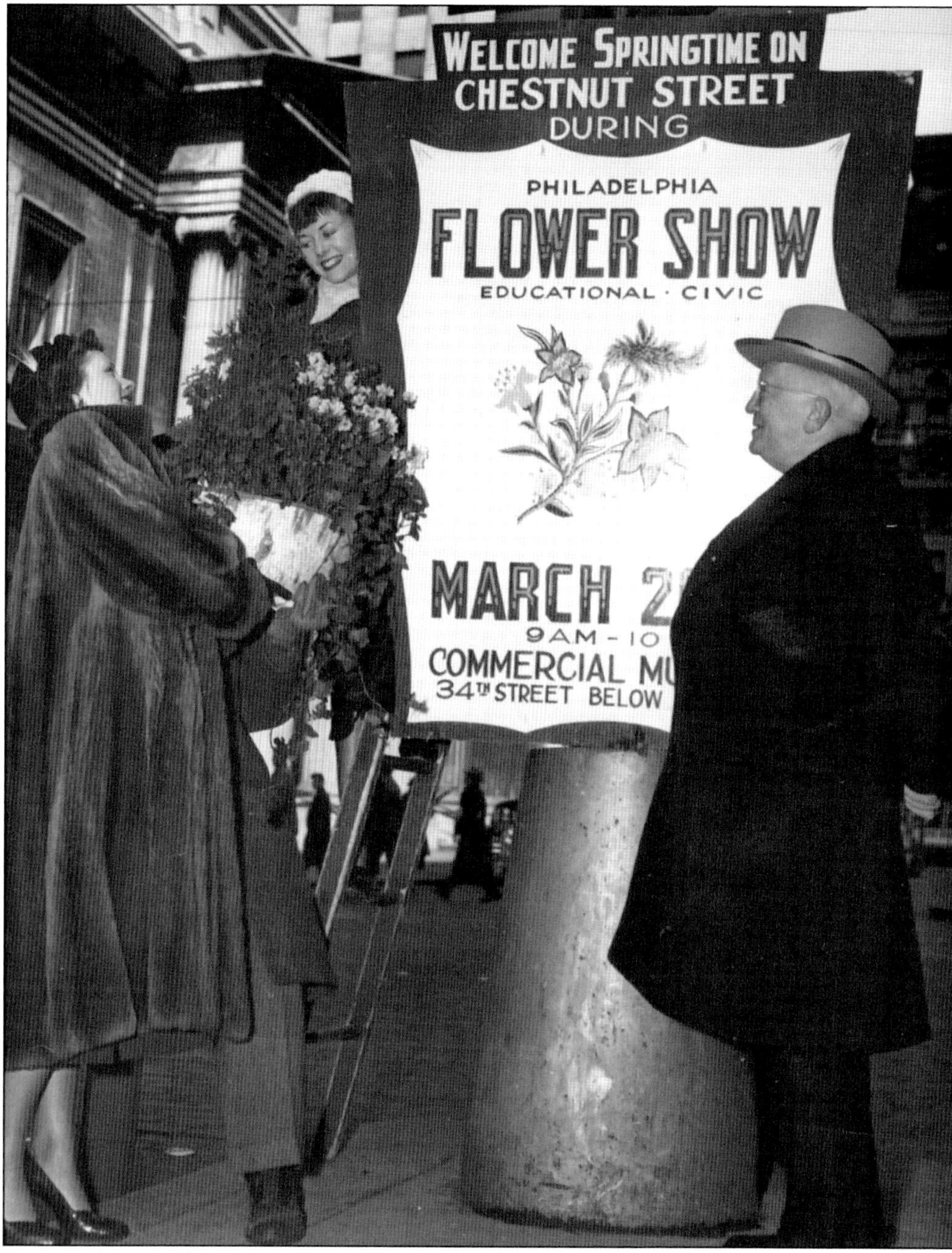

For several years, Chestnut Street shop windows were decorated for "Flower Day" to coincide with the opening of the show. Show officials judged these efforts and awarded prizes to the shops with the best floral decorations. Chestnut Street was one of Philadelphia's main shopping streets in the 1950s. The competition continues today as the region-wide Window Decorating Contest.

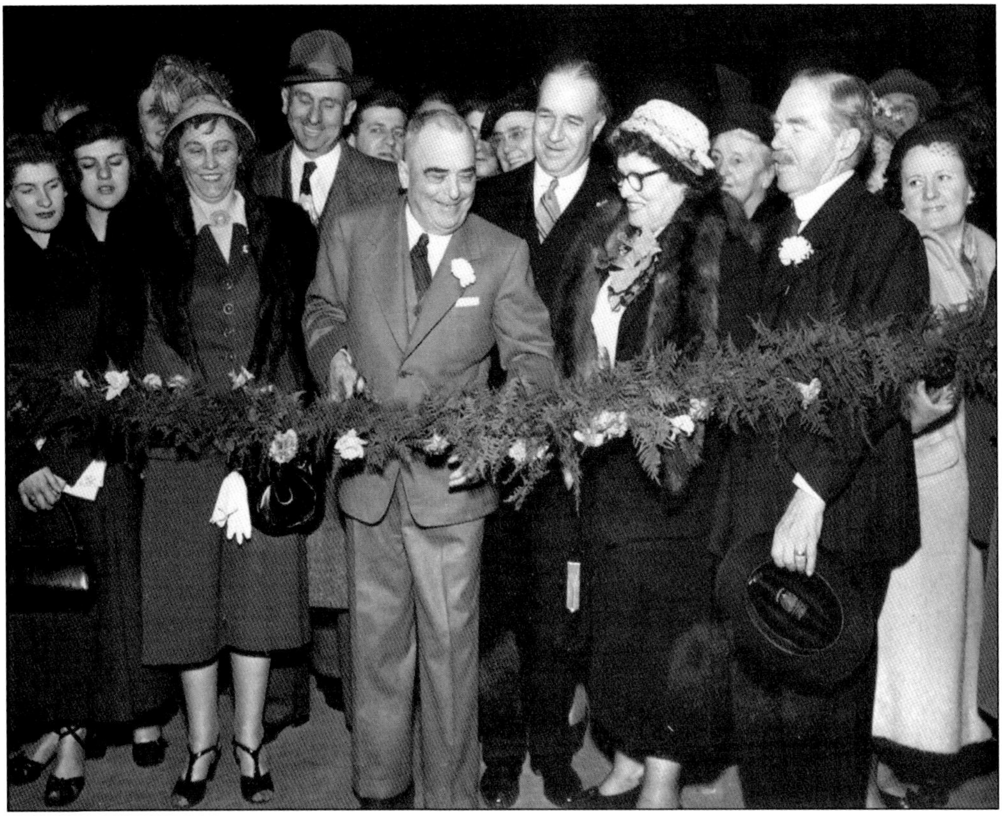

Cutting the ribbon at the 1950 show are (from the ribbon cutter at center to right) Philadelphia mayor Bernard Samuel; show president W. Atlee Burpee Jr.; Jean Duff, wife of Pennsylvania governor James H. Duff; and Lord Aberconway (holding hat), president of the United Kingdom's Royal Horticultural Society. Lord Aberconway (born Henry Duncan McLaren) was a noted horticulturist who judged the Philadelphia Flower Show that year.

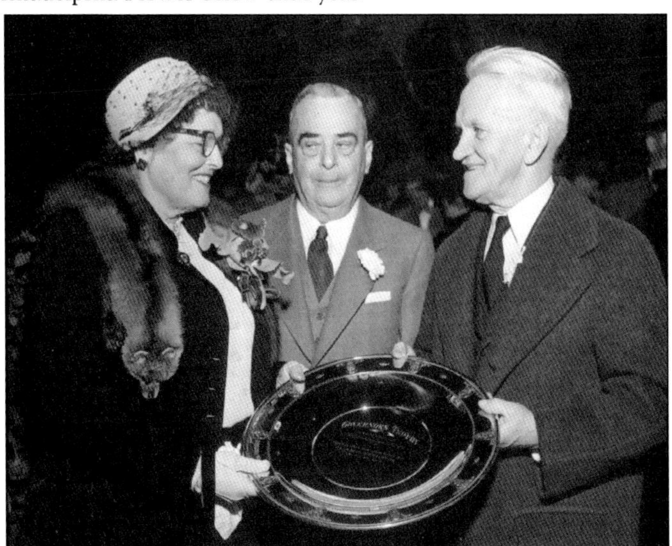

Jean Duff (left) presented the Governor's Trophy, an engraved silver plate awarded for the most meritorious exhibit in the 1950 show, to Arthur F. Paul (right) as Philadelphia mayor Bernard Samuel looked on. Paul created the Aisle of the Seasons, a 350-foot center aisle that displayed the floral life of the seasons and ended with a 30-foot waterfall set in a winter snow scene.

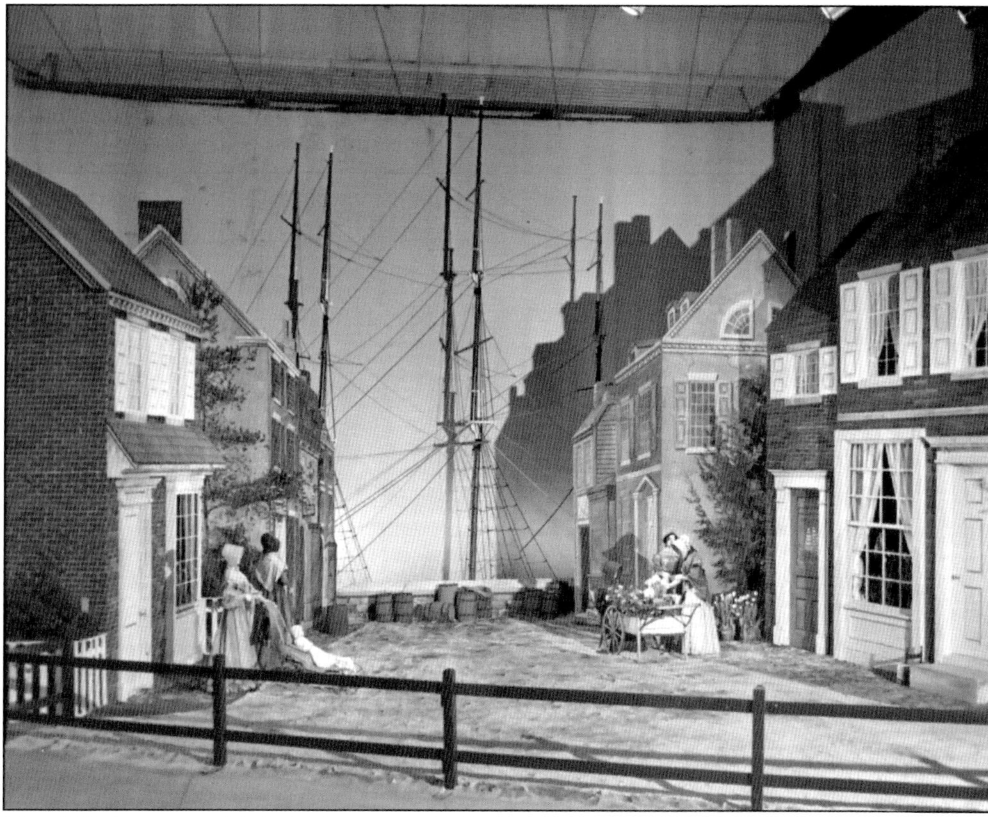

The 1953 theme was "Philadelphia circa 1827"; this part of the central aisle depicted Arch Street complete with dooryard plantings and flower-vendor carts. Designed by landscape architect Frederick W.G. Peck, the show celebrated PHS's 125th anniversary. As part of the celebration, PHS commissioned Peck to design the much-loved Azalea Garden in Philadelphia's Fairmount Park.

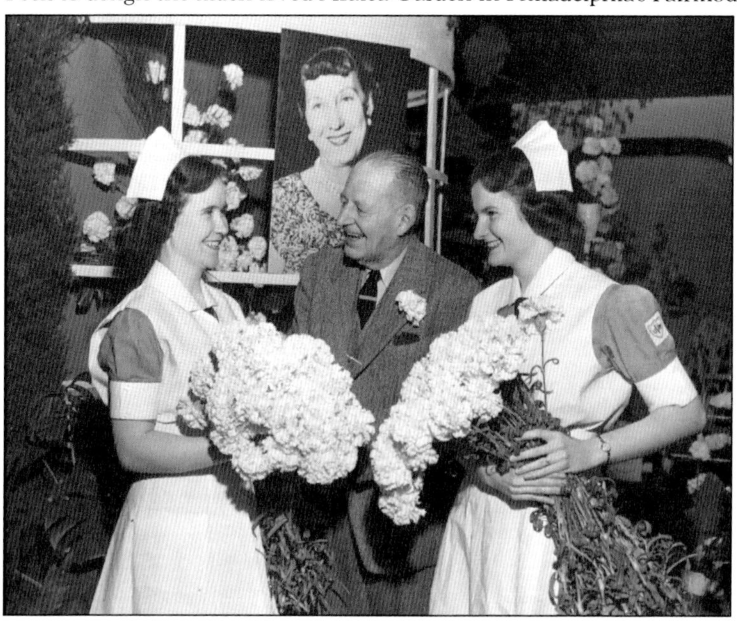

For many years, at the show's end, cut flowers were given to area hospitals. In 1953, nurses from the Children's Hospital received "Mamie Eisenhower" carnations from show official Harry M. Waterer (center). Over time, hospitals stopped accepting large donations of cut flowers, citing a lack of staff to care for and distribute arrangements to hospital patients.

In the 1950s, Chestnut Street shop windows were decorated for Flower Day to promote the opening of the show. Here, judges stand in front of Engel's, which, along with Lane Bryant and Saks Fifth Avenue stores, received silver trophies for outstanding floral window displays in 1954.

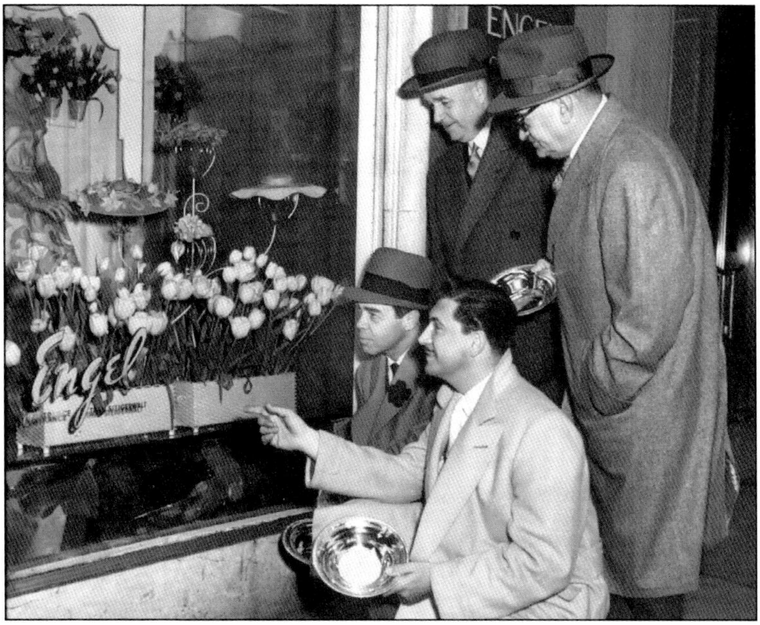

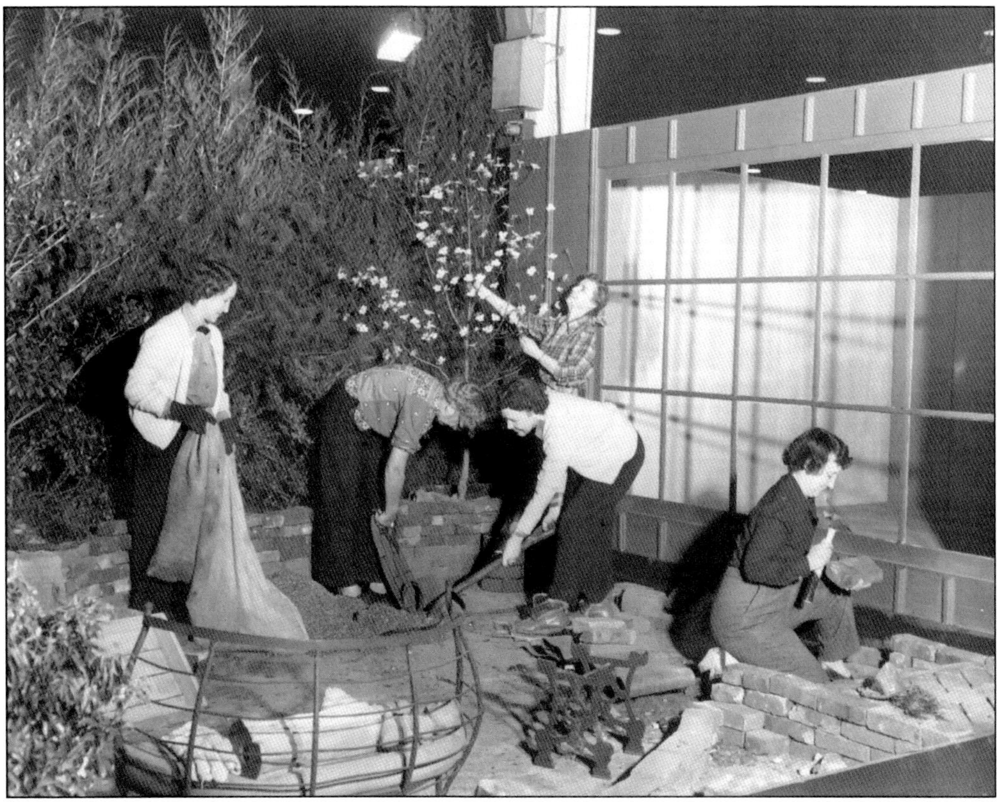

Here, members of the Spade and Trowel Garden Club of Kennett Square, Pennsylvania, are installing their 1954 exhibit. From left to right are Mrs. Thomas R. Jackson, Mrs. J.A. Almquist, Mrs. A. Duer Pierce, Mrs. William J. Scarlett (at tree), and Mrs. J.R. Wilson. Small gardens remain popular with visitors, who look for design ideas to incorporate into their gardens at home.

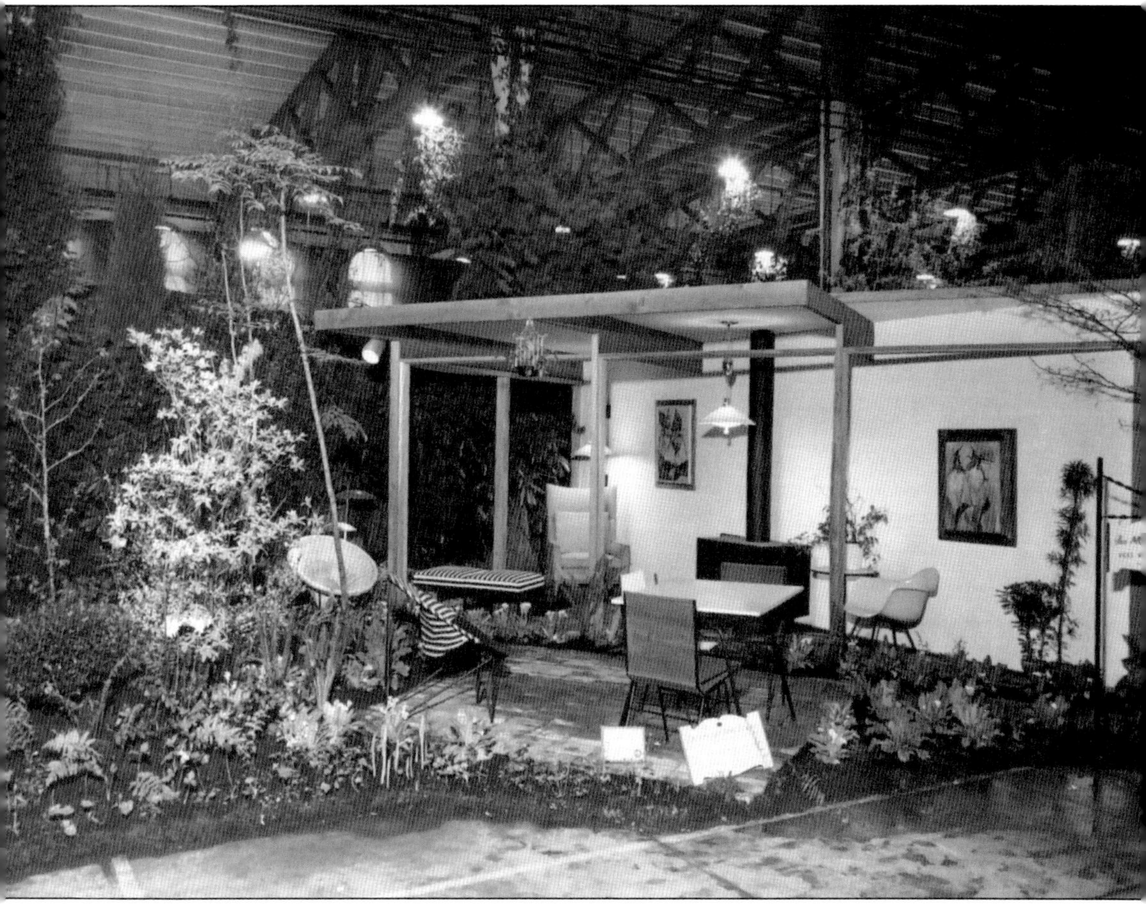

Vick's Wildgardens 1955 exhibit reflected the postwar trend toward relaxed suburban living. The mid-century modern living room and outdoor terrace—with an informal wild garden of flowering laurel, dogwood, and holly—were intended to show that people did not need to use concrete in their yards during the building of new homes.

In 1956, Sarah Groome won the Helen Hope Dechert Award for this arrangement. She submitted the entry to Class 516, Panorama of American Life, which called for an interpretive composition to suggest the work of an American artist. She placed R. Tait McKenzie's bronze sculpture *Winded* in counterpoint to the driftwood.

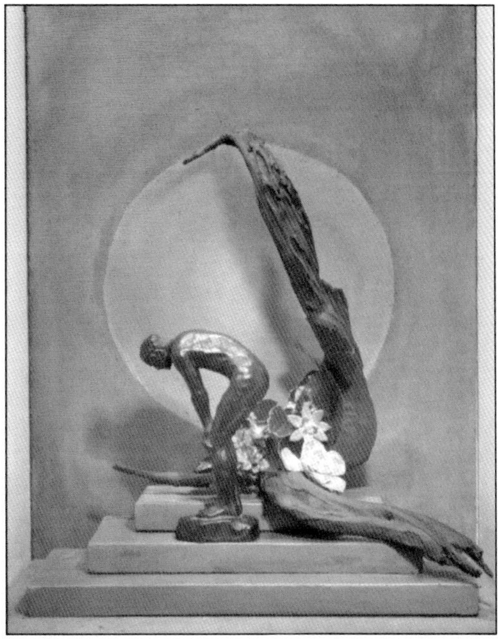

Aristide Maillol's *Pomona*, the Roman goddess of orchards and abundance, was a fitting choice to display at the 1956 Philadelphia Flower Show. Maillol cast this 67-inch-tall bronze figure in 1937. R. Sturgis and Marion B.F. Ingersoll purchased it in Paris in 1955 and gave the work to the Philadelphia Museum of Art.

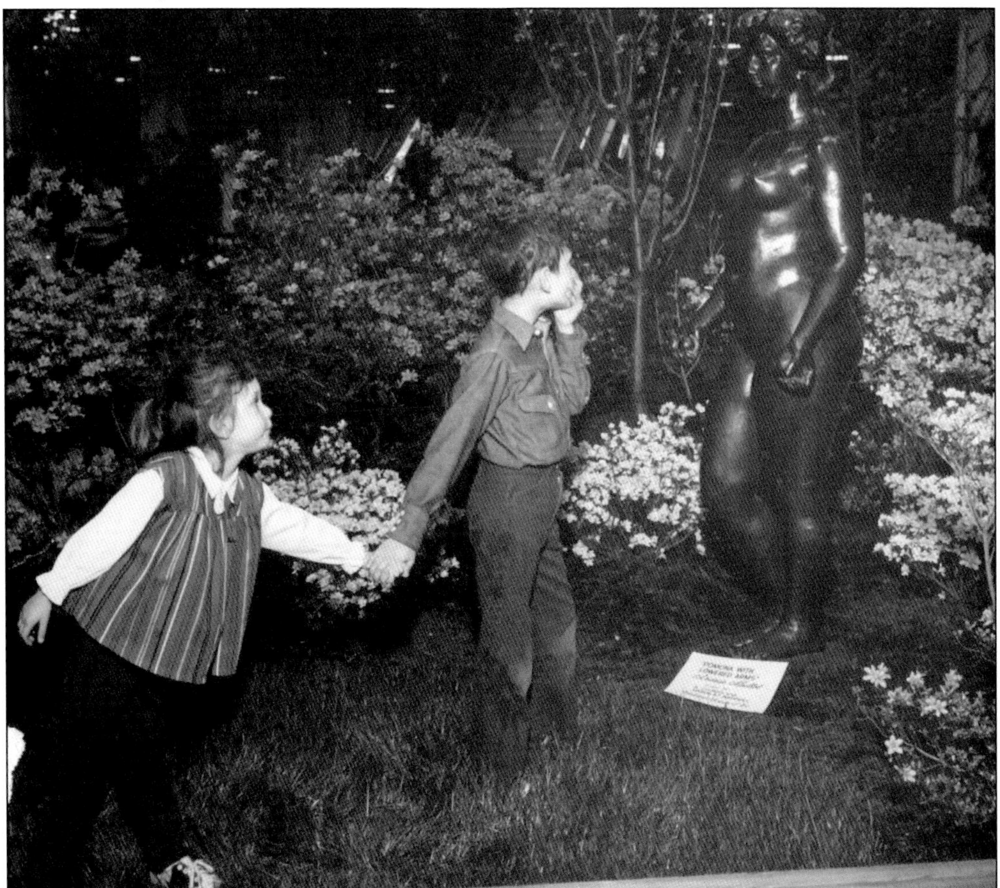

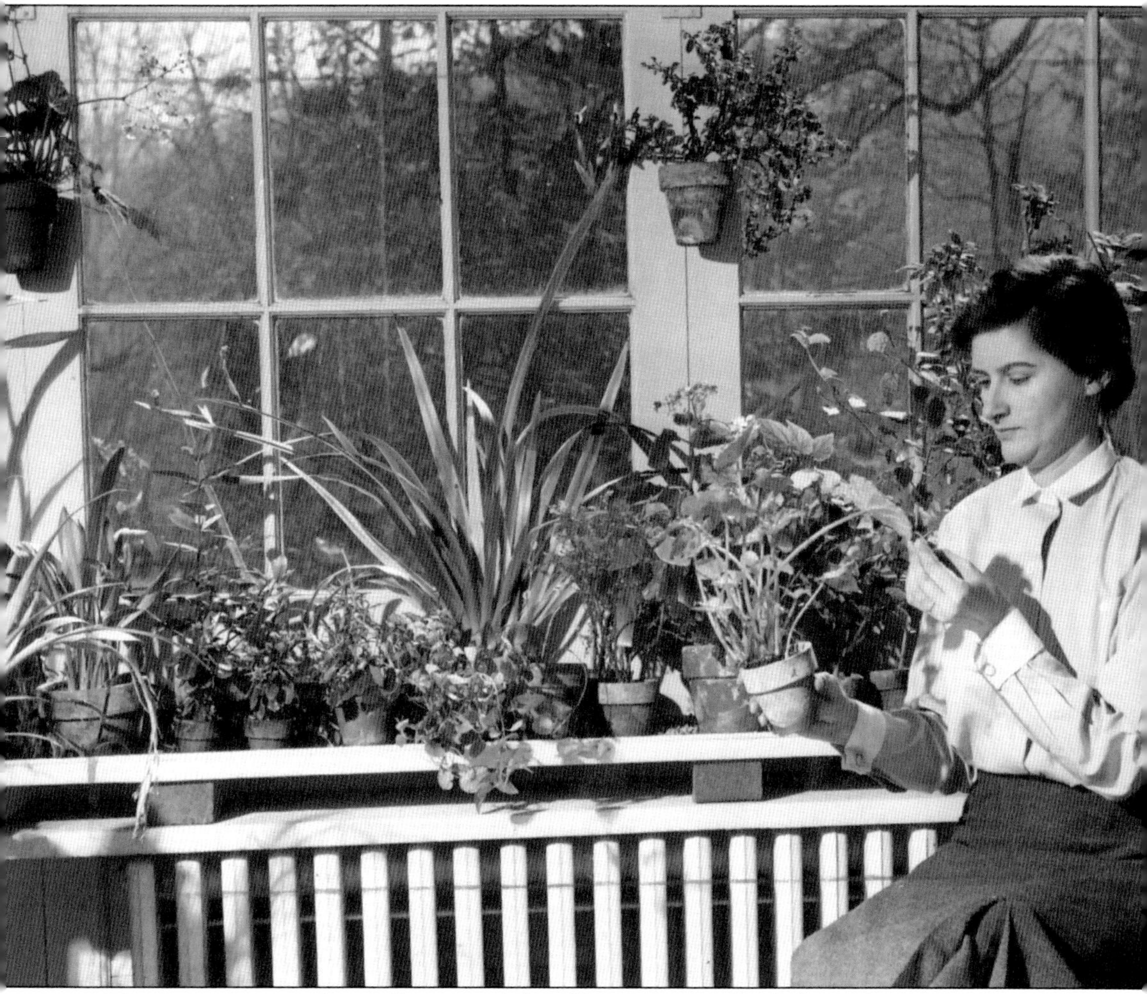

This prize-winning plant collection exhibited by Ernesta Ballard, shown here, in 1956 was the inspiration for something new to the show: horticulture classes staged in an area known as the Horticourt. Prior to the 1950s, amateur entries consisted of "artistic classes" (mostly flower arrangements) and "garden classes," in which clubs installed gardens and competed with each other. After starting from a small but promising showing of 78 horticultural entries in the late 1950s, participation in the present-day Horticourt has grown to 2,000 entries on each of the three judging days.

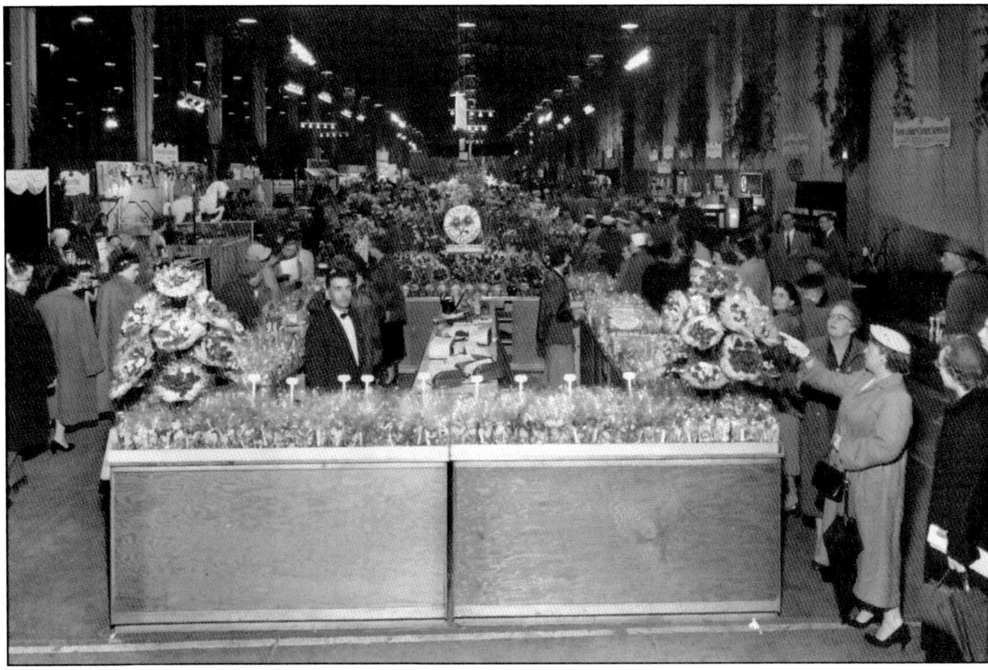

For 45 years, Philadelphians bought their African violets from Tinari's popular booth, a fixture from 1950 (in the Commercial Museum) until 1995, the last year the show was held in the Philadelphia Civic Center. The Marketplace area has expanded considerably since this 1954 show.

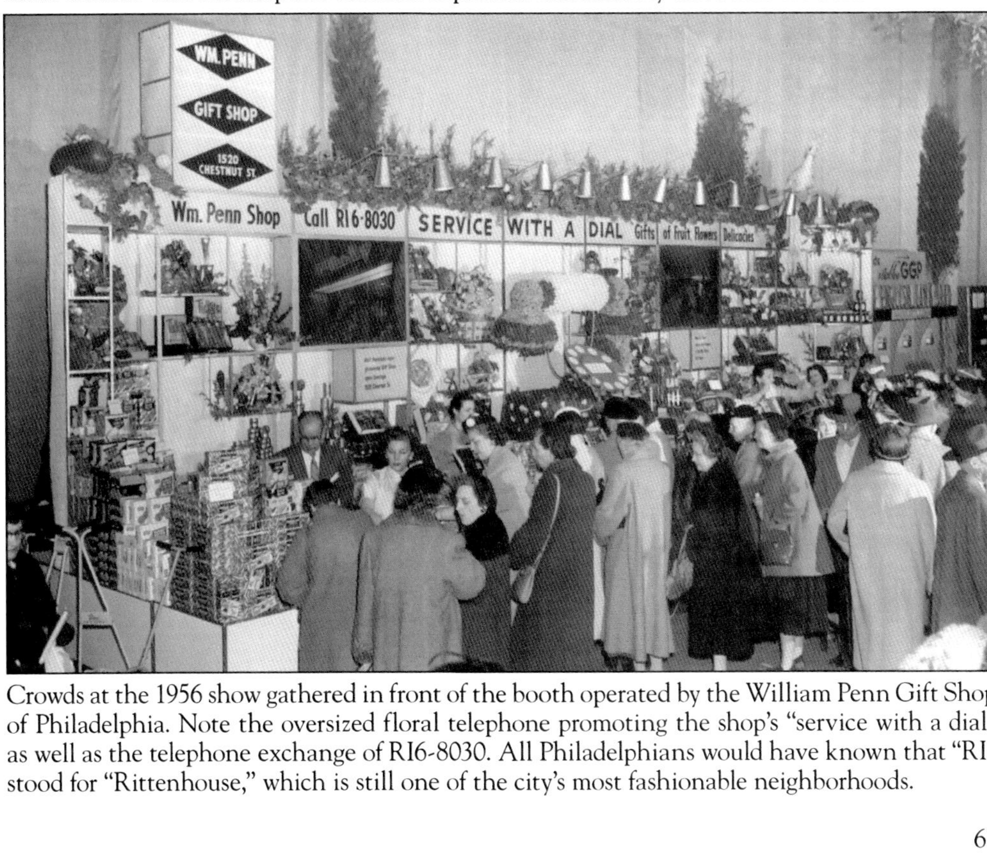

Crowds at the 1956 show gathered in front of the booth operated by the William Penn Gift Shop of Philadelphia. Note the oversized floral telephone promoting the shop's "service with a dial" as well as the telephone exchange of RI6-8030. All Philadelphians would have known that "RI" stood for "Rittenhouse," which is still one of the city's most fashionable neighborhoods.

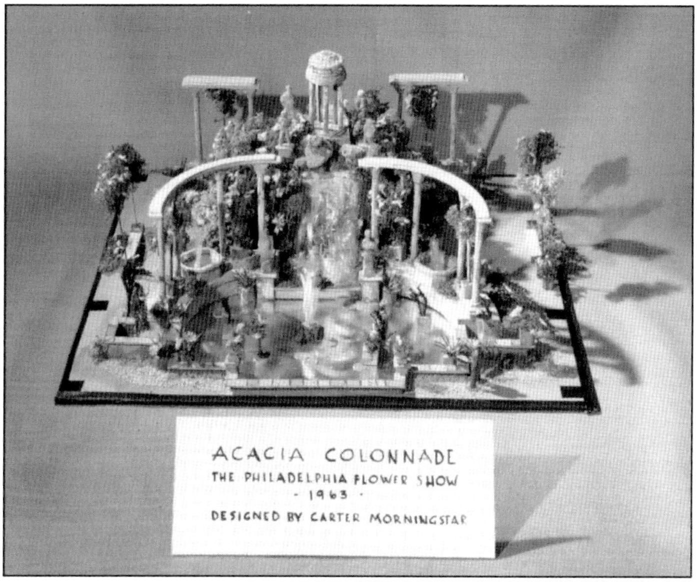

Designers often created models before building large exhibits. In 1962 and 1963, J. Liddon Pennock Jr. arranged to have Broadway set designer Carter Morningstar design the show's central feature. The Neoclassic colonnade featured a 40-foot waterfall, a sculpture, and an acacia collection belonging to Robert and Marion Stone of Marion, Massachusetts.

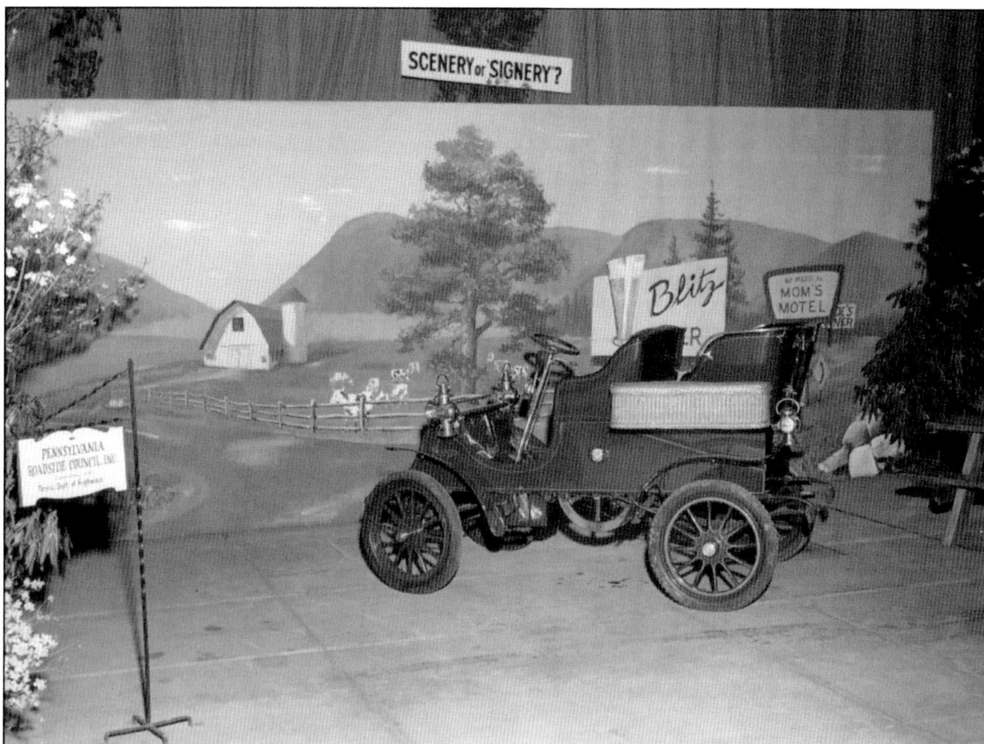

This 1963 exhibit from the Pennsylvania Roadside Council, titled "Scenery or Signery?", sent a message to the public that highway billboards were eyesores. The Pennsylvania Roadside Council, founded in 1939, was an outgrowth of the Garden Club Federation of Pennsylvania. It is now known as the Pennsylvania Resources Council and is one of the oldest citizen action environmental groups in Pennsylvania.

Three

CIVIC CENTER

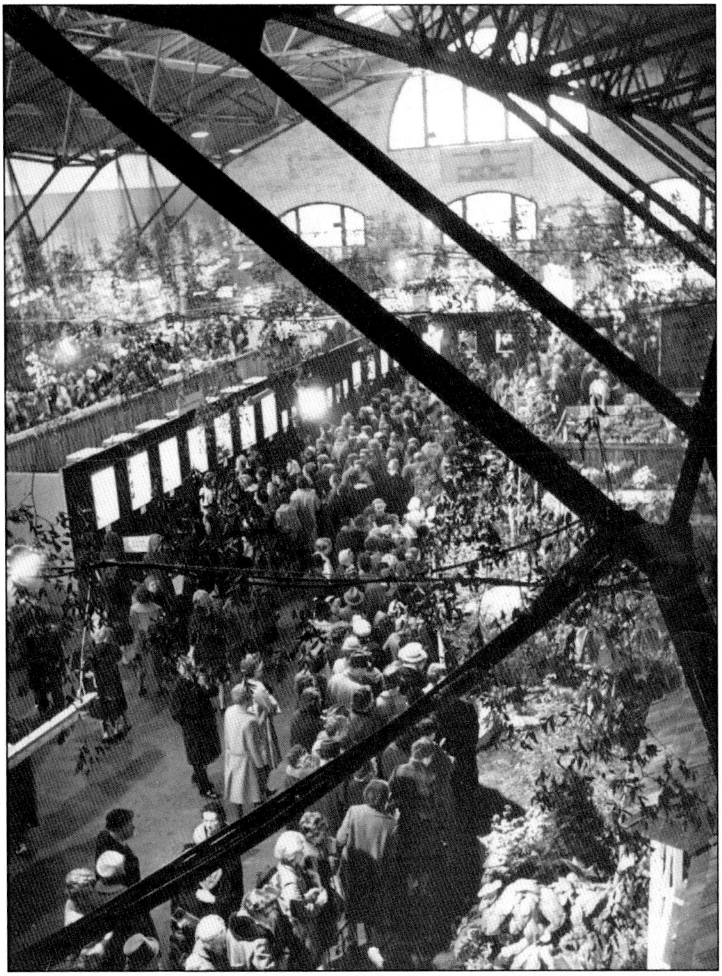

In 1964, the city announced plans to tear down the Commercial Museum to build a new Philadelphia Civic Center. Philadelphia Flower Show, Inc., opted to suspend shows for three years until the new exhibition space was completed. Under the strong leadership of Ernesta Ballard, PHS produced the 1965 show without the participation of "the Incorporators." This pivotal show was staged in the 23rd Street Armory (shown here). From then on, the Philadelphia Flower Show was under PHS management.

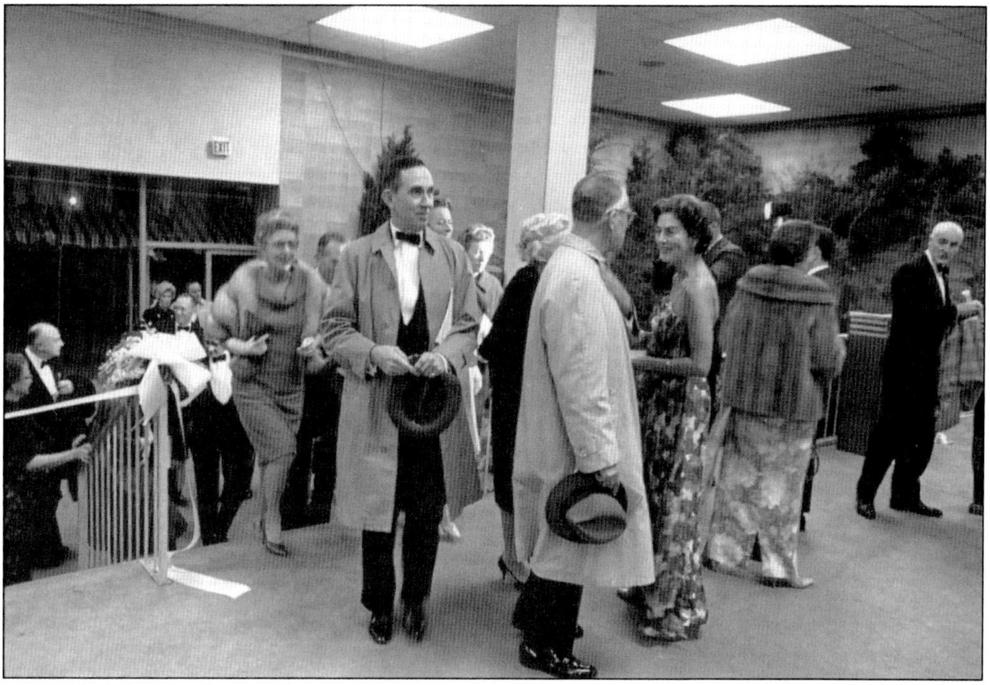

Noel Clark (in the flowered evening dress), wife of Pennsylvania senator Joseph Clark, is shown here just after cutting the ribbon that opened the 1966 show. The first Philadelphia Flower Show Preview Dinner was held that year, drawing 600 guests at a charge of $25 per person. The 1966 and 1967 shows were held in the basement of the Philadelphia Civic Center, as the main exhibition hall was still under construction.

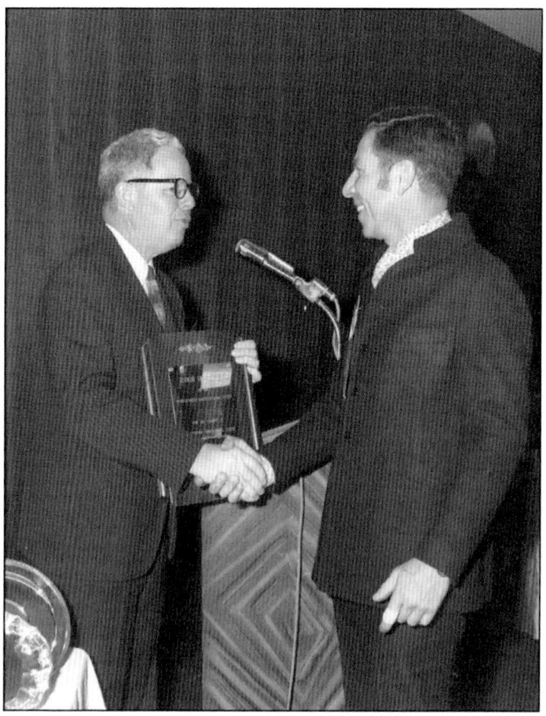

In 1969, PHS president George Clark (left) congratulated Lee Raden for the first of many awards Raden won over his 40-year involvement with the show. Raden was a legendary exhibitor who won numerous awards in the competitive classes, particularly for his alpine plant entries. Friendly and gregarious with an outsized personality, Raden inspired horticulturists young and old to exhibit. In 1998, he won the PHS Distinguished Achievement Award for his lifetime role as a "horticultural pied piper."

From the late 1940s through the 1970s, Gimbels Department Store and, later, the *Philadelphia Bulletin*, sponsored a Flower Show poster contest open to area art students. The poster created by the talented winner was printed as that year's official show poster. This poster was the winner for the 1968 show.

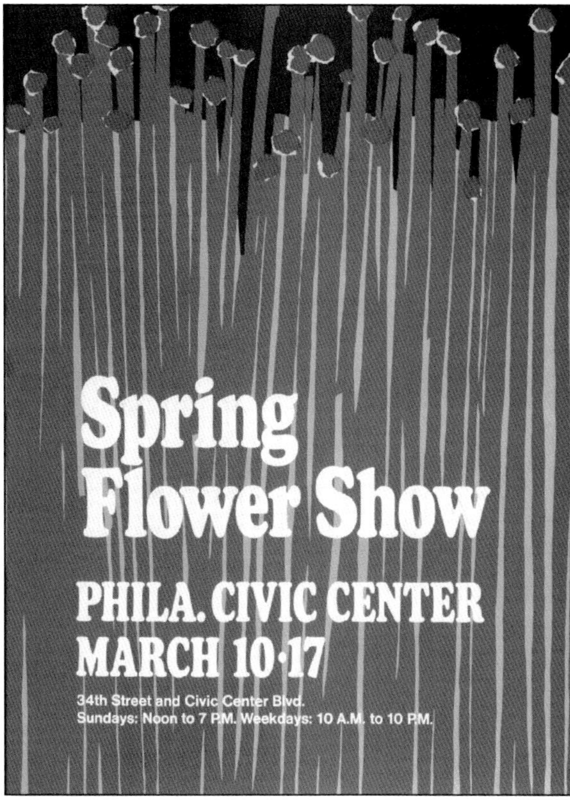

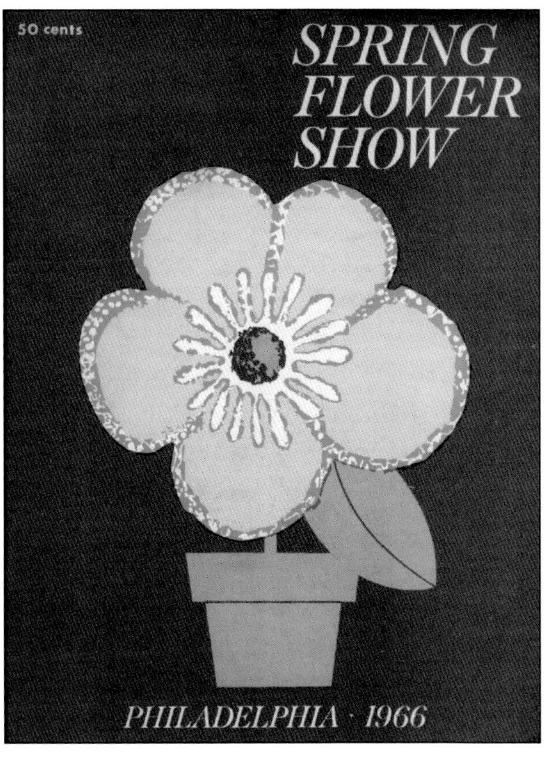

From 1966 through 1997, PHS produced a Flower Show program. The first program contained 57 pages and black-and-white photography; the last one was a 109-page souvenir edition in full color. Both contained the all-important floor plan, but later programs also included in-depth articles on the making of the central feature as well as detailed descriptions of major exhibitors' displays. Today, local newspapers produce detailed programs.

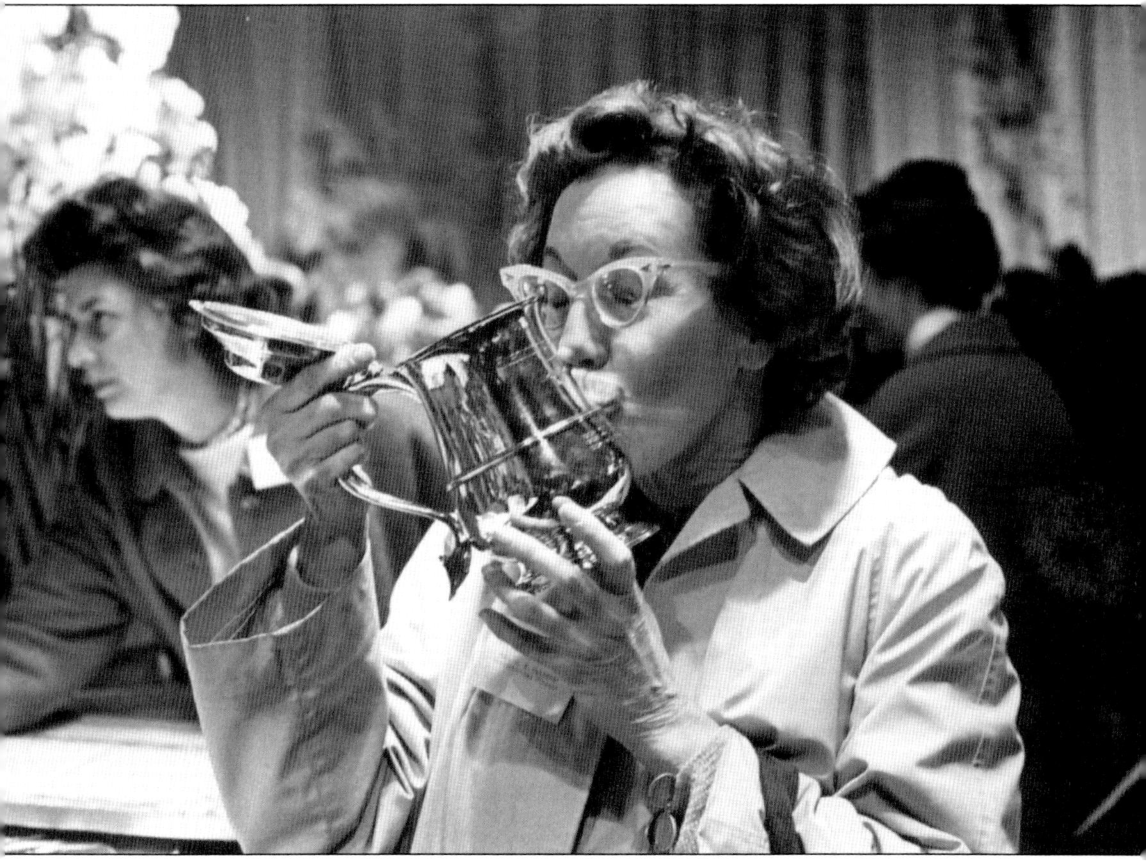

Joy Mackinney, 1970 Philadelphia Flower Show horticultural sweepstakes winner, kissed her trophy at the awards luncheon. This win was not beginner's luck; Mackinney won the society's sweepstakes trophy each year from 1962 through 1966 and again in 1969 and 1970. Horticultural sweepstakes winners are competitors who accumulate the greatest number of points in the horticulture classes over the course of the week.

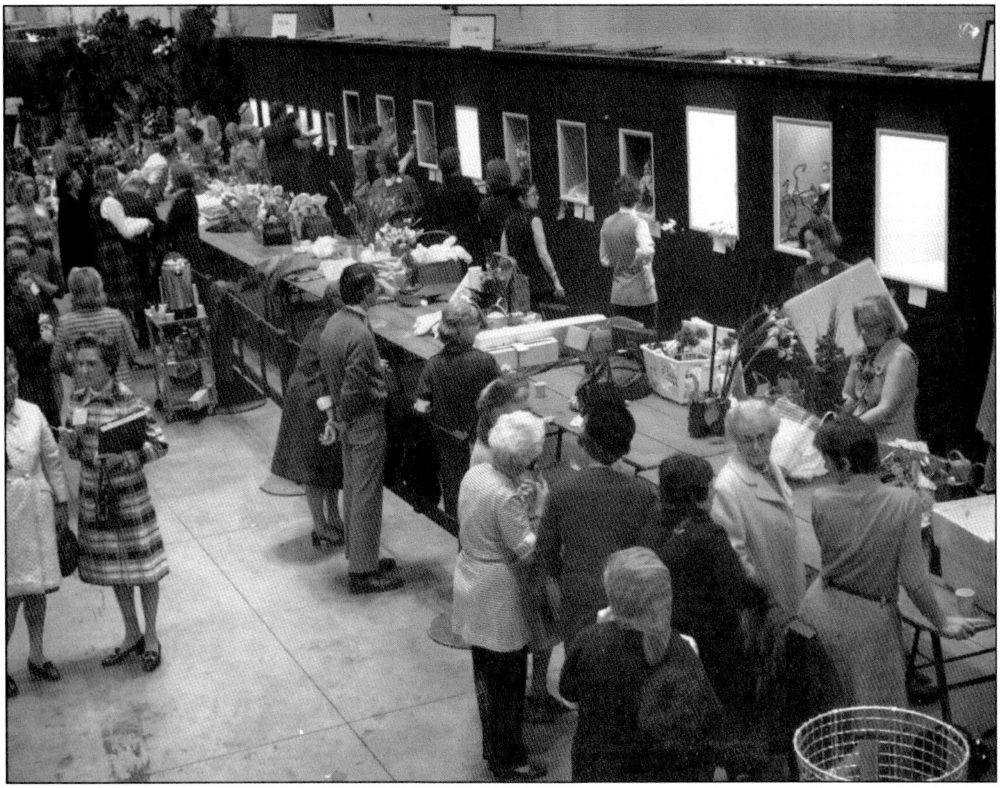

Competitors worked against the clock to install their creations in the time allotted—only two hours—before the judging began for the 1971 show. Exhibitors had everything they needed: flowers, accessories, tools, and—of course—coffee and conviviality. Part of the glue that holds the Philadelphia Flower Show together is the kibitzing among participants.

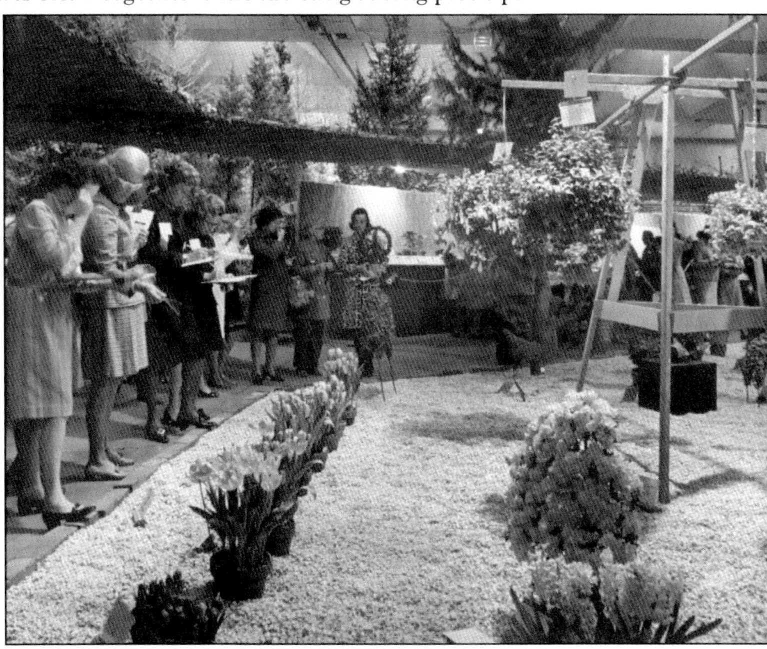

In this image, judges at the 1972 show deliberate on criteria (still used today) such as the plant's overall condition, its distinctiveness, and degree of difficulty in growing. Judges come from all over the country. They are not paid for their efforts; they consider it an honor to be asked to judge the Philadelphia Flower Show.

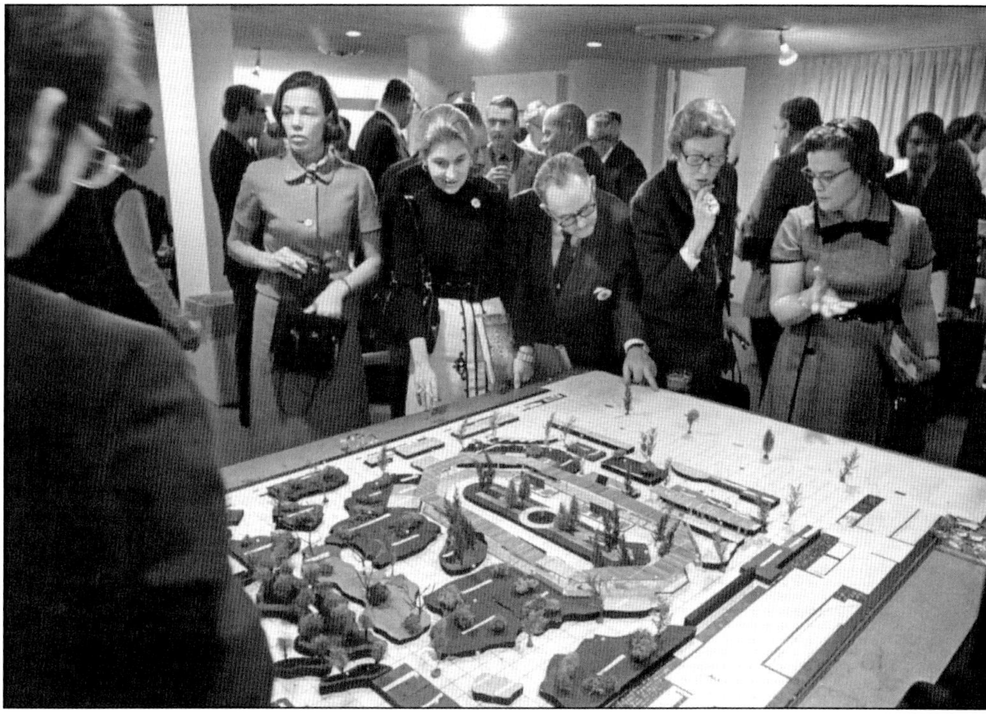

Architect Edward Semanko designed the 1972 show, shown here on a scale model. The man leaning over the model is show manager James McCarvill, who, after a career with RCA organizing trade shows, joined the Philadelphia Flower Show in 1966. Together with Ernesta Ballard, McCarvill nurtured the show through its most critical growth period.

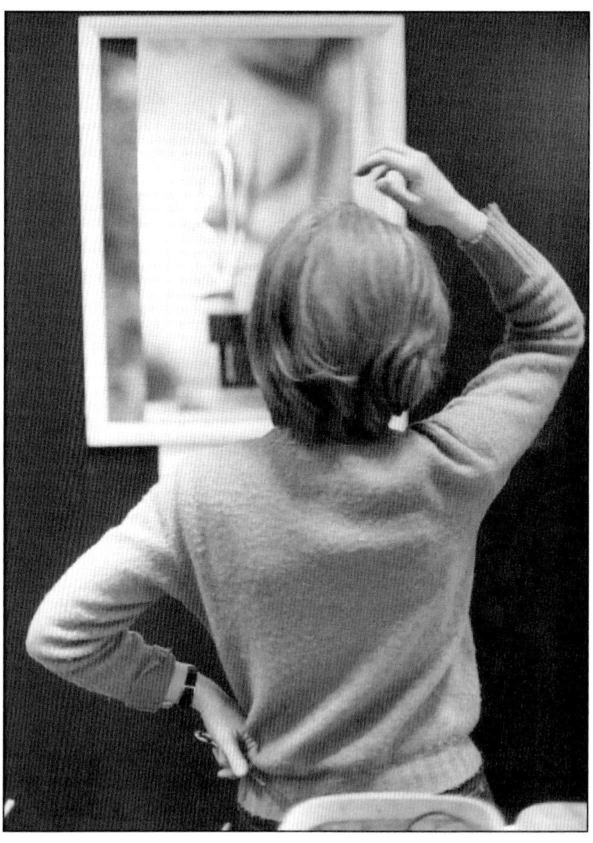

With scissors in hand, this exhibitor at the 1972 show studies the niche she was installing. Perhaps she just trimmed a tiny leaf or cut the background fabric so that it fit perfectly into the space. She must have been contemplating every detail of her design to make sure it was perfect in hopes that the judges would award her a blue ribbon.

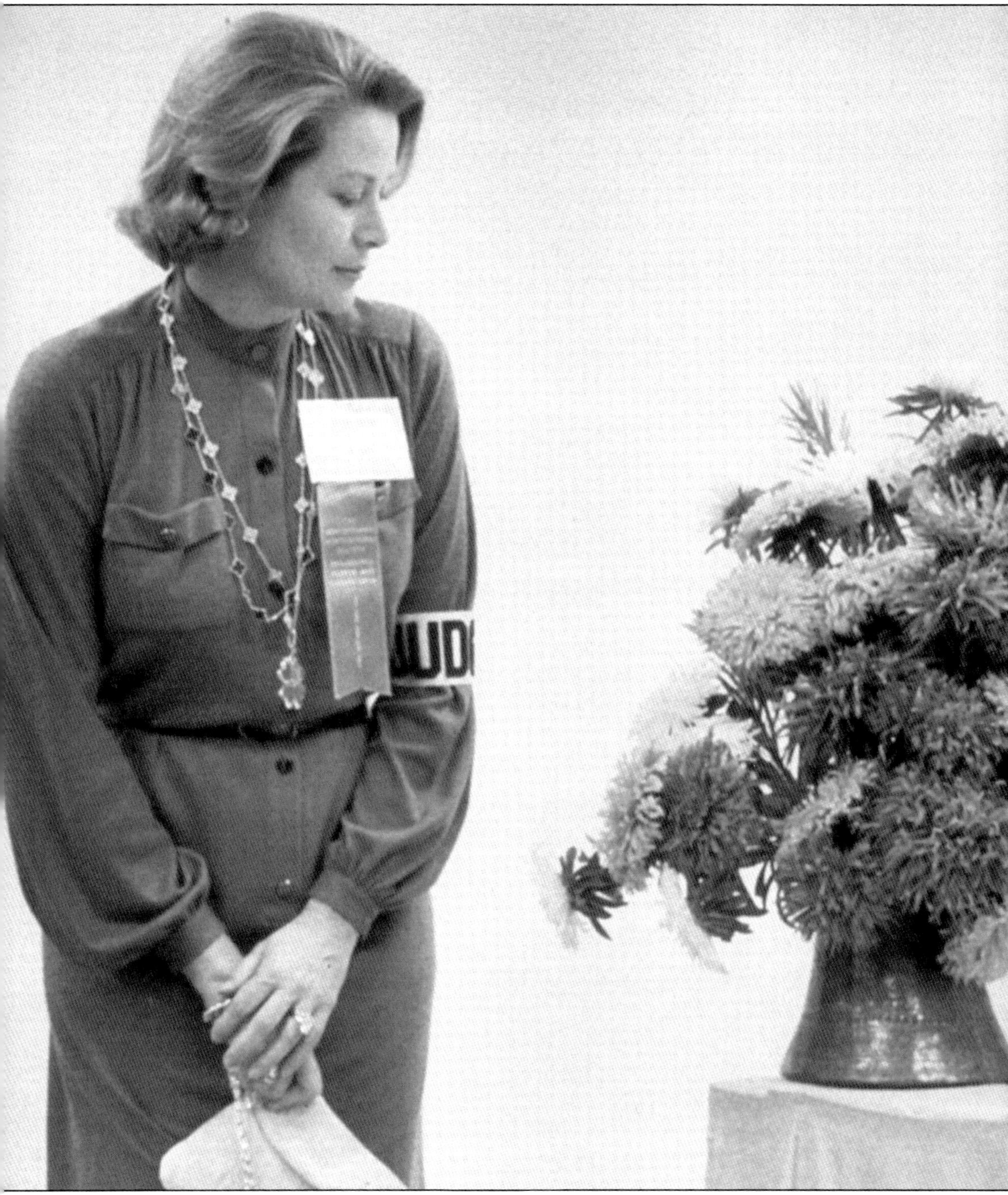

Show organizers wanted to invite a special guest to judge the 1976 show held in the year of the nation's bicentennial. They were delighted when Princess Grace of Monaco accepted their invitation. A Philadelphia native, the former Grace Kelly was a practitioner of the floral arts and studied the art of pressed flower compositions with Katie King, a longtime show competitor.

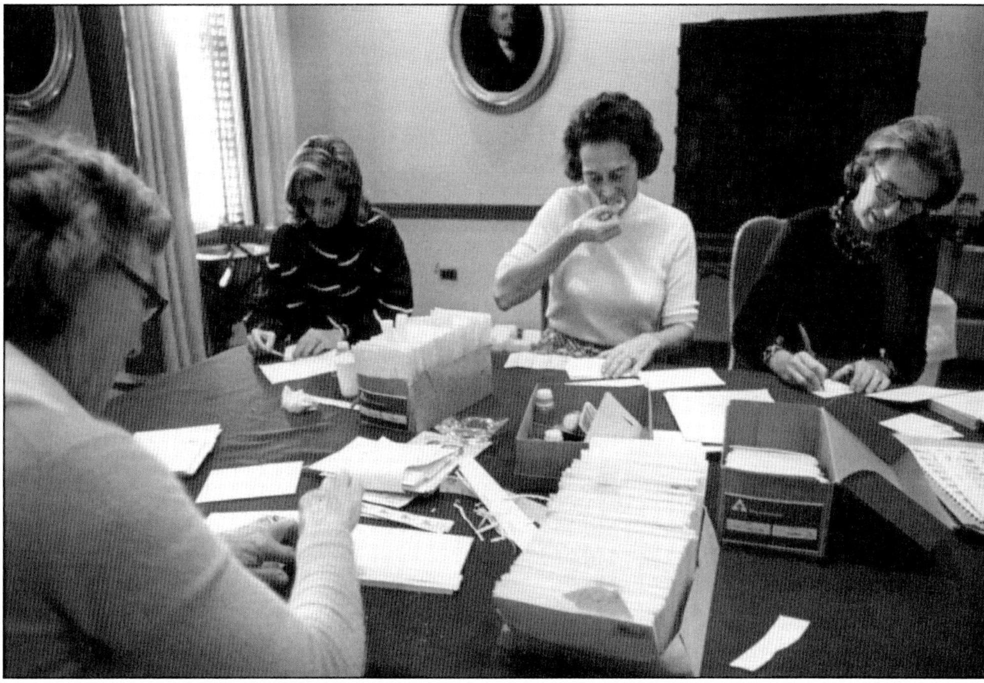

Decisions about suppliers, costs, decor, menus, seating, and the logistics of the 1973 Preview Dinner were made by the hardworking Preview Dinner committee. Jean Bodine, chair of the committee, is at far right. Volunteers, operating in many capacities, have always been and continue to be integral to the success of the Philadelphia Flower Show.

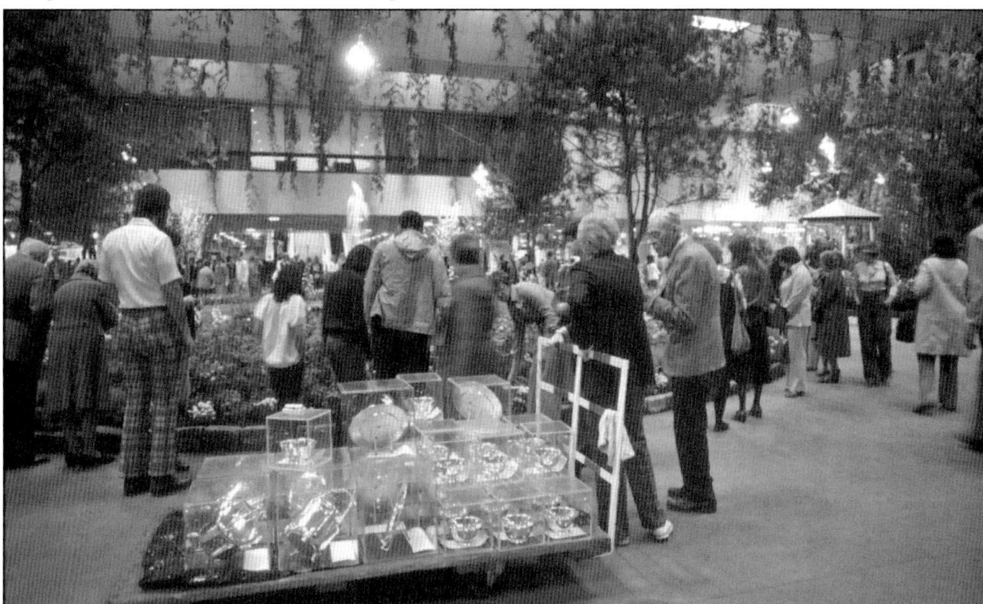

Many of the people dedicated to the show work behind the scenes. Members of the trophy committee, shown in this photograph from the 1977 show, inventory and organize the trophies, unpack and polish them, and place them on the winning exhibits. Their work ensures that an admiring public recognizes exhibitors' talents.

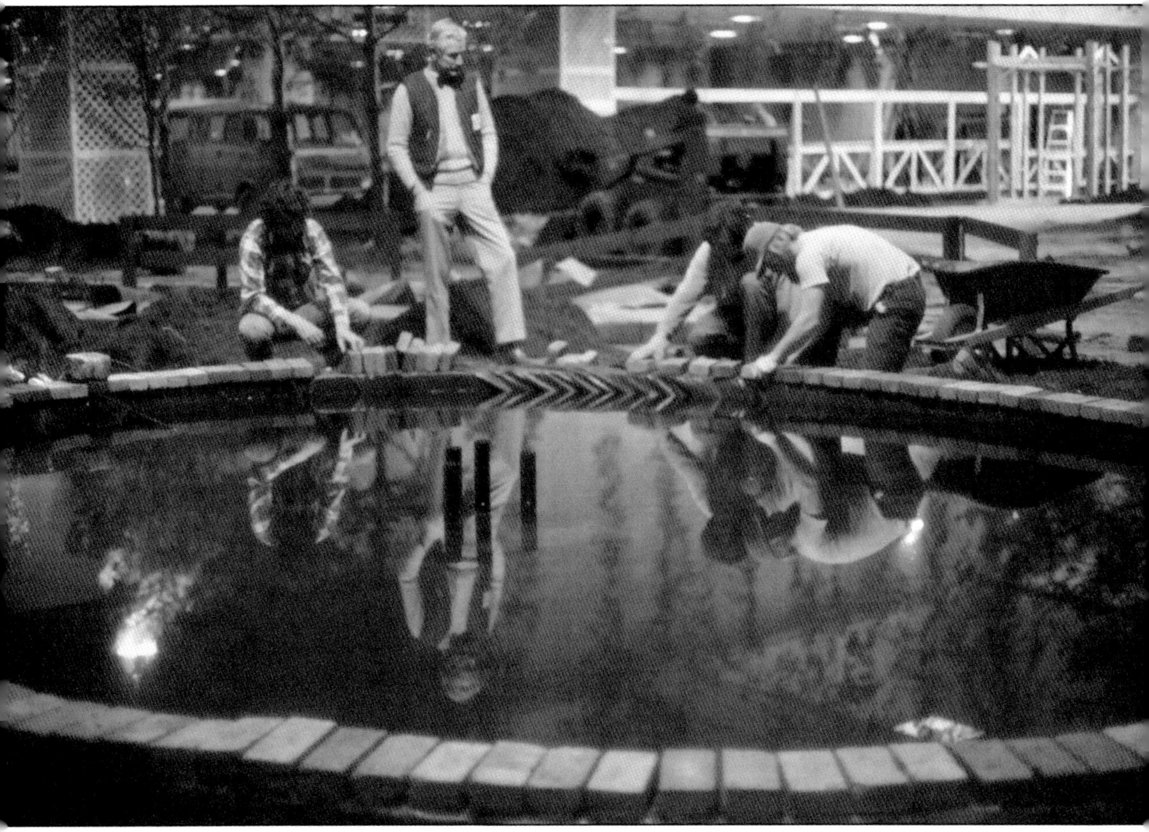

J. Liddon Pennock Jr. (standing) is pictured on the floor during set-up for the 1977 show. Known as "Mr. Flower Show," Pennock was active in all areas of its production for more than 50 years. He was mentor to many and friend to all. The 1991 show, with its theme of "Endless Spring," was dedicated to Pennock's endless enthusiasm for the Philadelphia Flower Show.

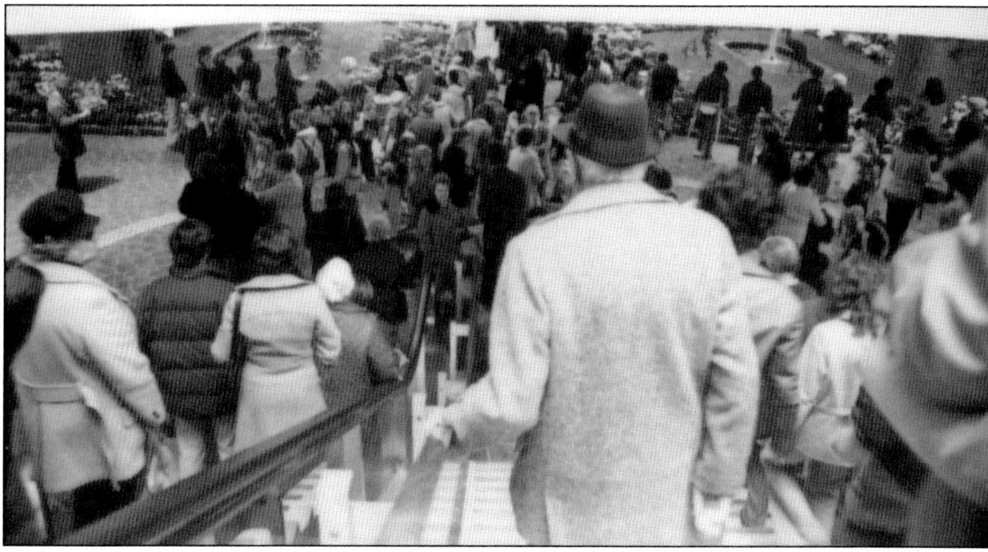

Today's visitors old enough to recall Philadelphia Flower Shows held in the civic center often say that their most evocative memories are of descending the escalator to enter the show. Riding down the escalator was a sensory experience; visitors could see the colorful central feature before them, and about halfway through the 12-second ride, they would be invigorated by the heady fragrance of hyacinths in bloom.

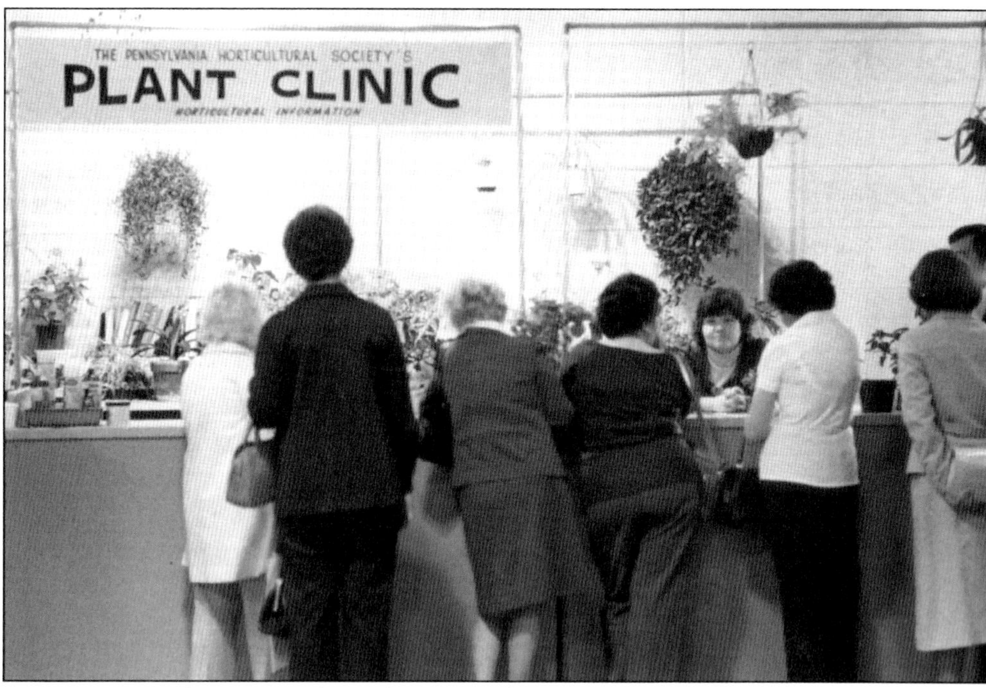

Visitors eager to learn more about the extraordinary plants on exhibit gathered around the PHS Plant Clinic at the 1979 show as staff member Patricia Schrieber dispensed gardening tips. Horticultural education has always been a strong component at the Flower Show. Today's shows include a busy plant information booth staffed by knowledgeable volunteers.

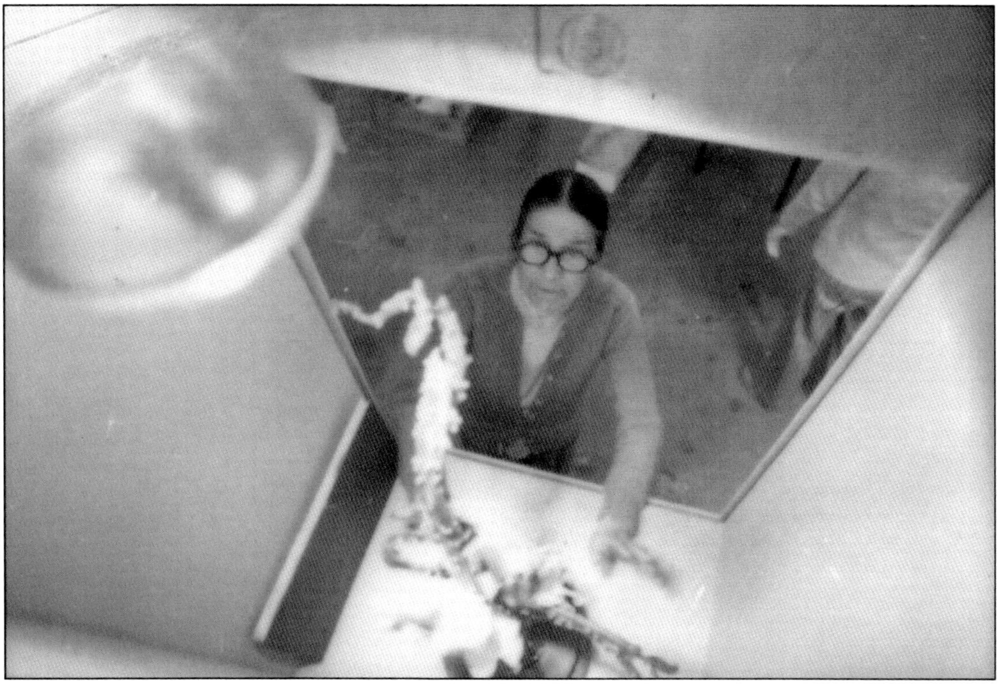

Sarah Groome was a venerable, award-winning exhibitor who held weekly workshops in her home to encourage niche competitors to enter the show. She also had a sense of humor. For a 1961 composition, she chose to do an interpretation of fish chowder. She used a background and floor of sea toast (crackers once made by Keebler), a cardboard fish covered in aluminum, onions, potatoes, parsley, and a soup tureen.

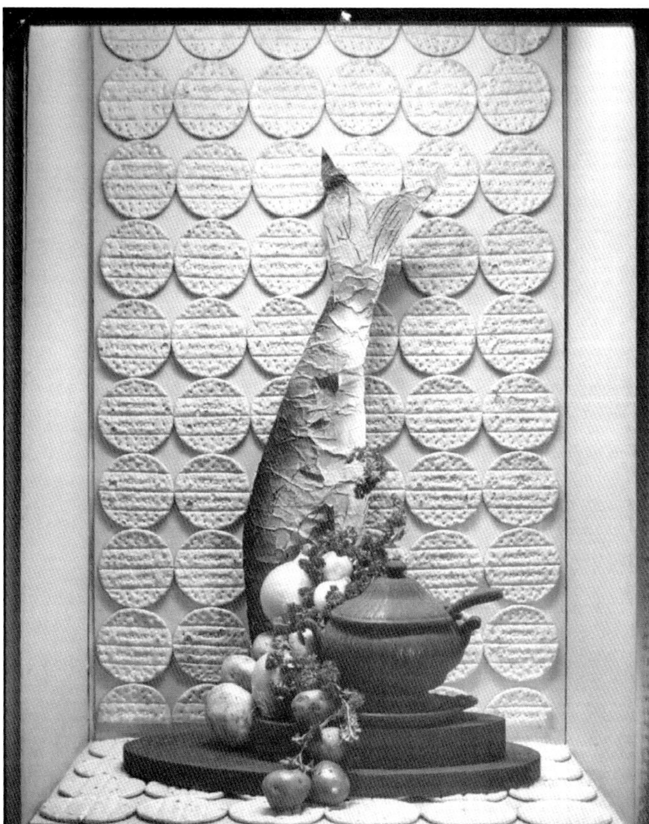

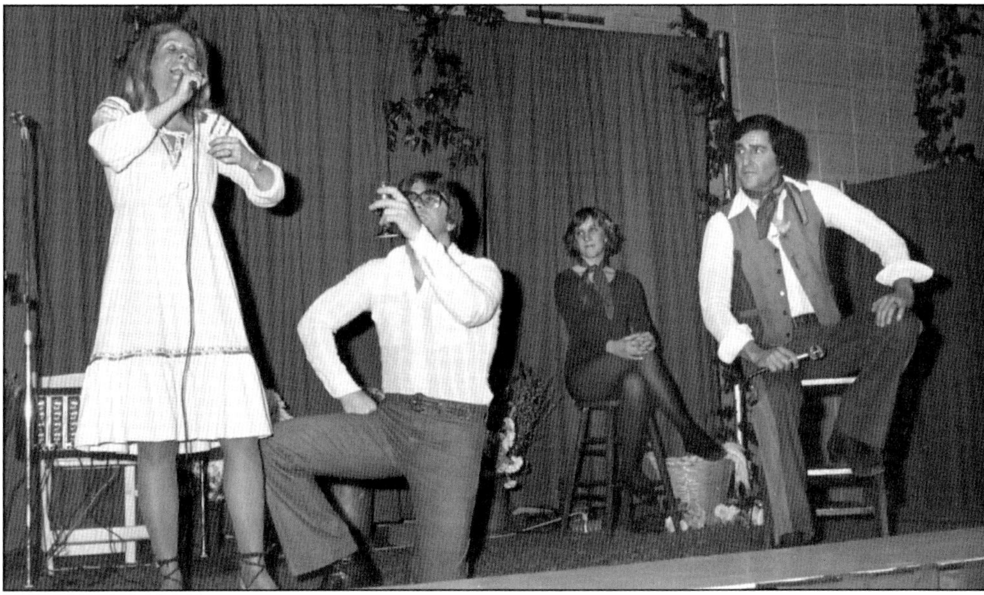

During the 1978 Philadelphia Flower Show, Morgan Ruth and Donna Bates Ruth wrote and performed a musical comedy called "Flourish" as a toast to PHS's 150-year history. Donna was also the voice behind the show's promotional "jingle" heard for many years on local radio stations. From left to right are Donna Bates Ruth (now Donna Cockenberg), Kerry Ziegler, Amanda Ruth, and Morgan Ruth.

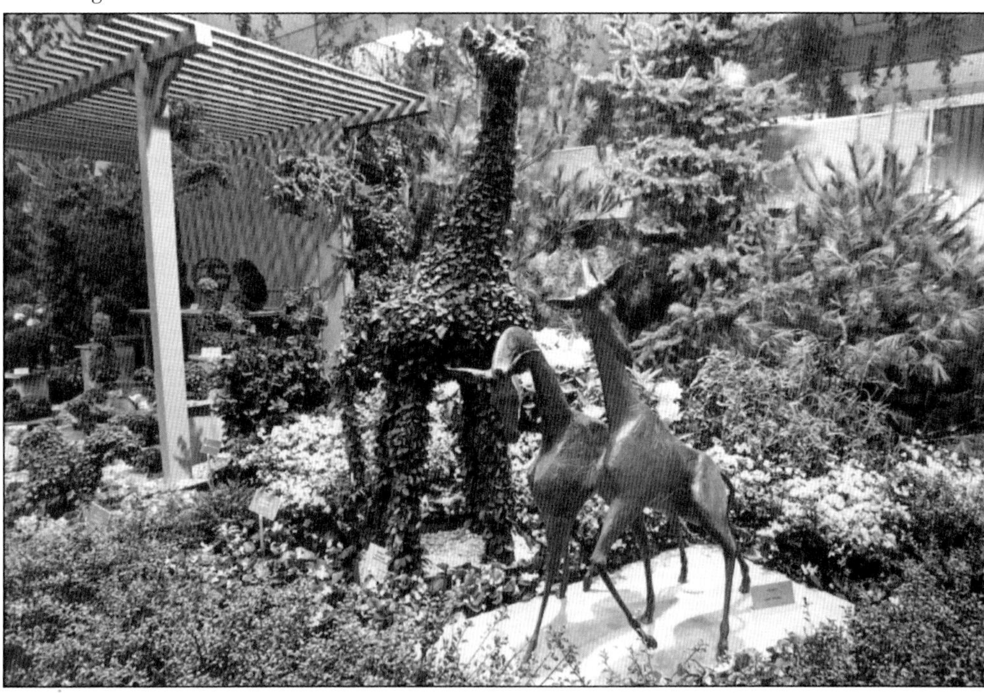

Artist Henry Mitchell's 45-inch-tall bronze sculpture *Giraffes* shared the stage with ivy topiary cousins in this 1979 Philadelphia Zoo exhibit. Mitchell was well known for his charming public art displayed throughout Philadelphia. His works include a child-friendly sculpture meant for fun and climbing and his *Impala* fountain, an iconic landmark at the Philadelphia Zoo.

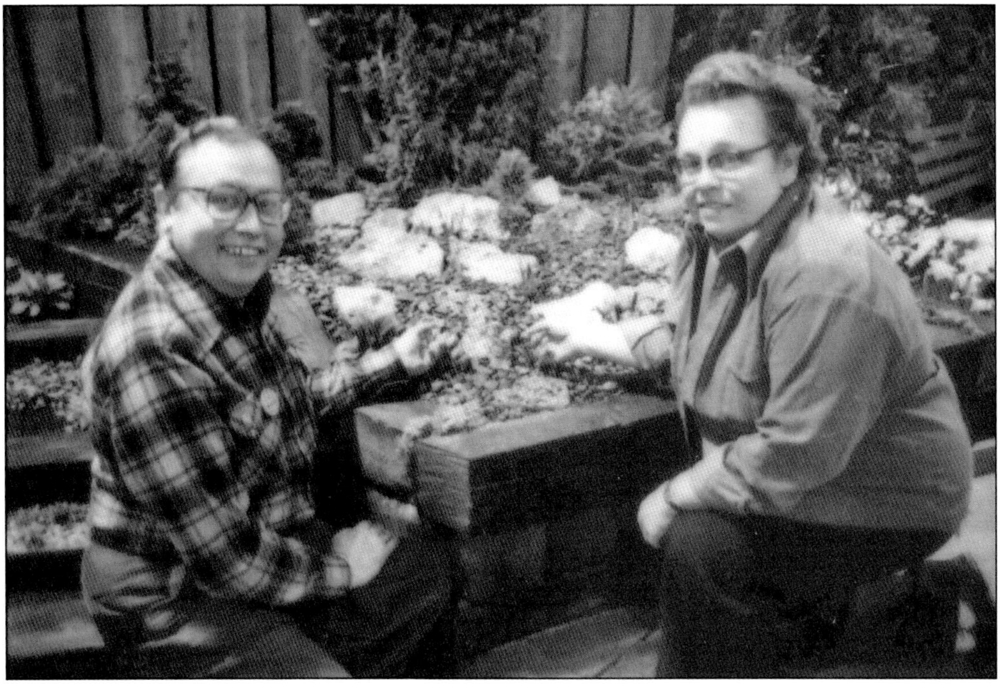

Rock garden society volunteers and husband-and-wife team Alan and Charlotte Slack helped install this 1980 exhibit. Plant society exhibits are important educational opportunities that let visitors ask questions and meet plant experts. Alan has played many roles at the show; he chaired the horticulture classes committees and served on the Flower Show Executive Committee and PHS Council.

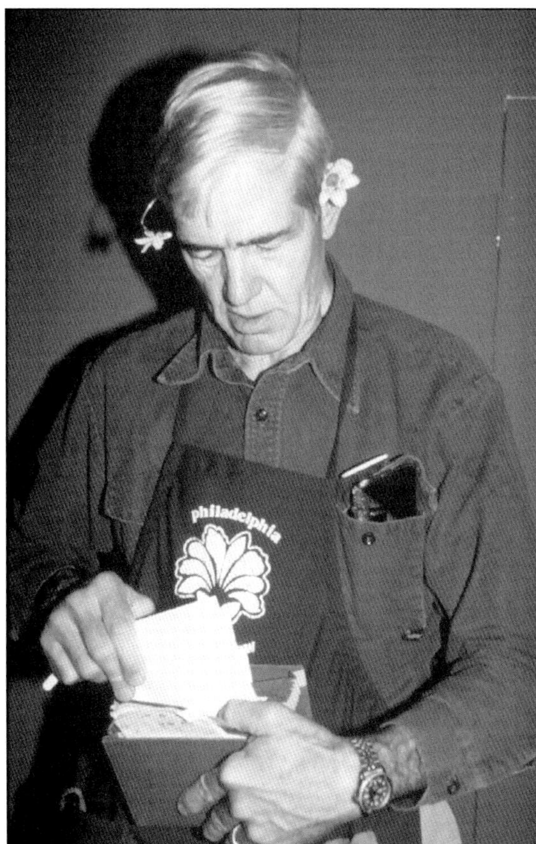

Walt Fisher has won many blue ribbons for his forced bulbs exhibits. He has also chaired the Philadelphia Flower Show and appeared yearly in demonstrations on the show floor to teach visitors how to grow bulbs. With his camera in hand, Fisher is the show's unofficial chronicler of the hundreds of exhibitors, staff, and volunteers who make up the Flower Show family.

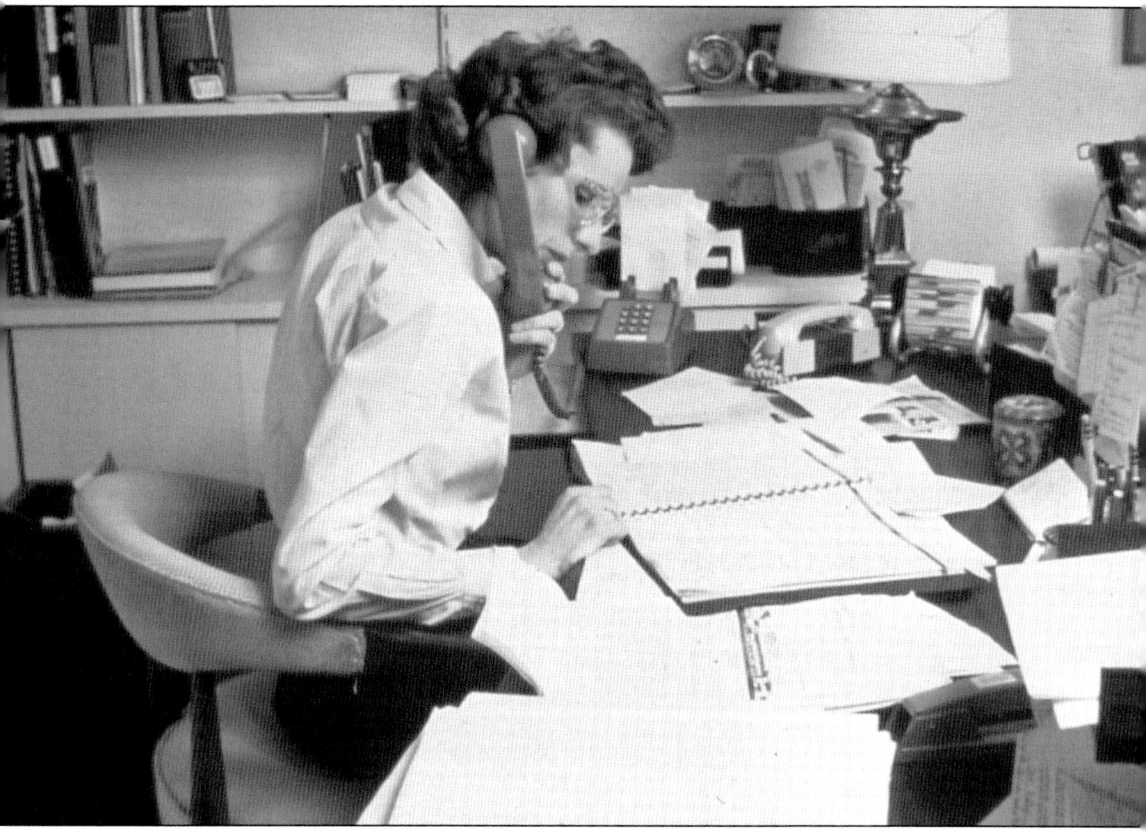

Jane Pepper joined PHS in 1979 and became president in 1981. She and designer Ed Lindemann led the Philadelphia Flower Show for the next 25 years. Pepper brought an excellent sense of business, exceptional people skills, and international connections. Lindemann's talents were in the creative and aesthetic realms. Together, they made an excellent team supported by dedicated staff and volunteers.

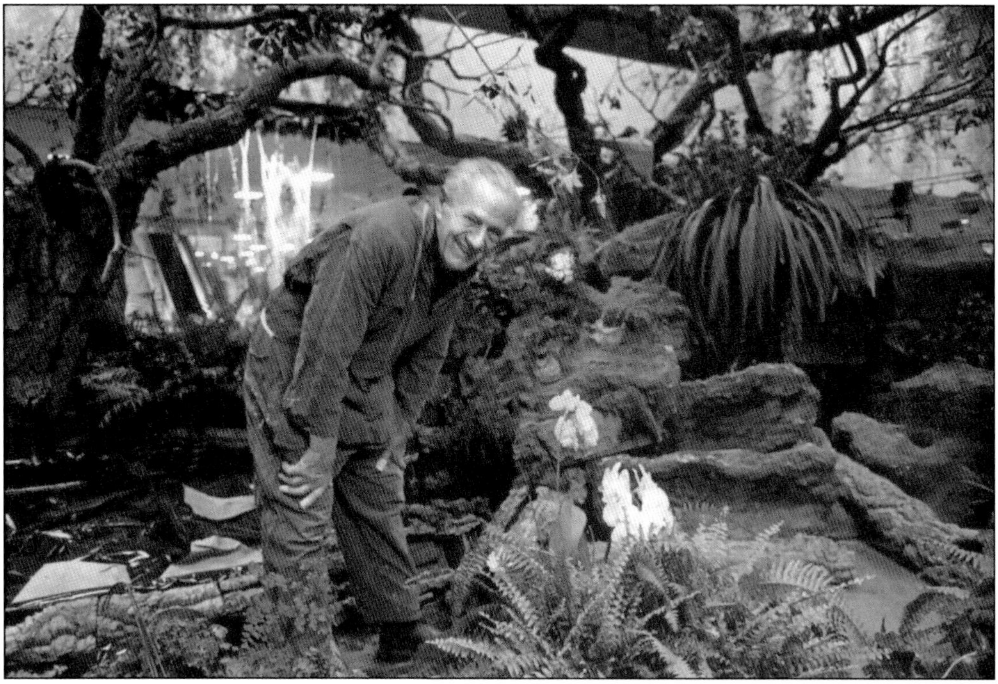

George Off, owner of Waldor Orchids, is shown here in his 1982 exhibit. While Waldor Orchids has been exhibiting under that name since 1970, Off exhibited from the 1930s to the 1950s with his Brighton Florist business; he rarely missed a year from 1970 until his death in 1987. The 1988 show was dedicated to his memory. His son Walter continues the family tradition of exhibiting in the show.

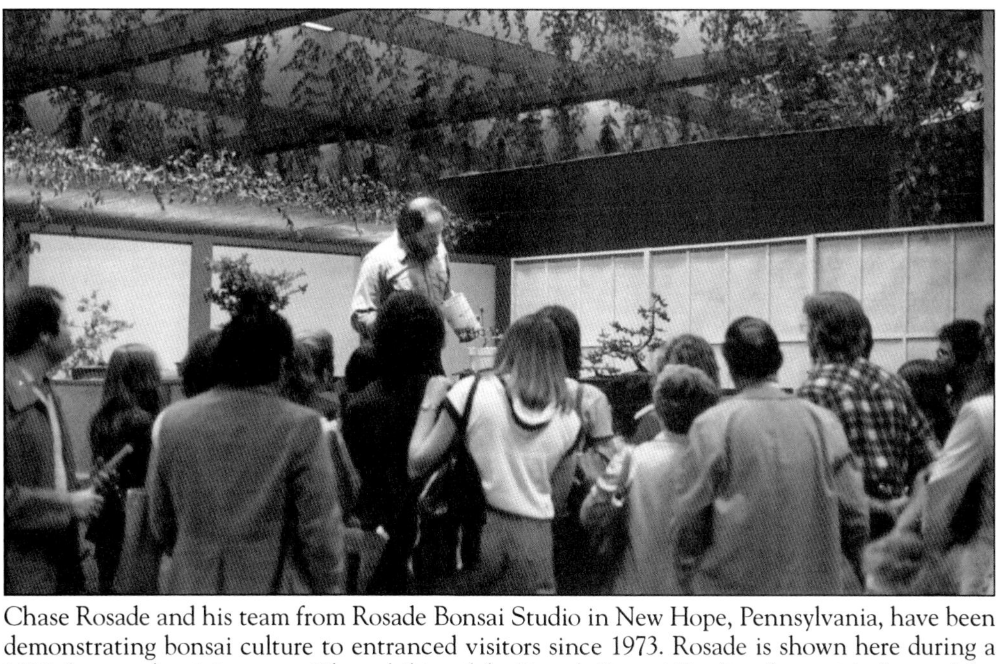

Chase Rosade and his team from Rosade Bonsai Studio in New Hope, Pennsylvania, have been demonstrating bonsai culture to entranced visitors since 1973. Rosade is shown here during a 1982 show at the civic center. The exhibits of the Rosade Bonsai Studio, along with those of the Pennsylvania Bonsai Society, are perennial favorites among visitors to the show.

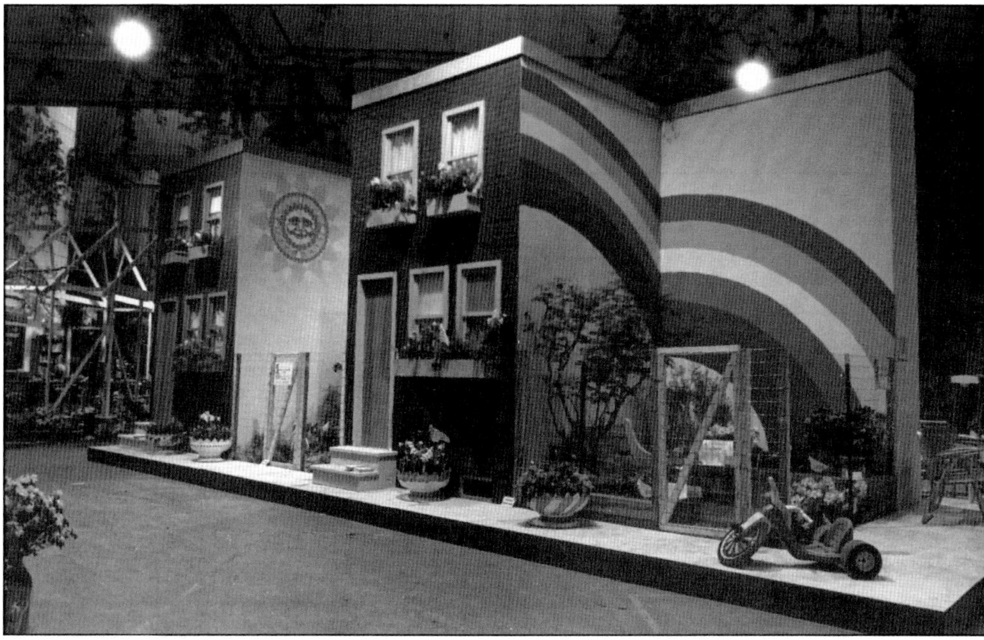

The first year PHS staged an exhibit to showcase Philadelphia Green, its urban gardening program, was 1983. This exhibit featured a typical Philadelphia street of row houses decorated with colorful window boxes, containers made from recycled automobile tires, a corner sitting garden, and a community vegetable garden planted in the vacant lot between the two houses.

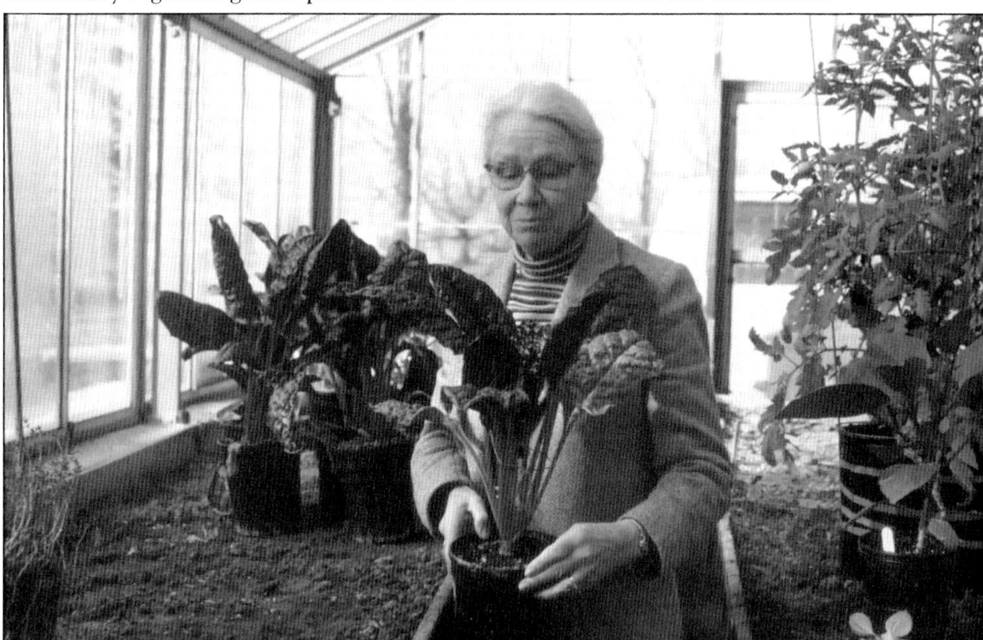

For the 1983 show, the vegetables that appeared in the Philadelphia Green exhibit were grown by Lois Burpee, widow of David Burpee (of the Burpee seed company), at her home, Fordhook Farm, in Bucks County. Lois Burpee supported PHS urban greening efforts and offered the use of Burpee's greenhouses to grow the vegetables.

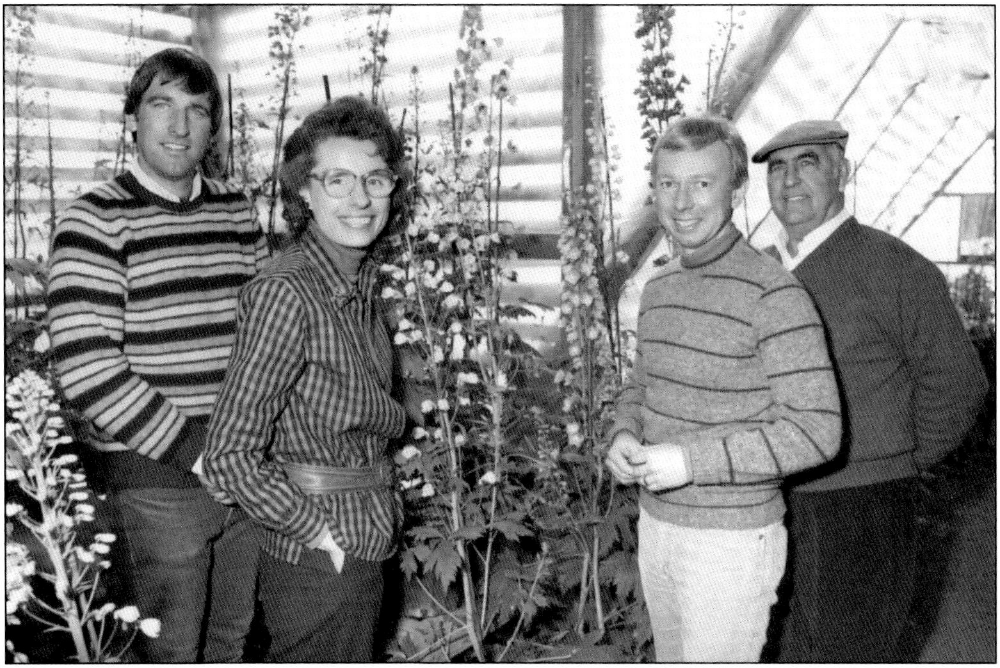

Pictured here are, from left to right, Chuck Gale; Jane Pepper, PHS president and show manager; Ed Lindemann, show designer; and Charlie Gale, Chuck's father. The group is in the Gale Nurseries greenhouses examining plants for the 1985 British-themed central feature. The Gales first created a rendering to show how visitors would walk through their exhibit, which consisted of a knot garden; 61 varieties of perennials, biennials, and annuals; and a rose garden. Planning for the growth and forcing of the plants is complex; some plants are sown as early as two years before their exhibit debuts.

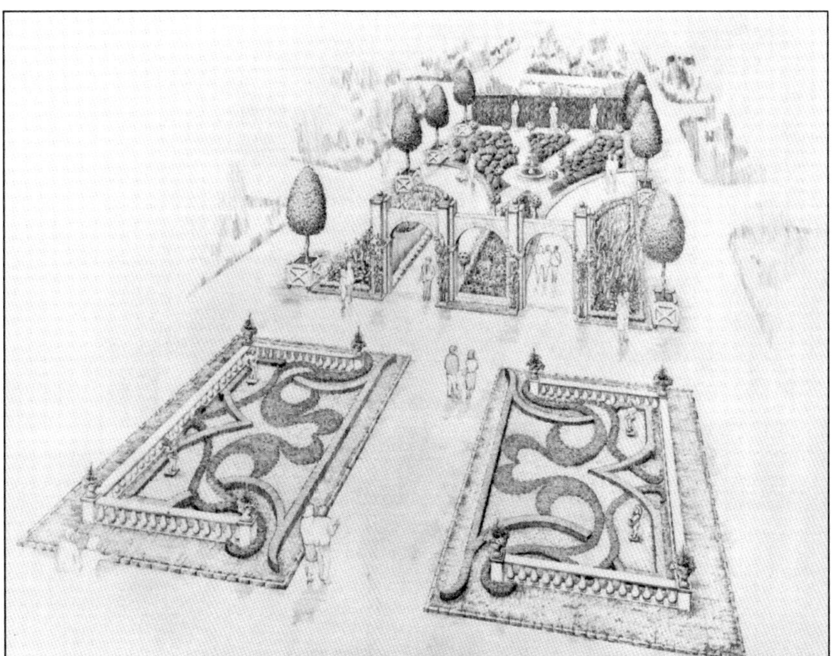

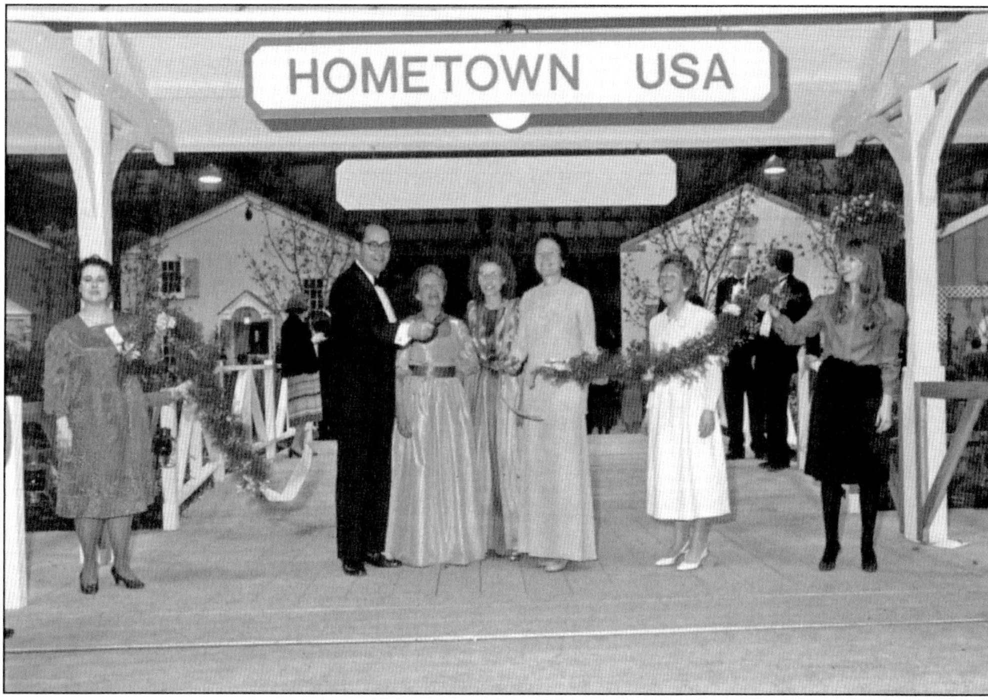

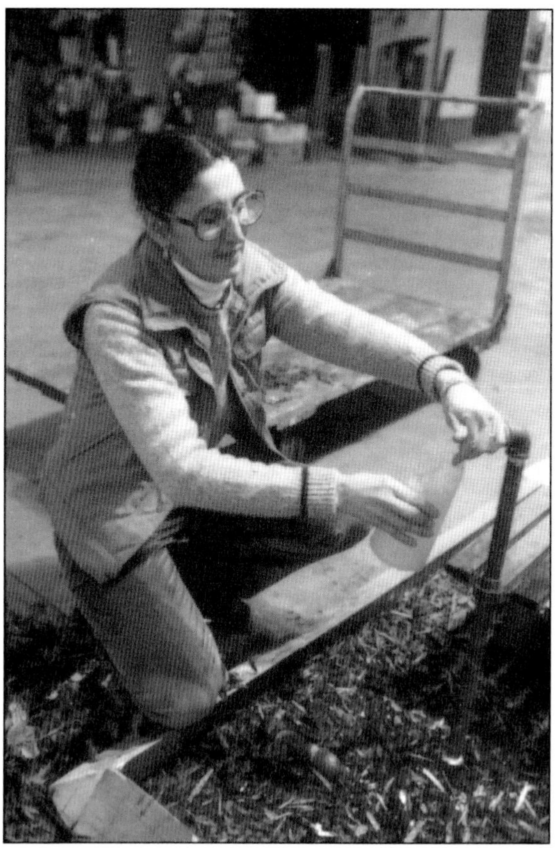

This photograph of the 1986 Preview Dinner ribbon-cutting ceremony includes, from left to right, Ellen Wheeler, Preview Dinner coordinator; Pennsylvania governor Richard Thornburgh; Preview Dinner chair Elizabeth Dolan; PHS president Jane Pepper; Ginny Thornburgh, wife of Richard; Mary Hyndman, Flower Show chair; and Lisa Stephano, public information coordinator.

Sylvia Lin exhibited in the show from the 1970s until 2010. She won the PHS Horticultural Sweepstakes 11 times, along with numerous other show awards and countless blue ribbons. Known as the show's "begonia queen," she grew and groomed her plants to perfection. She is shown during a 1985 show at the civic center, preparing to water her entries.

Here, Bruce Rawlings, of Robert W. Montgomery Landscape Nursery, is setting up the central feature, titled "Hometown USA," at the 1986 show held at the civic center. The exhibit featured a typical American hometown of the 1940s, complete with a park, pond, bandstand, and railroad station. A working locomotive and tracks were part of the staging.

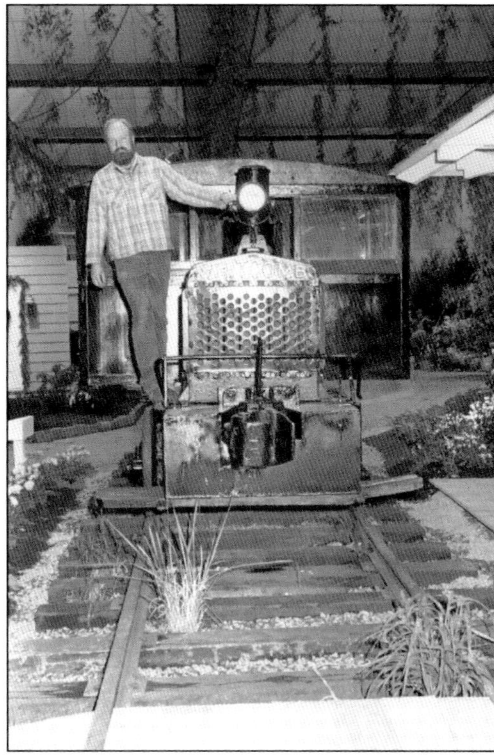

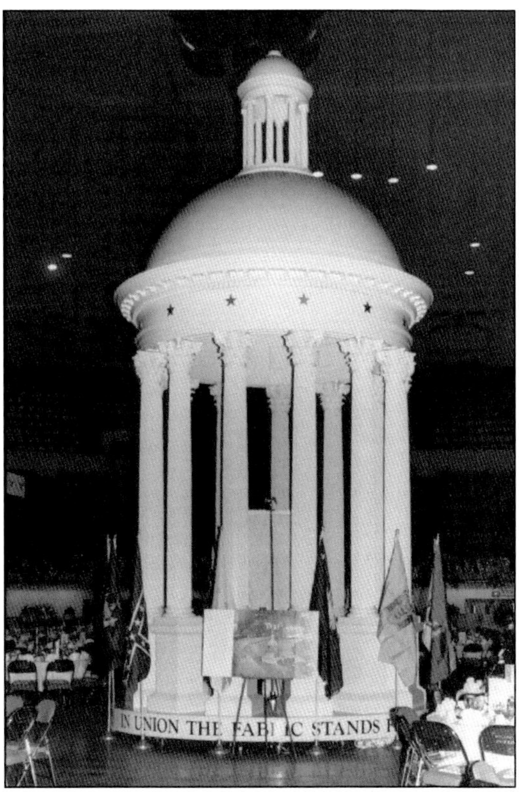

The 1987 Philadelphia Flower Show Preview Dinner was graced with a replica of Charles Willson Peale's "Grand Federal Edifice." The original edifice was paraded in the Grand Federal Procession in Philadelphia to celebrate the 1787 ratification of the United States Constitution. The display of the replica was one of several commemorative events held in 1987, the bicentennial year of the ratification of the Constitution.

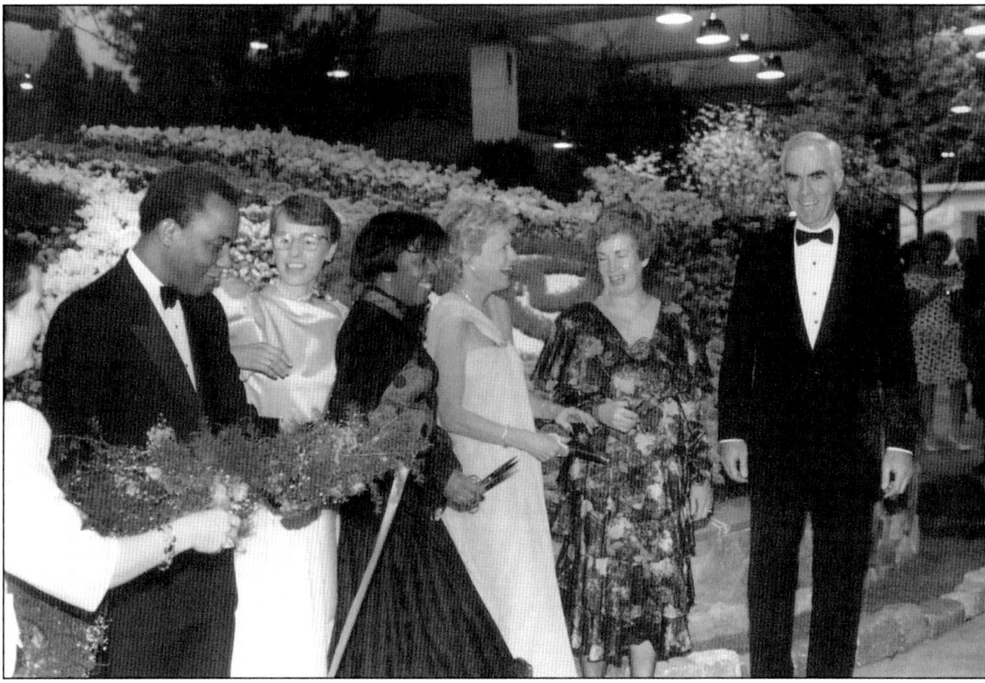

After the ribbon was cut, the 1989 Philadelphia Flower Show Preview Dinner festivities could begin. Pictured here are, from left to right, Philadelphia mayor Wilson Goode, PHS president Jane Pepper, Velma Goode, Preview Dinner chair Sallie Korman, Ellen Casey, and Pennsylvania governor Robert Casey. After a hectic set-up week, it was a treat to attend the Preview Dinner and see the now-completed, beautiful garden displays.

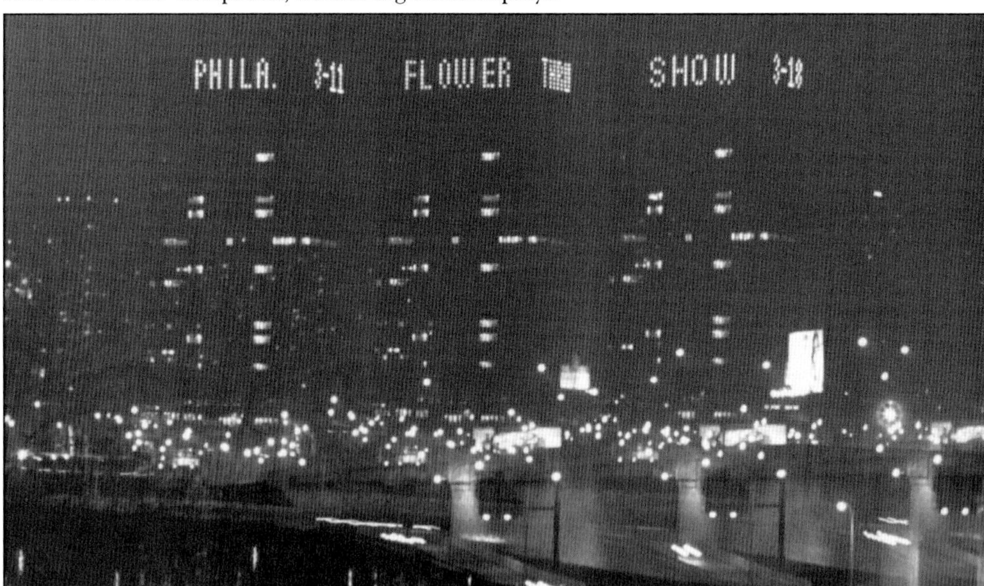

In this composite photograph, the Philadelphia Electric Company building is shown lighting up the sky with the 1990 show dates. PECO (formerly Philadelphia Electric Company) has helped promote the Flower Show since 1970 by emblazoning the dates in lights around the top of its building at 2301 Market Street. The company now uses a more energy-efficient LED lighting system.

From the 1980s forward, the Philadelphia Flower Show became more international as organizers began to work in partnership with horticultural organizations from other countries and to invite talented designers from afar to participate in the Philadelphia shows. These efforts drew visitors from abroad; the show is now both a local tradition and a must-see event for worldwide flower lovers.

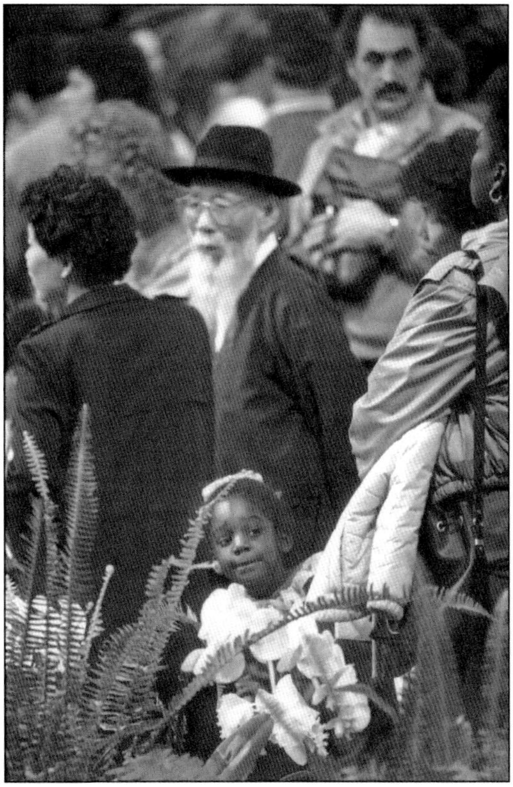

Im Wha Kong, the state flower arranger of South Korea, is shown below making preparations for her display on Korean flower arranging in the late 1980s. Im exhibited for many years, traveling at her own expense and bringing her beautiful handmade pottery to incorporate into her creations.

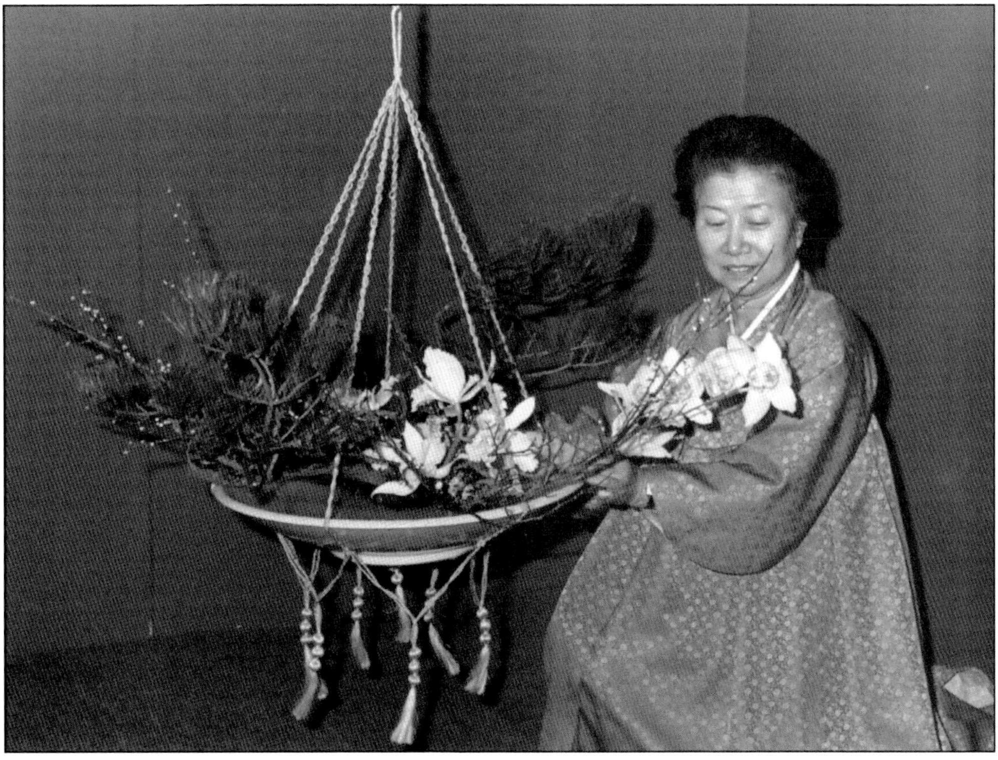

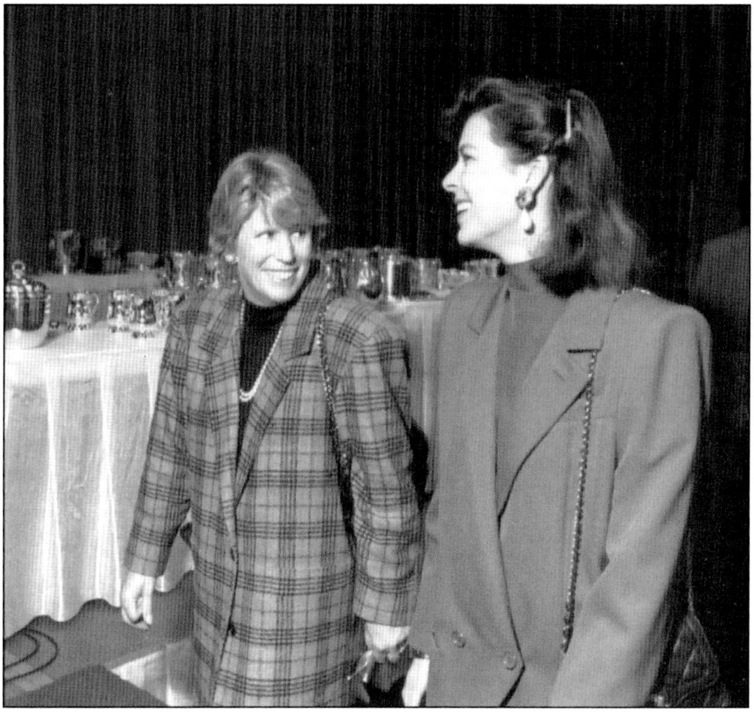

Marban Sparkman (left) president of the Garden Club of Philadelphia, accompanied Her Serene Highness Princess Caroline of Monaco to the 1990 awards luncheon. That year, the Garden Club of Monaco and the Garden Club of Philadelphia worked together to create a major exhibit.

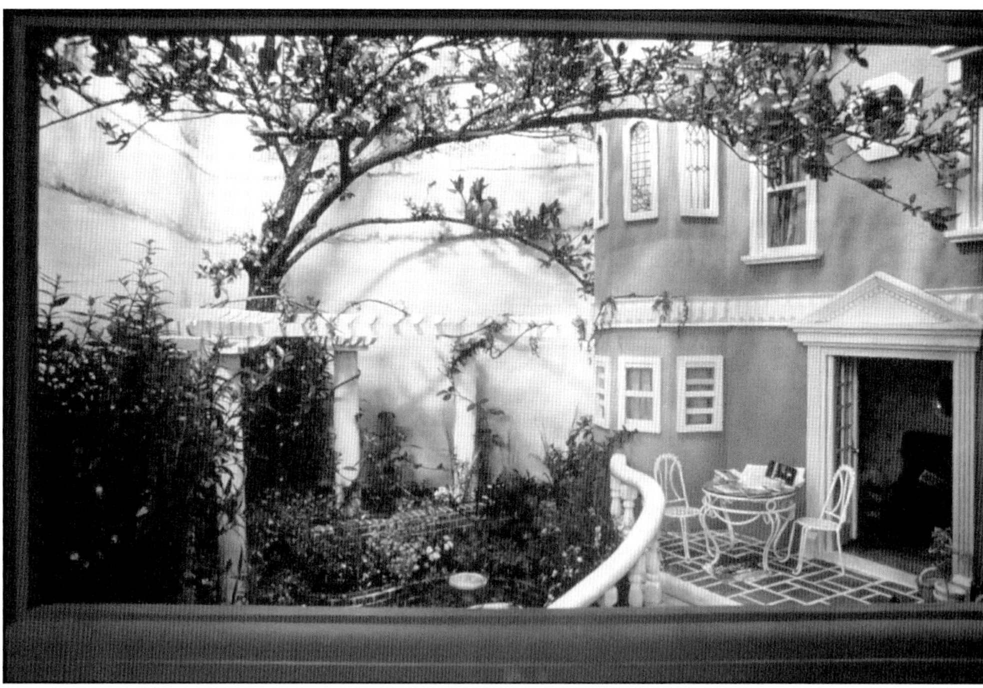

The miniature settings in 1990 focused on that year's Monaco theme. This entry by Anne Vallery, Gia DeGenova, and Barbara Olejnik in the Miniature Setting class, A Day on the Town, was whimsically titled "Weed Rather Be at a Matinee in Monaco." The judges praised this blue ribbon–winning exhibit for its rhythmic design and lyrical feeling.

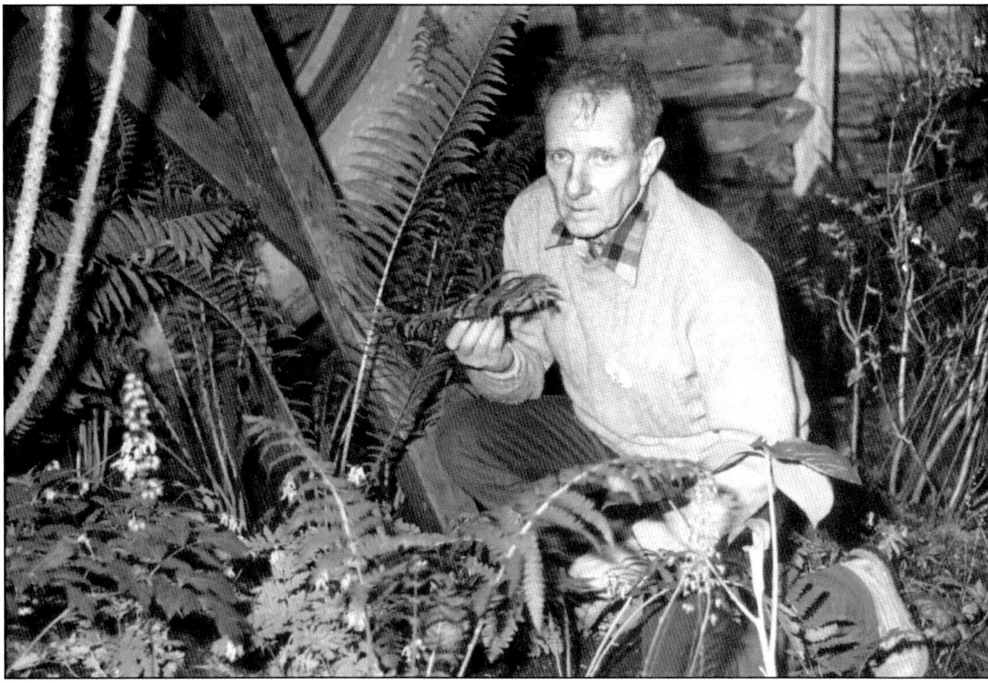

Al Vick, of Vick's Wildgardens in Gladwyne, Pennsylvania, exhibited at the show for more than 60 years, until 1993. His exhibits celebrated native wildflowers and woodland settings, evoking calm and tranquility for appreciative show visitors. An avid amateur photographer, Vick was often seen photographing the show during early morning set-up hours.

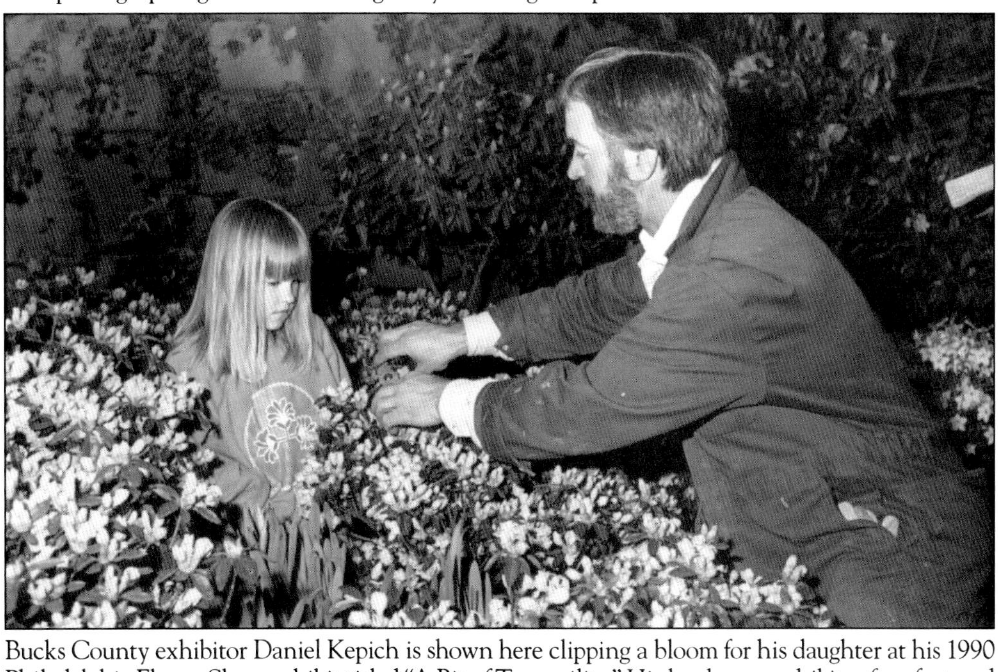

Bucks County exhibitor Daniel Kepich is shown here clipping a bloom for his daughter at his 1990 Philadelphia Flower Show exhibit titled "A Bit of Tranquility." His landscape exhibits often featured exquisite rhododendrons and azaleas rounded out with ferns and woodland flowers and complemented by rock and water; he always incorporated ideas that visitors could use in their own backyards.

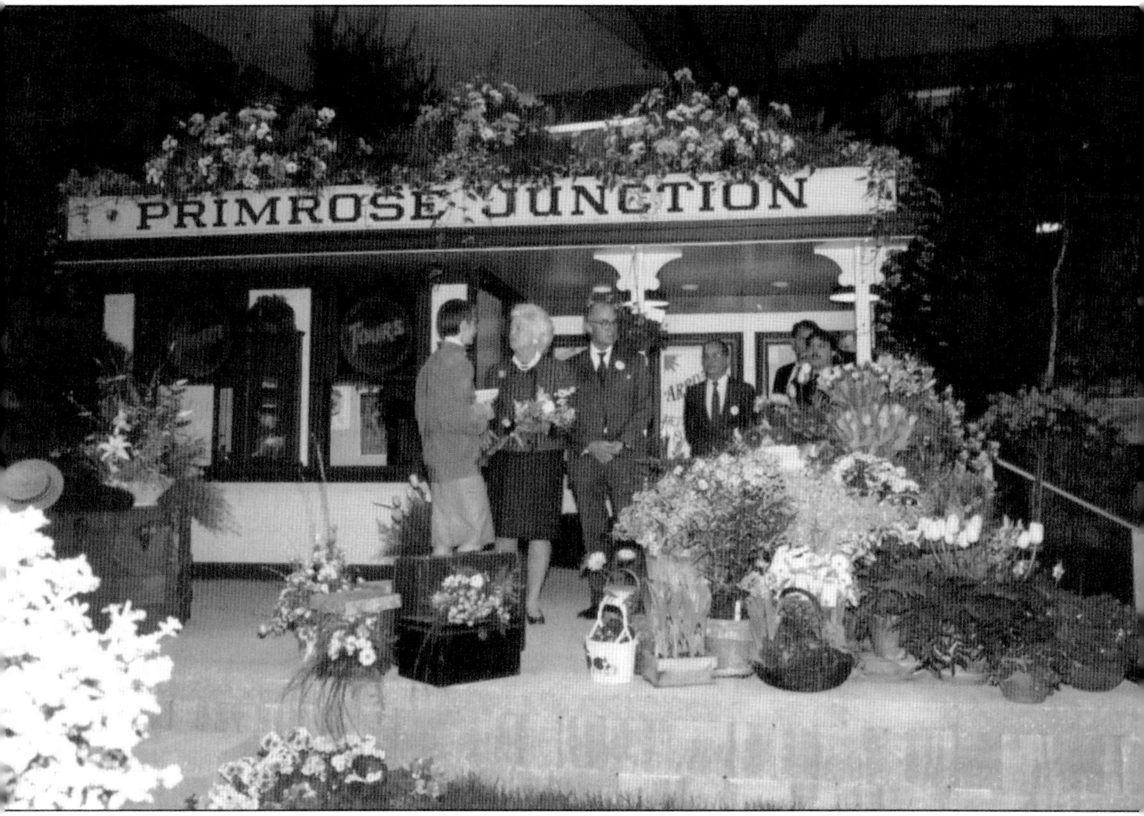

Barbara Bush visited an exhibit called "Primrose Junction" during her surprise midweek visit to the 1992 Philadelphia Flower Show—the perfect whistle-stop for a first lady. From left to right are Jane Pepper, PHS president; Bush; Morris Cheston, of the Flower Show Executive Committee; and exhibitor LeRoy LaBold. Secret Service men stood discreetly to the side.

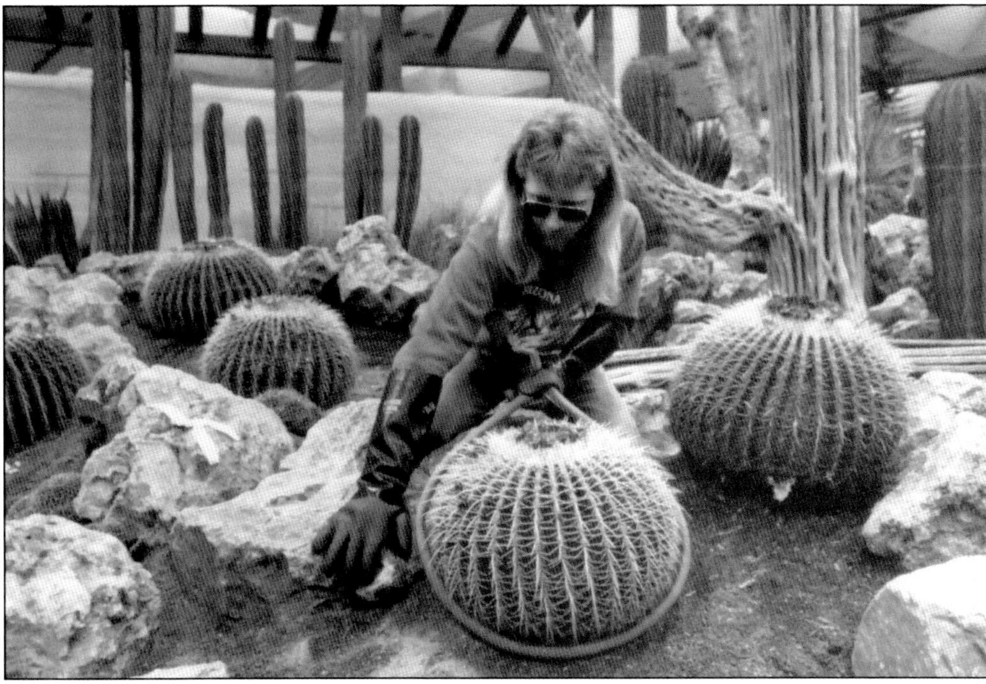

A worker at the 1992 show gingerly moves one of the 700 cacti shipped from the Southwest for that year's desert garden central feature. Giant cacti and yuccas were transported over 1,000 miles in heated trucks, wrapped in protective foam, and placed on large slings with braces and splints for protection. The exhibit, created by Robert W. Montgomery Landscape Nursery, took three years to plan and 75 people to execute.

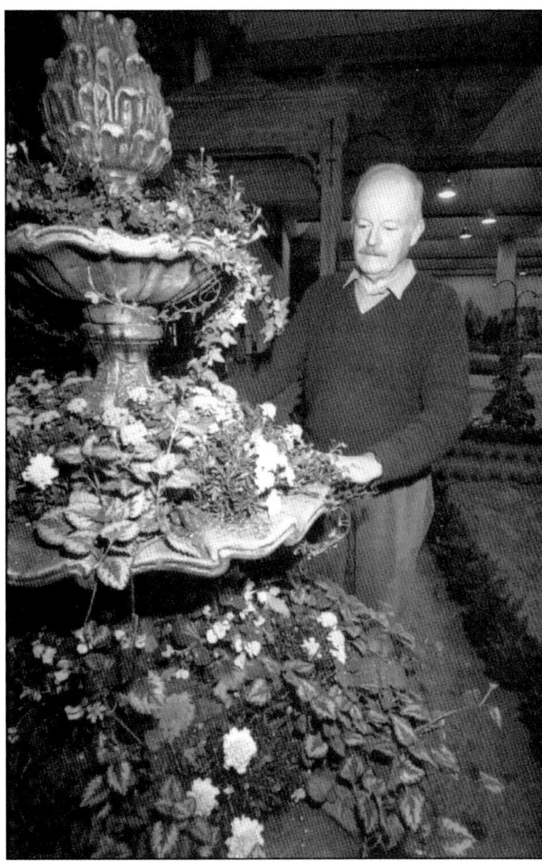

Chuck Rogers worked on an elaborate arrangement that was part of the 1992 Meadowbrook Farm exhibit titled "A *Great Gatsby* Garden." Inspired by the estate gardens of the 1920s, the exhibit's formal garden featured handsome belvederes, patterned garden beds, and terraces. Verdant topiaries and colorful hanging baskets, two iconic design elements of nearly every Meadowbrook Farm flower show exhibit, were part of this display.

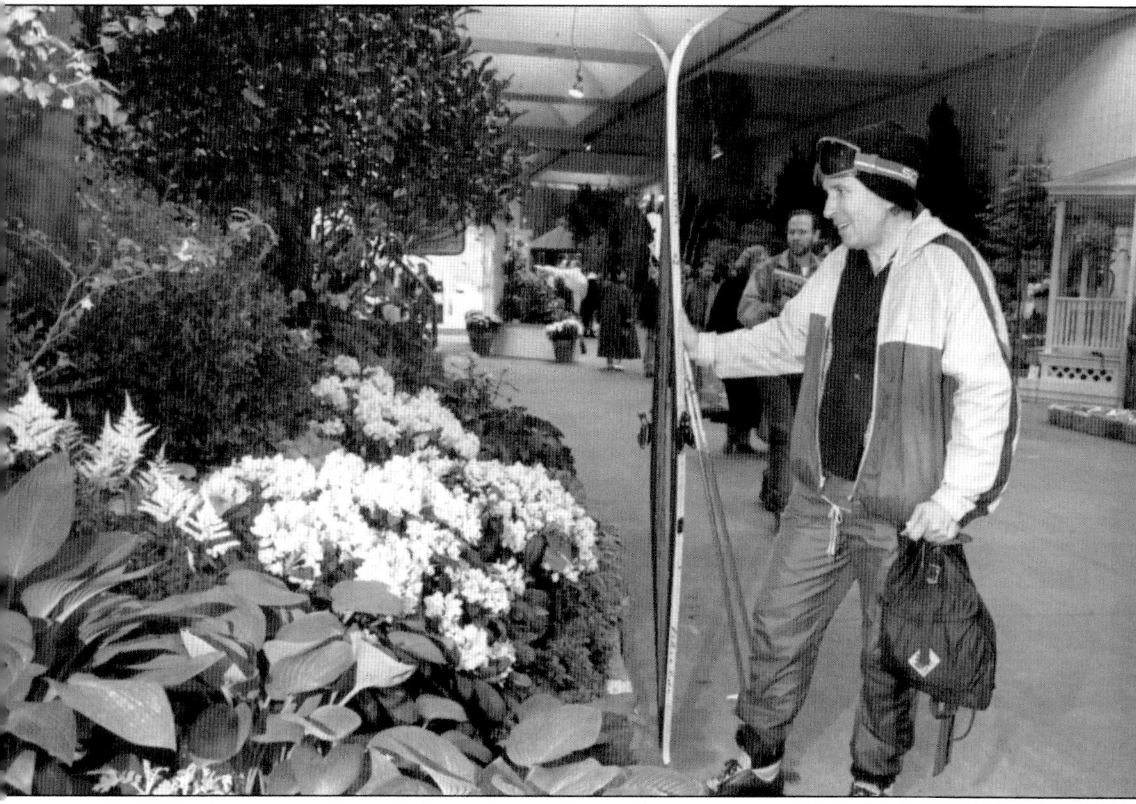

In 1993, a late-winter blizzard dumped more than a foot of snow on Philadelphia and shut down roads and railways. The show closed early, but not before Oleh Tretiak skied to the civic center from his home in the city's Art Museum neighborhood. After the forced closing of the show, civic center employees took pity on stranded exhibitors and PHS staff and supplied them with food.

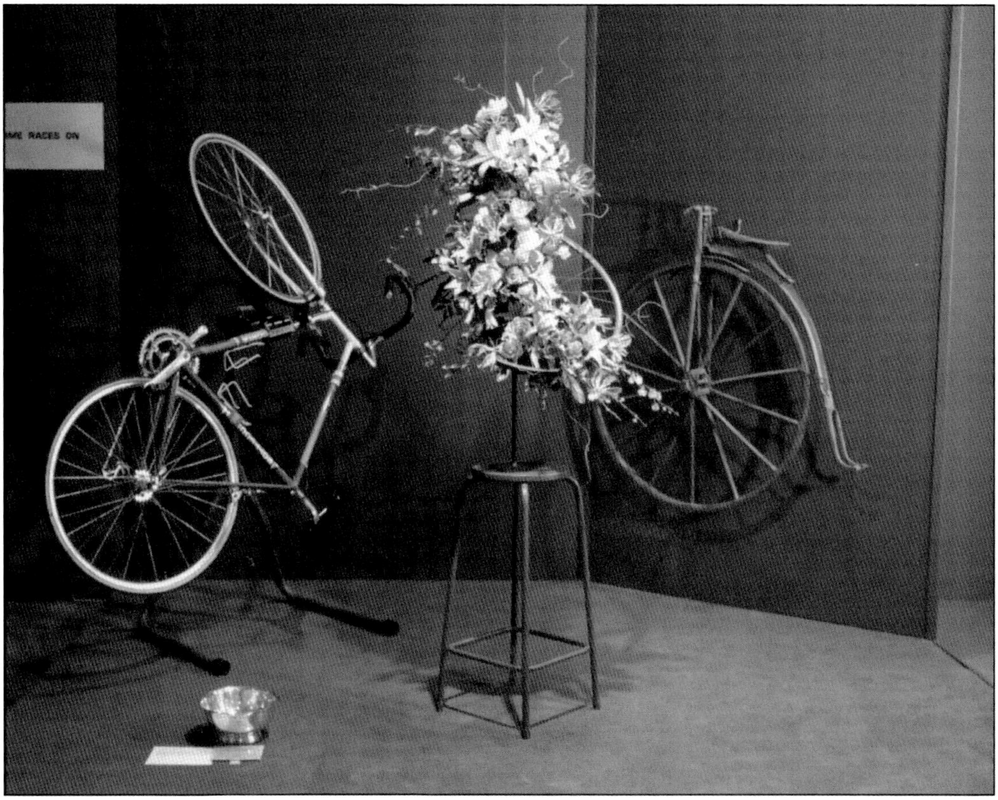

This 1993 room class required that entries interpret a "commercial enterprise then and now: a section of a commercial space depicting some sort of business." The Garden Workers exhibit, "Time Races On," depicted a bicycle shop then and now. "The choice of gear-like plants captured the sensation of cycling," wrote the enthusiastic judges.

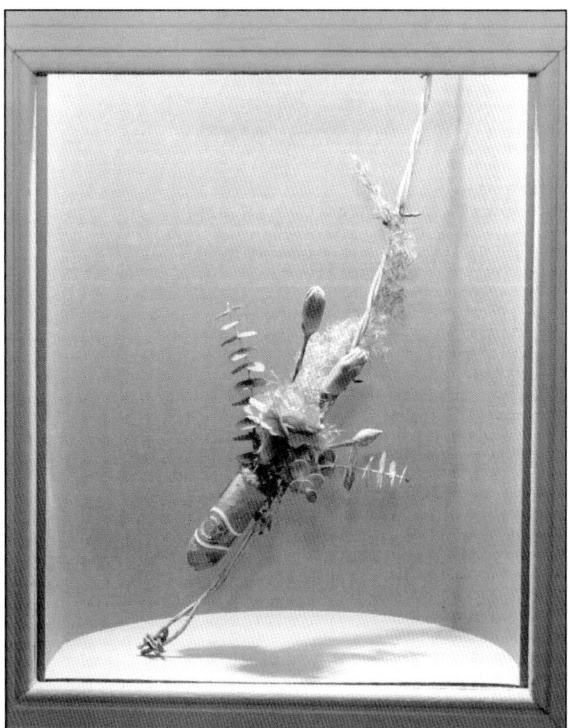

This 1993 niche category required competitors to create an arrangement that would interpret a famous quote. Using a mini carnation, eucalyptus, and part of a cigar, Pamela Danner interpreted Winston Churchill's unforgettable words, "We shall fight on the landing grounds, we shall fight in the fields and in the streets, we shall fight in the hills, we shall never surrender."

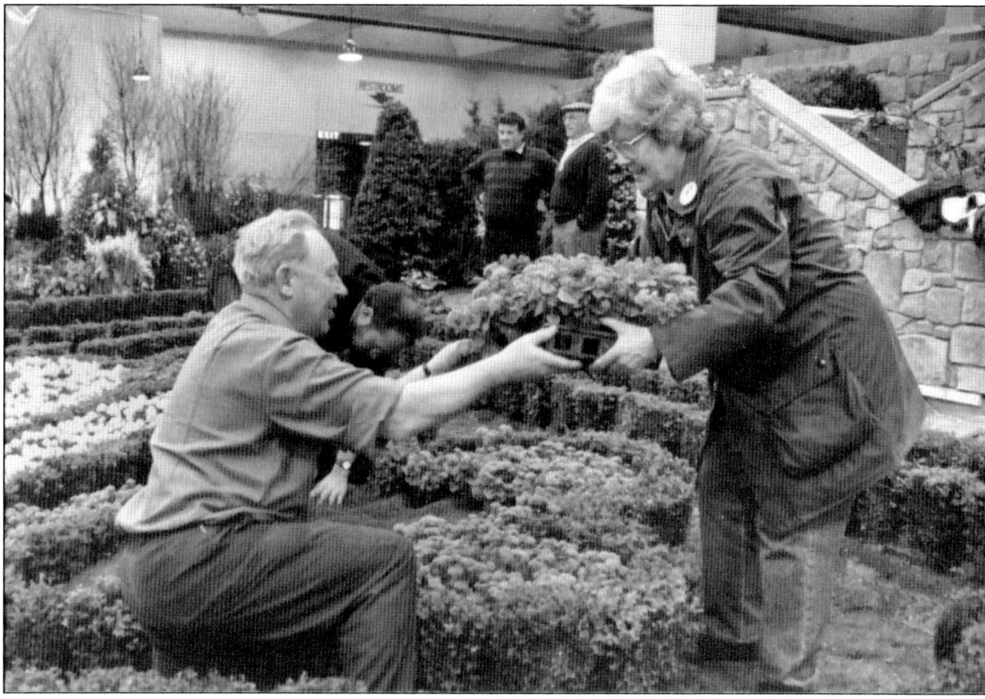

Pitmedden, a garden of the Scottish National Trust, inspired the central feature of the 1993 show. Pitmedden's head gardener, Ian Ross, left, is handing plants to Elizabeth McLean, project manager for this exhibit, which required more than 2,000 plants for its colorful floral carpet. A garden historian, McLean was charged with ensuring that this replica of Pitmedden's 17th-century parterre was correct in every detail. She visited Scotland to study and photograph the original gardens.

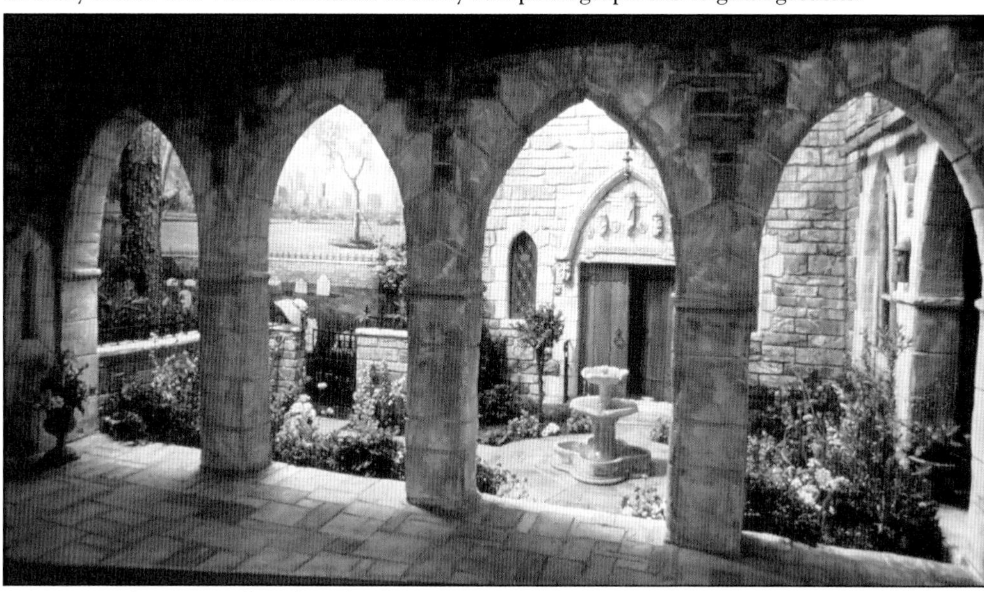

In 1993, Midge Ingersoll and Evelyn Seaton created their first miniature exhibit and won Best in Show for that category. Miniatures are installed in boxes measuring 36 inches wide, 22 inches deep, and 42 inches high; the viewing public sees them through a frame 12 inches high and 22 inches wide.

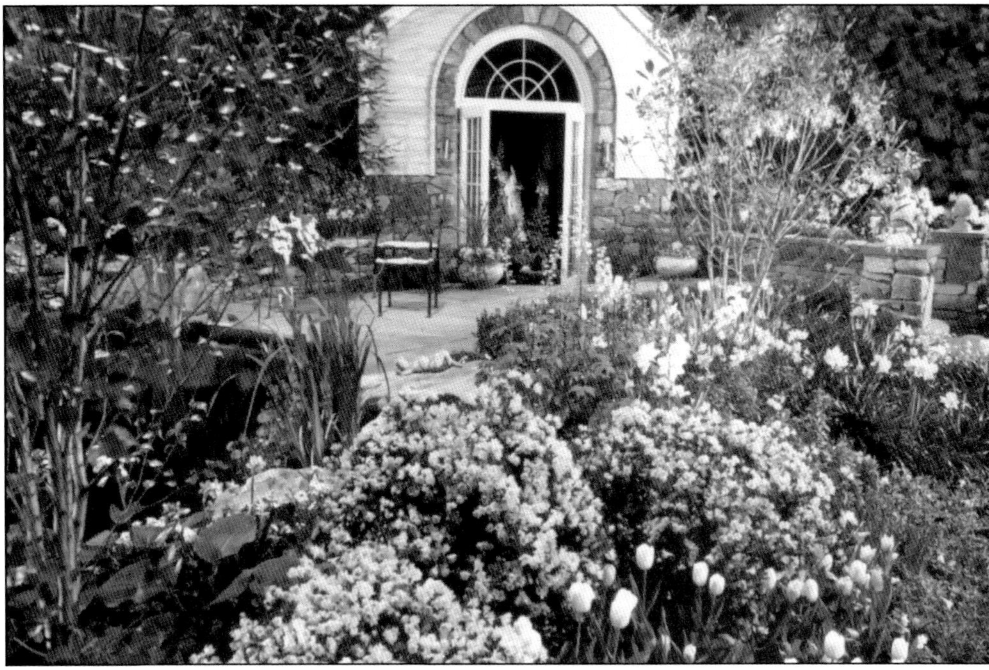

Signature Landscape & Design of Downingtown, Pennsylvania, and Romano's Landscaping of Pitman, New Jersey, worked together to create this 1993 exhibit inspired by a historic, renovated Chester County springhouse. The springhouse replica was set in a naturalistic backdrop of native rhododendrons and hostas. Delphiniums, astilbes, and azaleas surrounded a flagstone terrace.

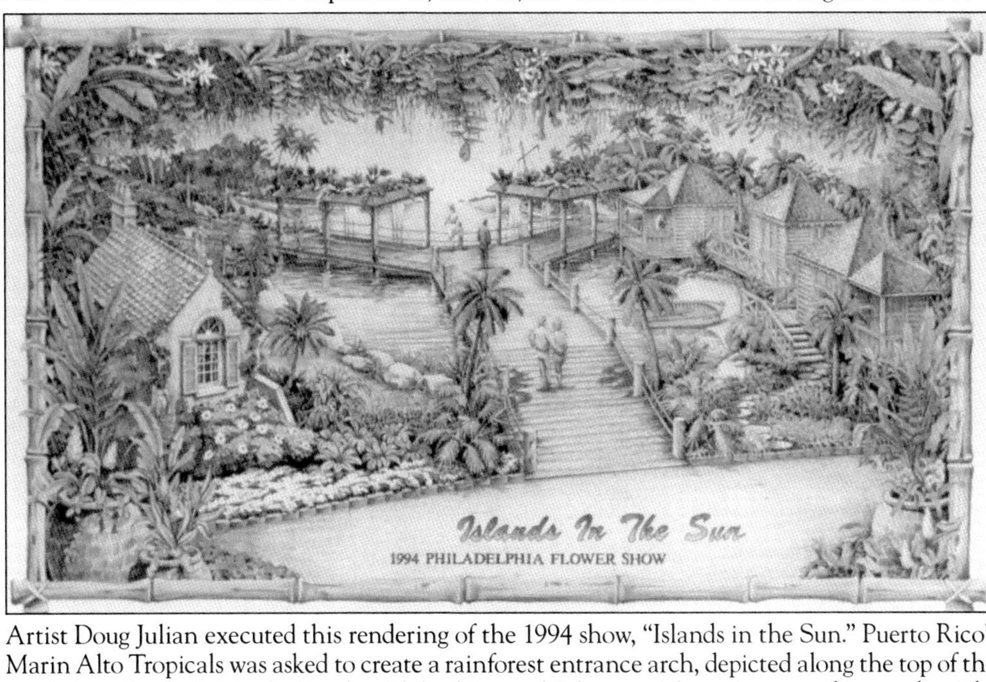

Artist Doug Julian executed this rendering of the 1994 show, "Islands in the Sun." Puerto Rico's Marin Alto Tropicals was asked to create a rainforest entrance arch, depicted along the top of the rendering. On the left is the Garden Club of Bermuda's house with a cottage garden; on the right is the Barbados Horticultural Society's Victorian island bathhouse. Waldor Orchids' orchid-filled haunted shipwreck is shown in the lagoon.

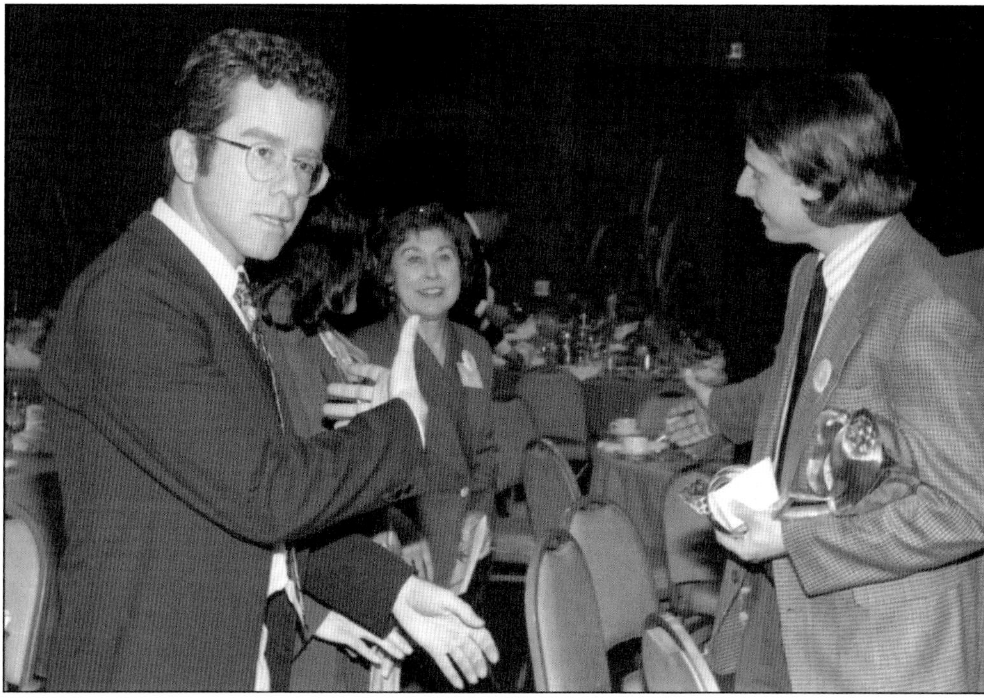

Two talented growers and exhibitors, Ray Rogers (left) and Ken Selody, are pictured at the 1994 awards luncheon. Selody, with trophy in hand, won the PHS Horticultural Sweepstakes that year; Rogers won that honor the year before and has won nearly 400 blue ribbons for his exquisitely grown entries.

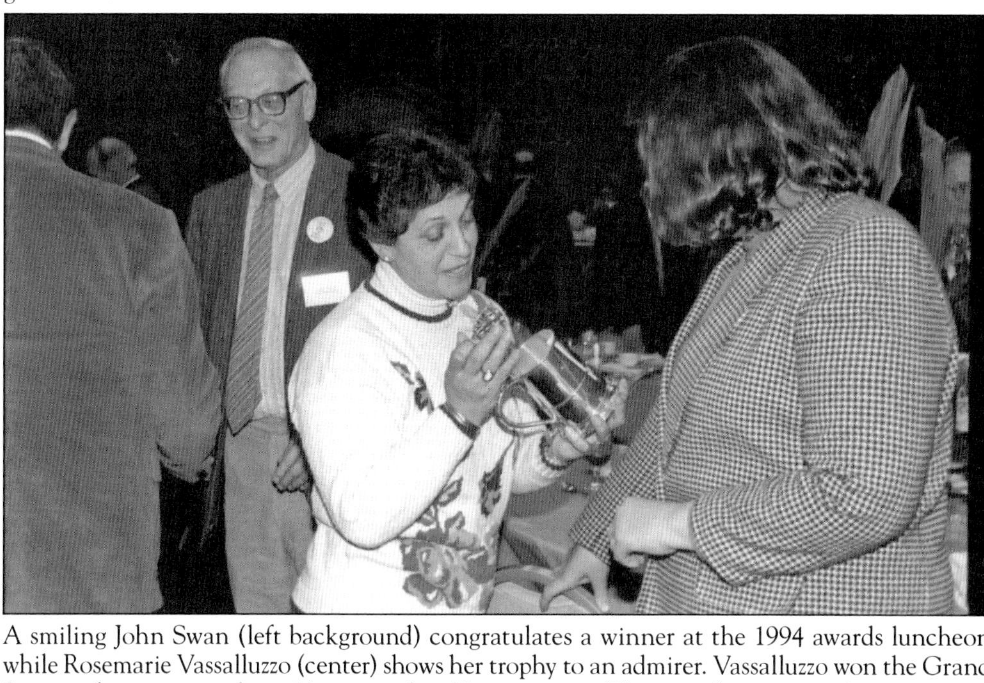

A smiling John Swan (left background) congratulates a winner at the 1994 awards luncheon while Rosemarie Vassalluzzo (center) shows her trophy to an admirer. Vassalluzzo won the Grand Sweepstakes an astonishing 14 times in her 30-year career. This award is given to the competitor who accumulates the most points in both the artistic and horticulture classes.

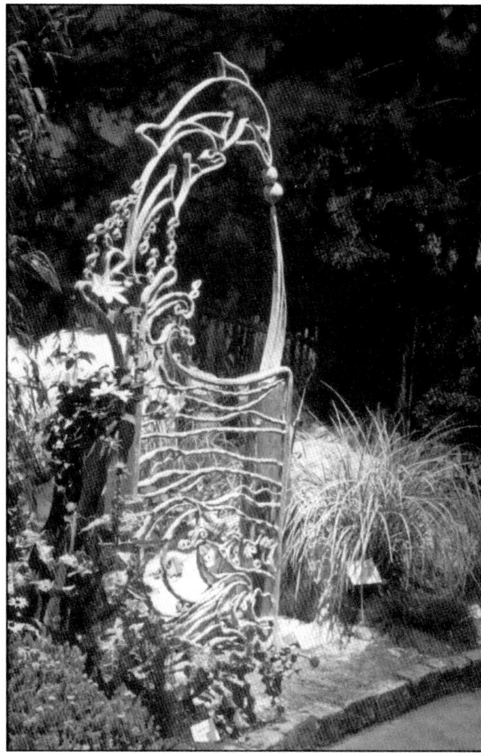

Stoney Bank Nurseries won a silver trophy for this Sand Castle exhibit in 1994. Show visitors were invited to look through this charming dolphin garden gate into a seaside garden. While the exhibit evoked sensations of warmth and sunshine with its sand dunes, ornamental grasses, and perennials, preparing the display was agony; the winter of 1994 was an especially frigid one that included power losses from severe ice storms. Jack Blandy (pictured below), the owner of Stoney Bank, waited in line for hours for kerosene in order to keep his greenhouse at a temperature of 50 degrees, a mere eight degrees above the danger zone for his plants.

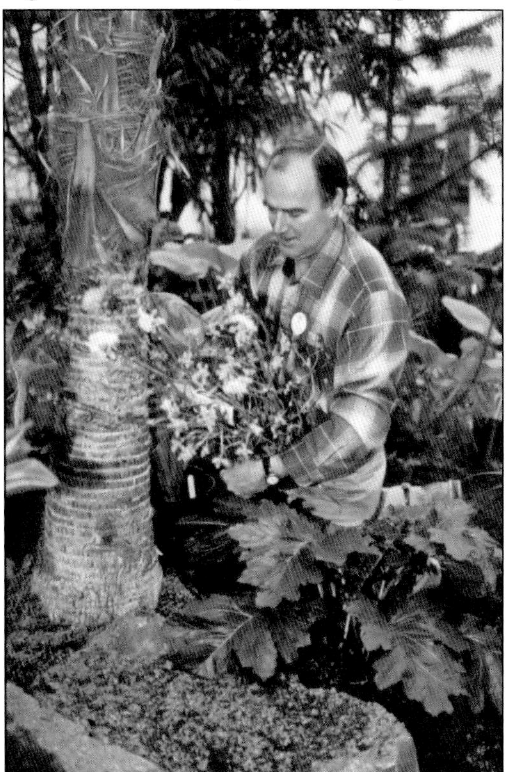

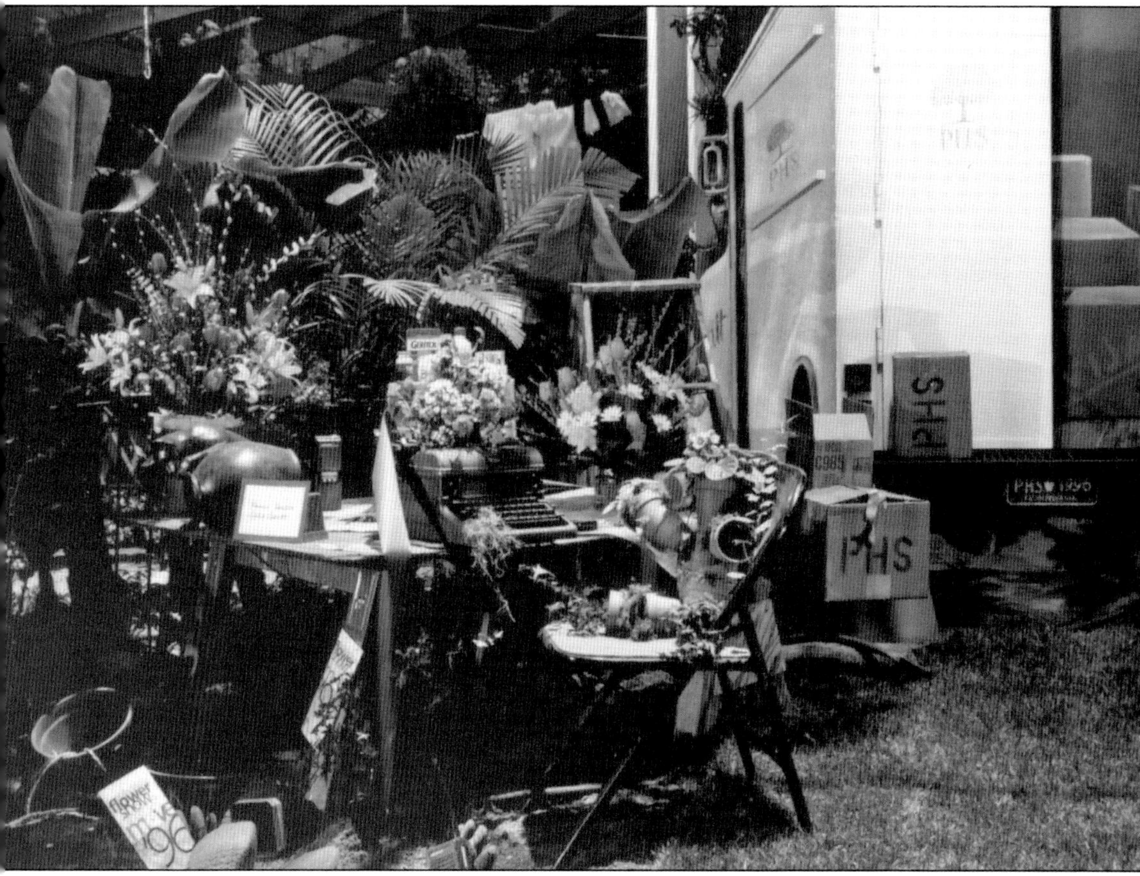

With packing boxes and a moving truck, this segment of Robertson's Flowers of Chestnut Hill's five-part central feature exhibit at the 1995 Philadelphia Flower Show depicted the act of moving out of the Philadelphia Civic Center after 30 years of great shows there. Robertson's has provided the floral arrangements for the Preview Dinner since the early 1970s and has been a major exhibitor for many years.

Four

Pennsylvania Convention Center

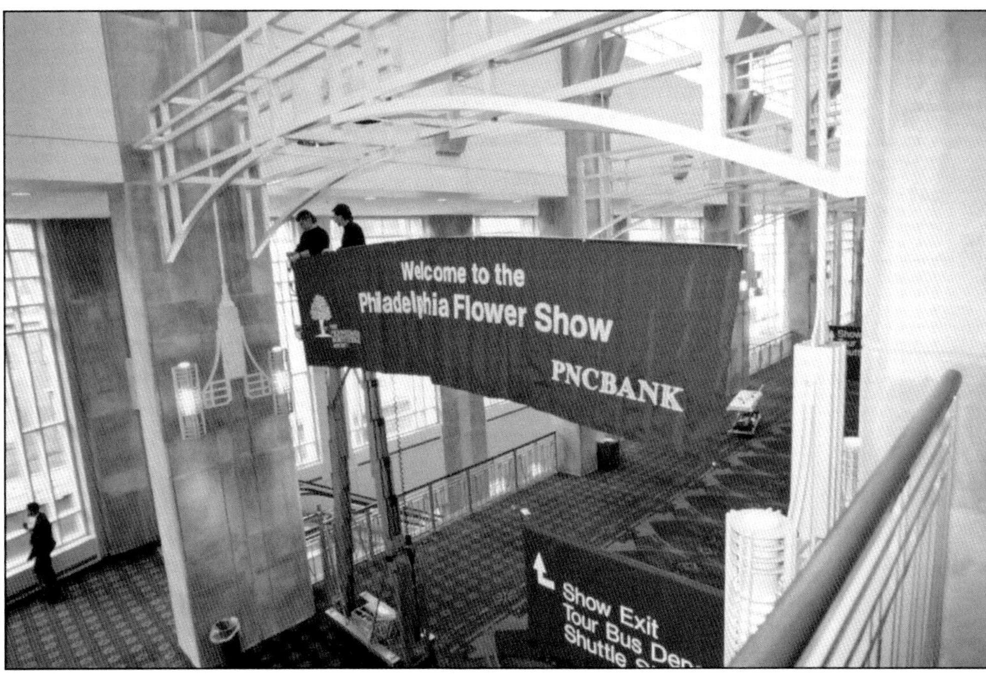

A big change came in 1996, when the Philadelphia Flower Show moved to the new Pennsylvania Convention Center in downtown Philadelphia after 30 years at the civic center. The Pennsylvania Convention Center covered 33 acres, and auxiliary space included rooms for culinary and flower arranging events. Show visitors had all of Philadelphia's amenities within walking distance. The show finally had a stage befitting its grandeur.

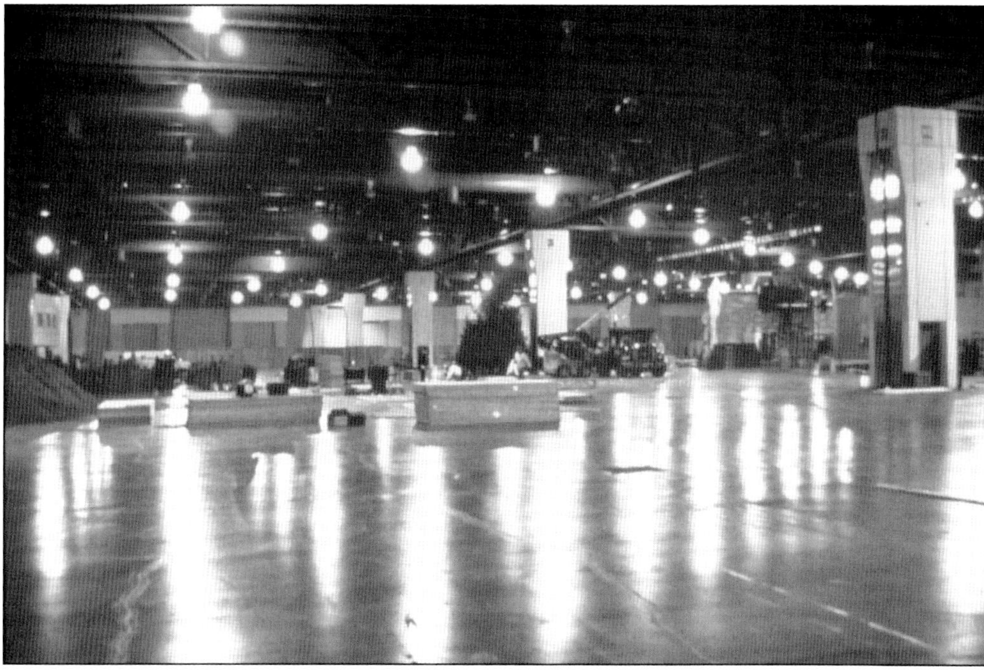

The move from the civic center to the Pennsylvania Convention Center in 1996 meant an increase of exhibition hall space from 6 acres to 10. Aisles at the civic center were 20 feet wide; the new space allowed for aisle space of up to 45 feet. Ceiling height increased to 55 feet—a great improvement over the 27-foot-high civic center ceiling.

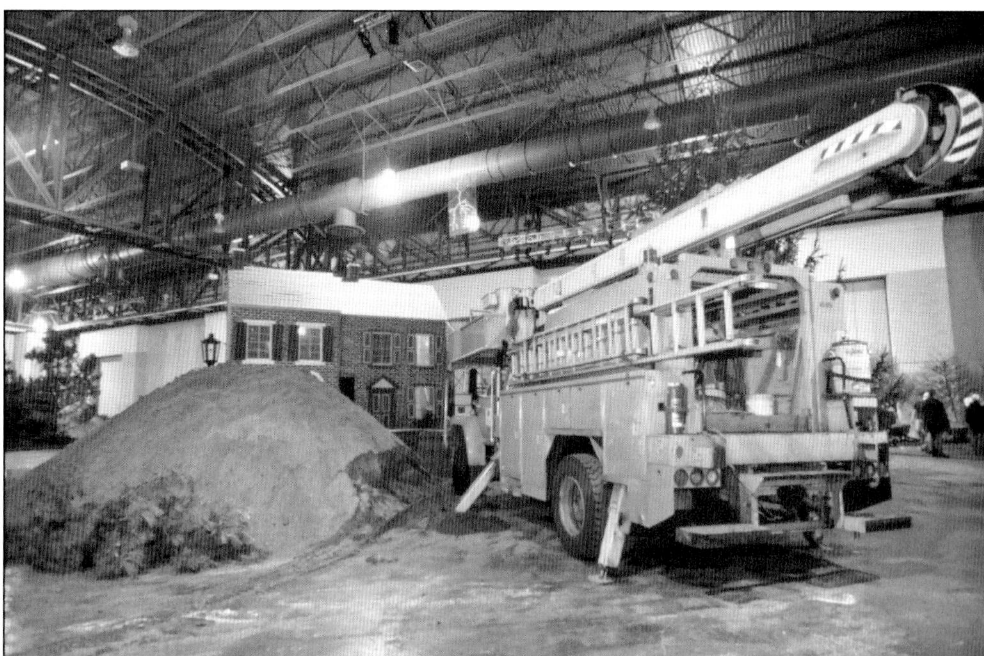

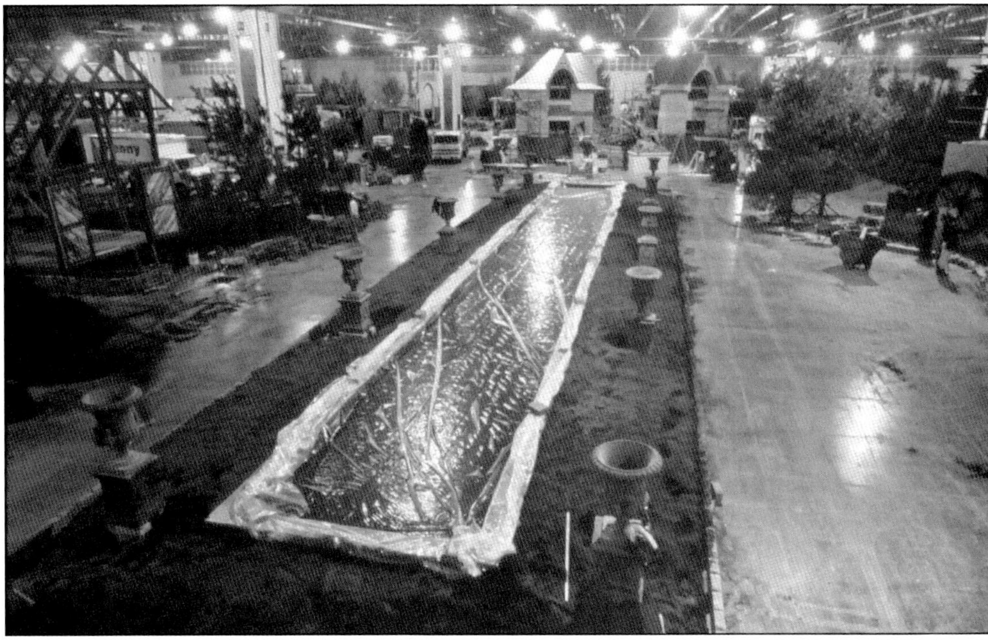

The first year in the new venue came with a surprise. Part of the central feature was a replica of the 1876 Centennial Pool in Fairmount Park. Upon installation, it was necessary to reduce the pool by 10 feet in length to allow enough space between the pool and the entrance doors for people to enter comfortably. Resizing the pool was easy; the bigger challenge was redesigning the elaborate bedding plant garden that was to surround it.

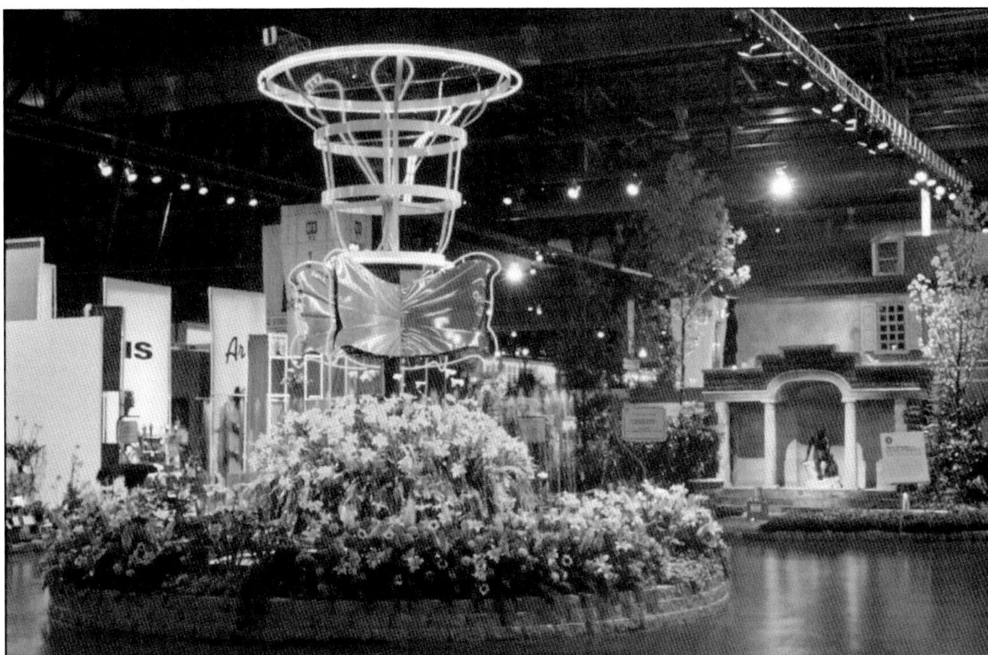

As part of the central feature of the 1996 show, floral designers Elverston Jordan teamed with sculptor Charles A. Szoradi to create a Liberty Bell Fountain exhibit. It was a fantasy interpretation of Philadelphia's famous bell made using plants, a neon-lit sculpture, and a fountain.

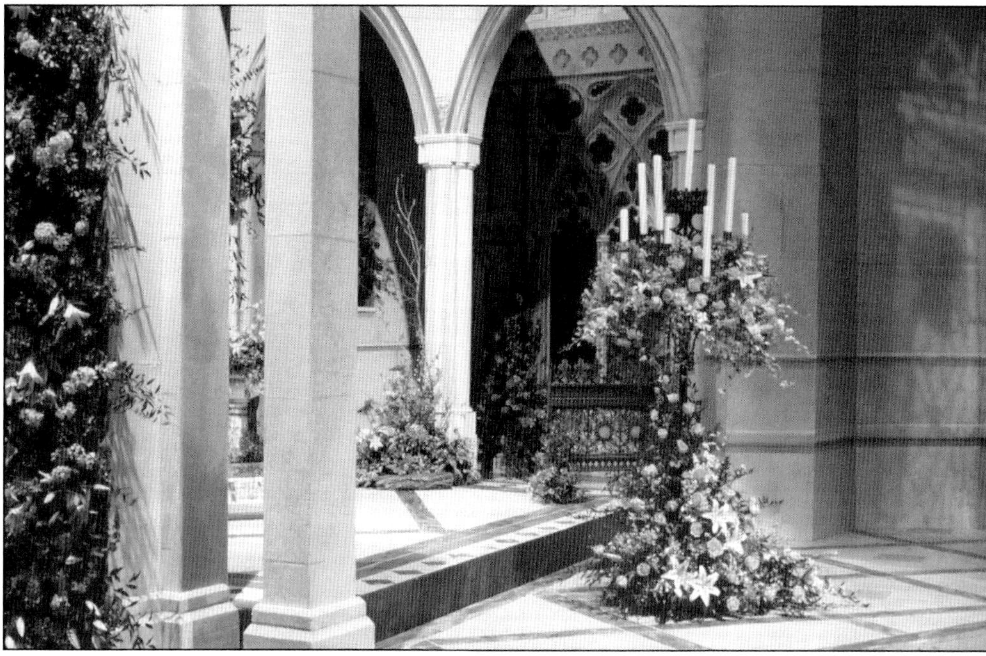

The Altar Guild of the Washington National Cathedral exhibited several times and was very popular with visitors. Guild designs were often sculptural as well as spiritual in their interpretations. This 1996 exhibit, "Divine Inspiration," captured the remarkable ambiance of the guild's heavenly arrangements against the backdrop of the cathedral's Gothic architecture.

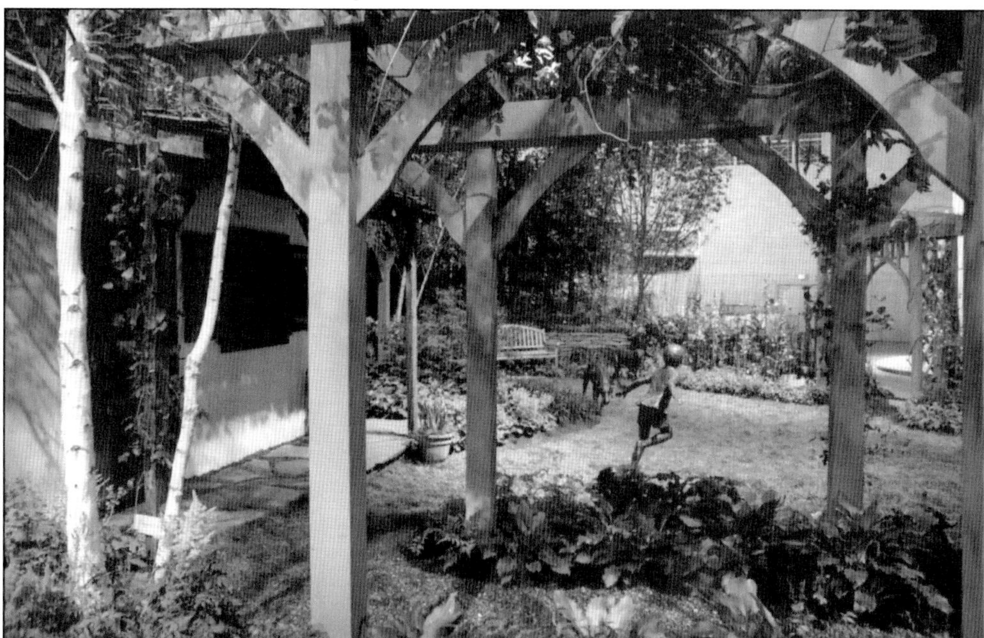

This lovely backyard retreat, titled "Simple Things," won J. Cugliotta Landscape/Nursery, Inc., the 1996 Best Achievement Award in the landscape category as well as the Pennsylvania Horticultural Society Council Trophy. The judges found "the large trees remarkably forced." J. Cugliotta exhibited at the show for more than 20 years.

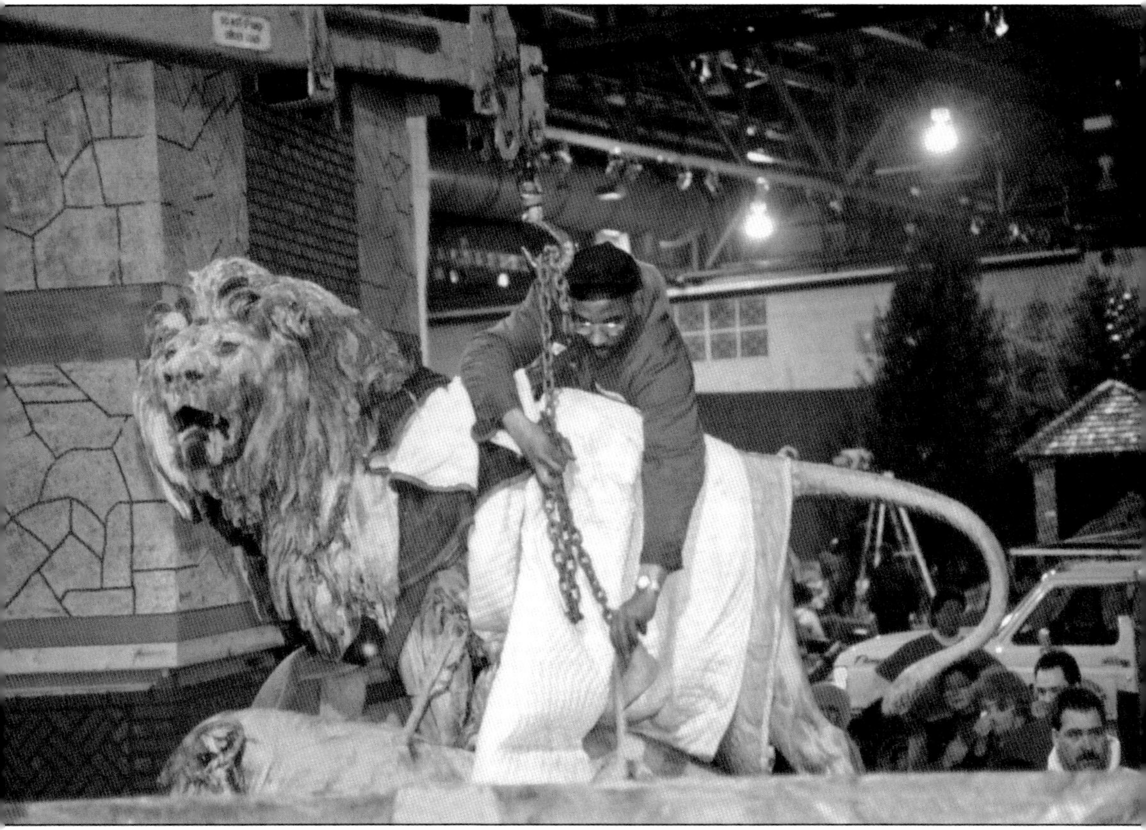

The 1996 show highlighted several of America's firsts that had origins in Philadelphia, including the Philadelphia Zoo. Show officials were thrilled to be able to borrow the zoo's Wilhelm Wolff sculpture, *The Dying Lioness*. This massive bronze work was first shown at the 1876 centennial and normally stands guard at the zoo entrance. A convention center worker made sure this 69-inch-tall treasure was firmly in place.

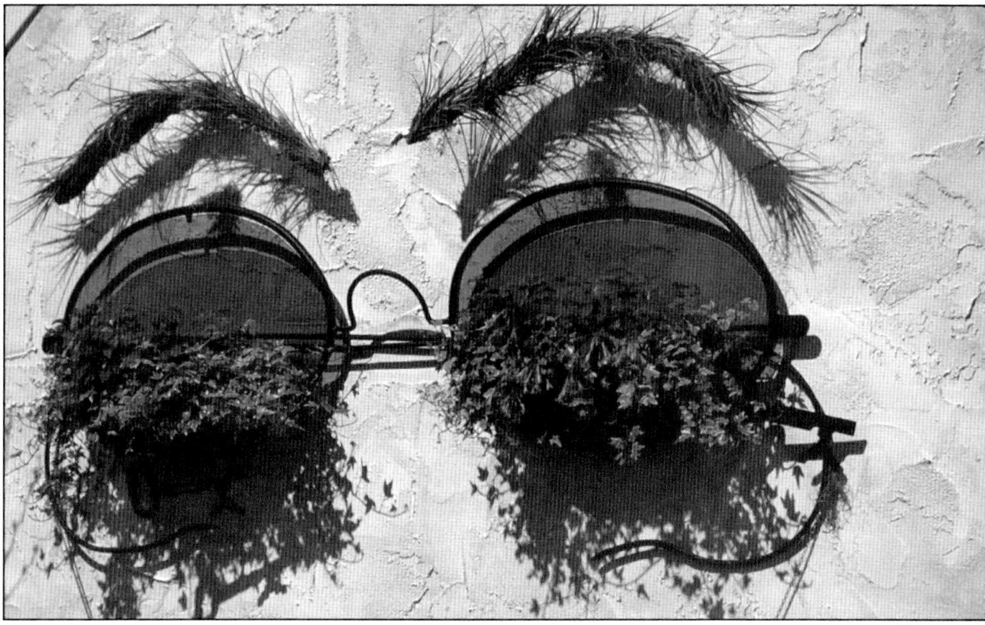

The 1997 exhibit by Robertson's Flowers of Chestnut Hill was a playful interpretation of that year's theme, "The Great Exchange—People, Places, and Plants." Visitors were invited to observe a birthday party celebration for Benjamin Franklin, one of Philadelphia's most famous citizens, as though he had been at the show all along. The party's "guest list" included notable figures from throughout the centuries.

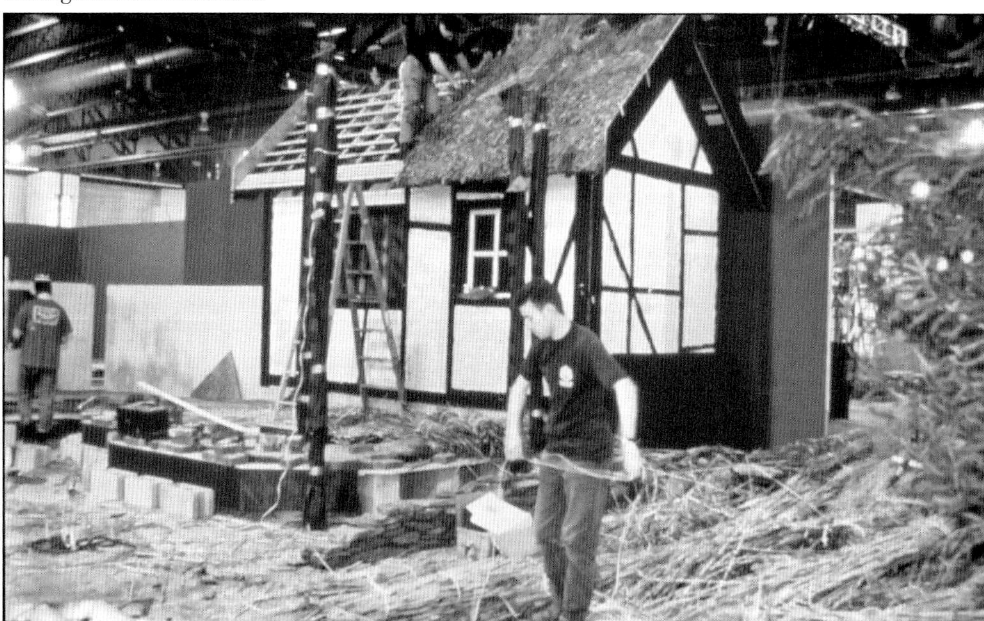

In 1997, the Williamson Free School of Mechanical Trades in Media, Pennsylvania, hosted this collaborative exhibit in which students from the Pershore College of Horticulture in England came to Philadelphia as guest exhibitors to work with Williamson on the display. A few years later, the Williamson students were invited by Pershore to exhibit at the Chelsea Flower Show in London.

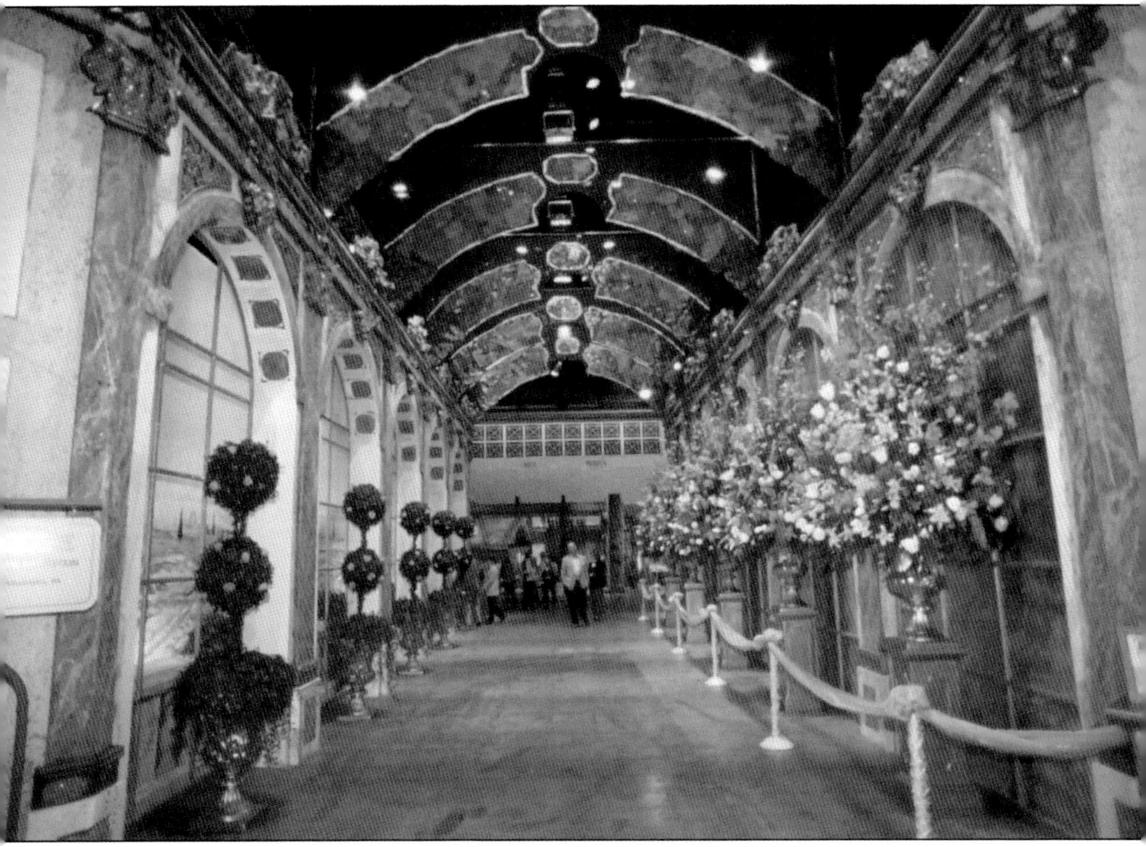

Philadelphia floral designer Jaime Rothstein created a replica of the Hall of Mirrors at Versailles in her 1998 exhibit. Only the topiary and 16-foot-high arrangements were real; the set was faux finished to imitate marble. That year, after the show closed to visitors, Rothstein married her husband in her exhibit during a ceremony witnessed by 300 guests.

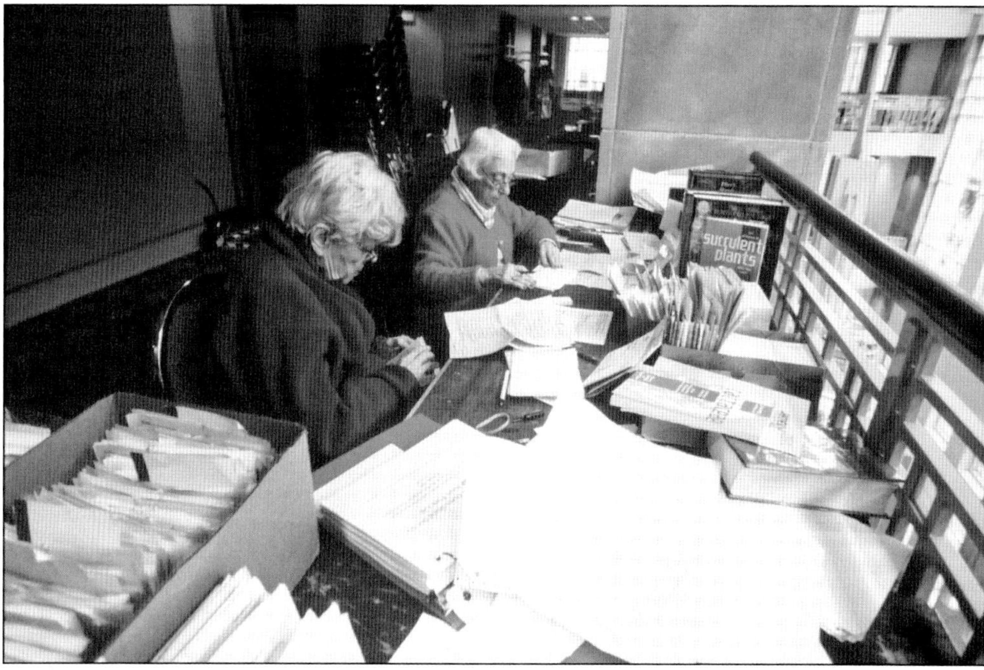

At the 1998 show, Elizabeth Farley (left) and Irene Slater consulted reference books to ensure that plant names submitted with entries were accurate and in agreement with current taxonomic practices. Every year, thousands of visitors study the plants and want to learn where to buy and how to grow them. Ensuring that visitors have accurate information is part of PHS's insistence on high standards for the show.

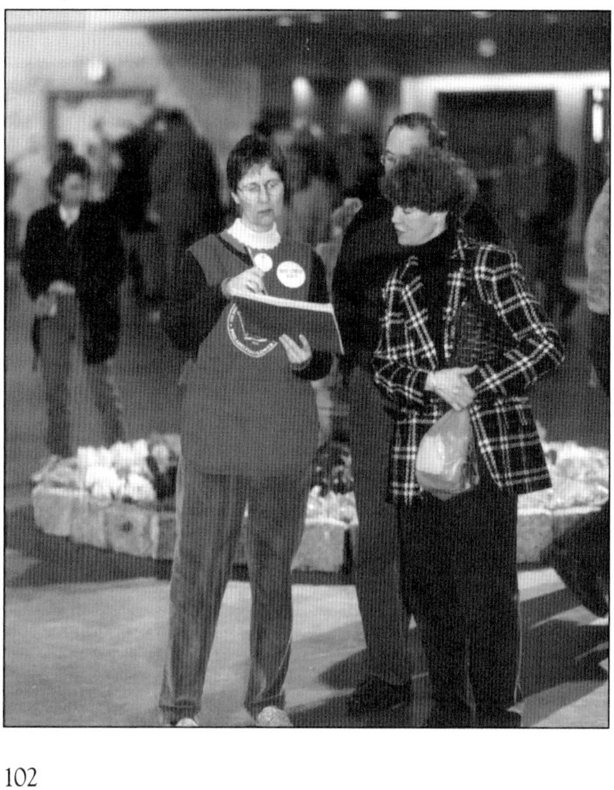

Volunteers have always been essential to the show's success. With the move to the much larger Pennsylvania Convention Center in 1996, show organizers recruited hundreds of visitor information volunteers, including Jane Alling (left), easily identifiable by her pink pinny. These friendly volunteer ambassadors help visitors find exhibits, reunite lost persons with loved ones, and put smiles on visitors' faces. Today's shows involve at least 4,000 volunteers.

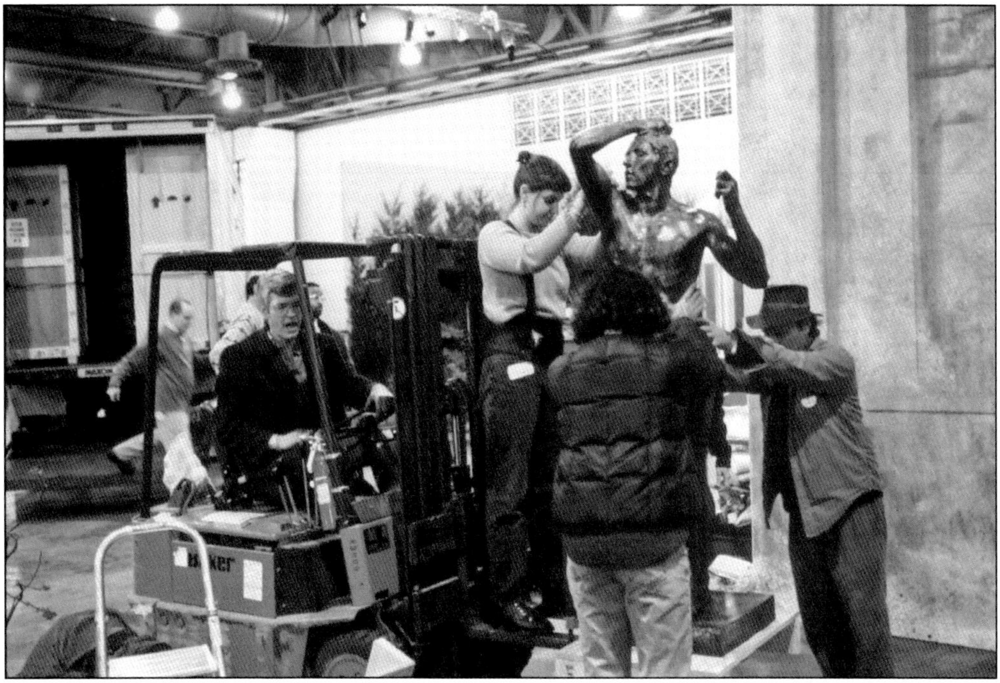

Above, from left to right, Philadelphia Museum of Art staff members Randall Cleaver, Sarah Thrower, Martha Masiello, and Andrew Lins carefully installed Rodin's sculpture, *The Age of Bronze*, at the Rodin Museum exhibit in the 1998 show. The exhibit (shown below) recreated Philadelphia's Rodin Museum, including its formal French garden and reflecting pool, as it appeared in 1929 based on an original three-dimensional model made for the museum's architects, Paul Cret and Jacques Gréber.

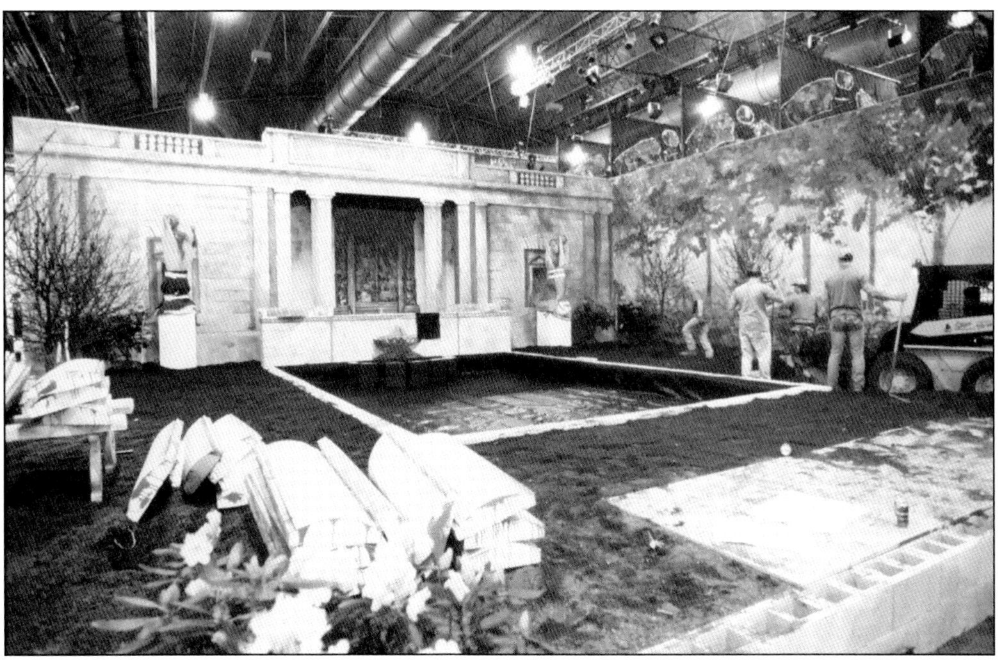

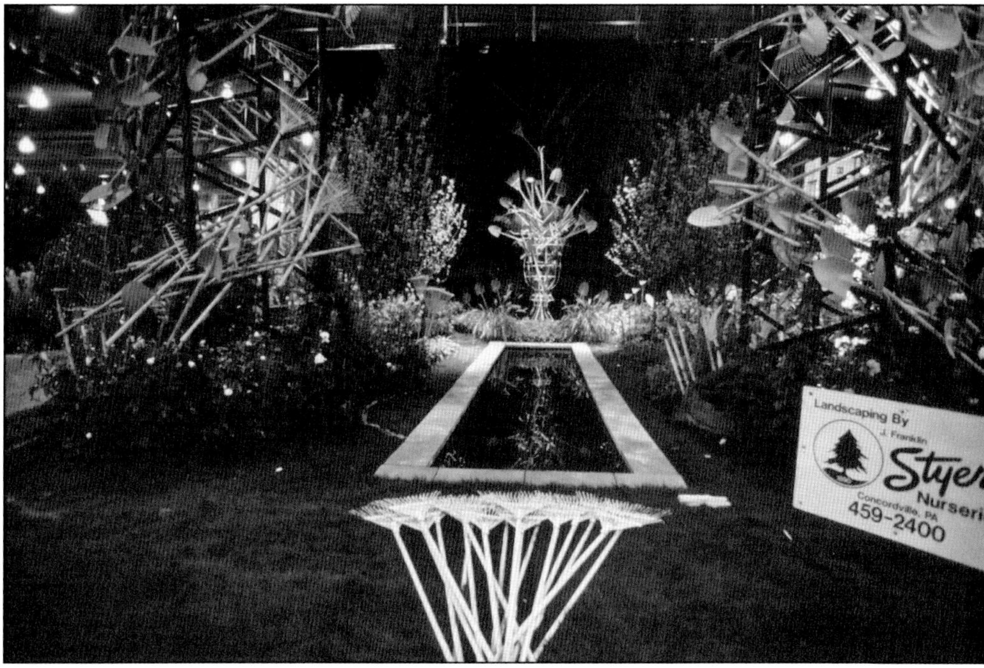

The 1998 show had a French theme, and Michael Petrie, designer at J. Franklin Styers Nurseries, created this "Tooleries" exhibit, a playful reference to the Tuileries Garden in Paris. It featured 500 painted garden tools in a rose garden, with a rake and shovel sculpture placed at the top of a reflecting pool. Petrie continues to exhibit under the name of his own business, Handmade Gardens.

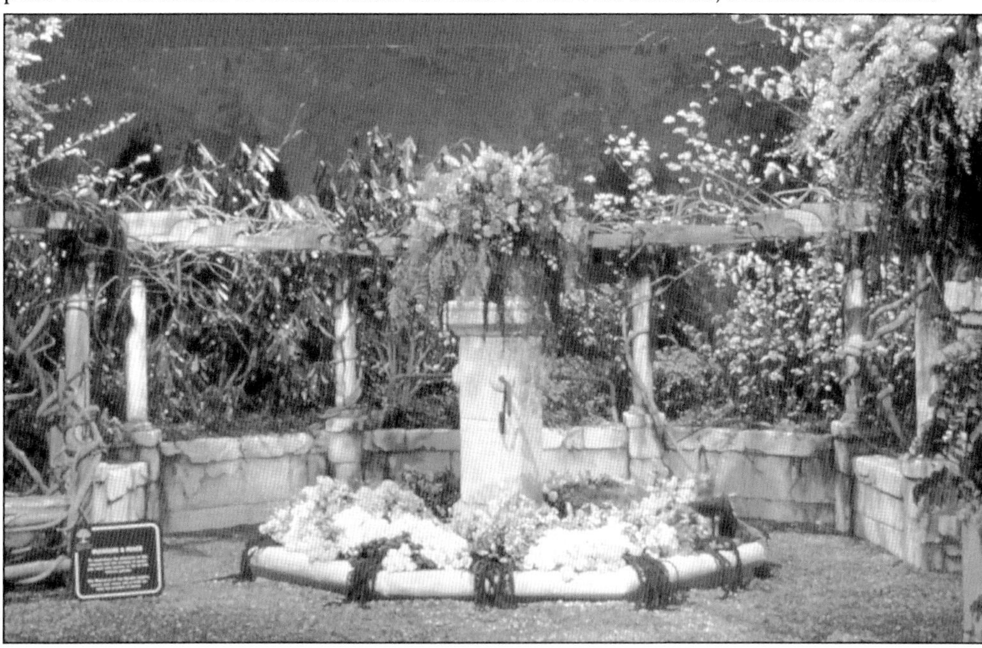

For the 2002 show, Jaime Rothstein worked closely with show designer Ed Lindemann to create the Peace Garden in response to the attacks of September 11, 2001. The exhibit depicted a garden setting that had become derelict but came back to life in the springtime, bringing a sense of renewal and hope for the future.

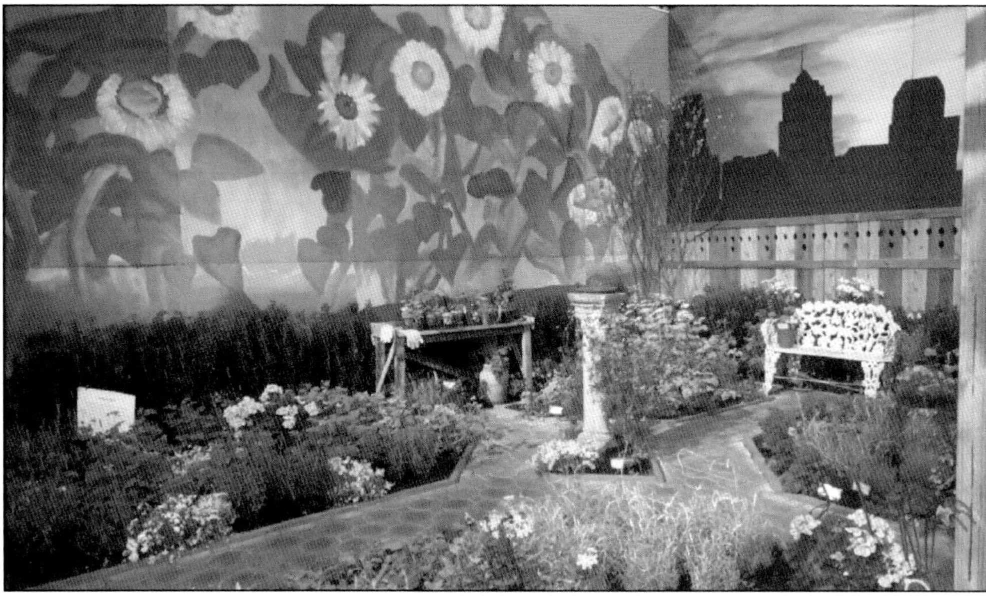

Students from Philadelphia's W.B. Saul High School of Agricultural Sciences presented their interpretation of the 2004 show theme, "Destination Paradise." Their display, "An Herban Paradise," featured a potpourri of herbs in a variety of settings, showing how an urban garden could be a feast for the eyes as well as the palate. Saul High School students have exhibited for more than 20 years.

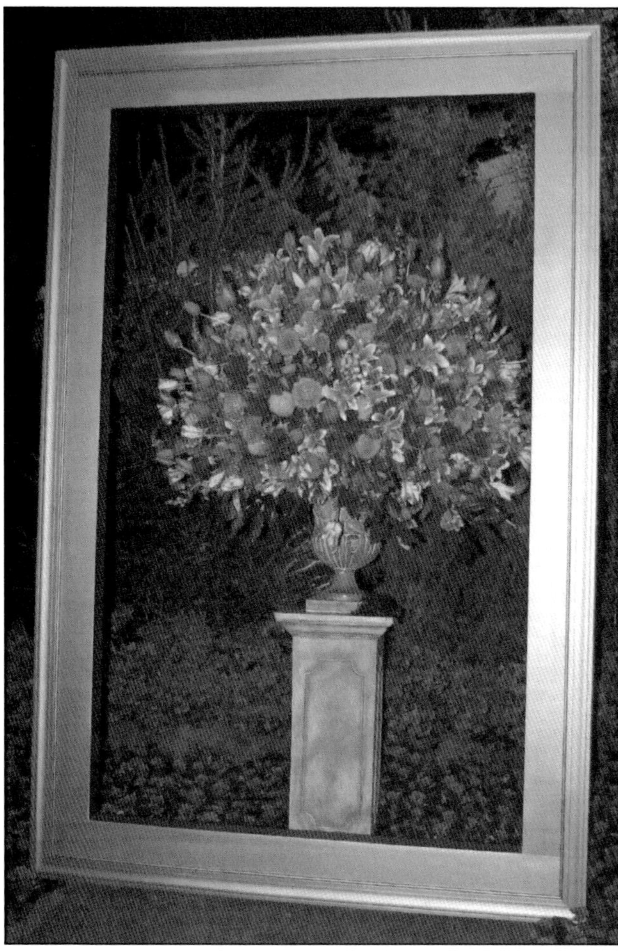

For the 2005 Philadelphia Flower Show, themed "America the Beautiful," Lamsback Floral Decorators of Philadelphia created this exhibit, "The Artist's Palette," using spectacular arrangements and creative use of artists' tools. The husband-and-wife team of Bob and Karen Lamsback was an integral part of the show for many years.

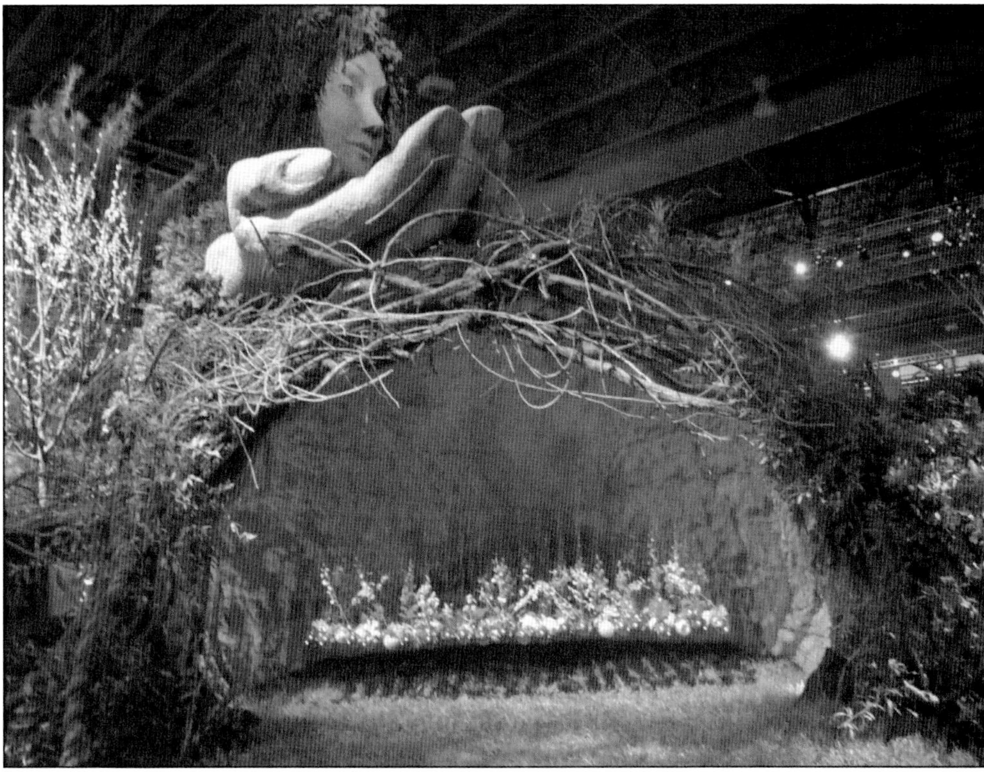

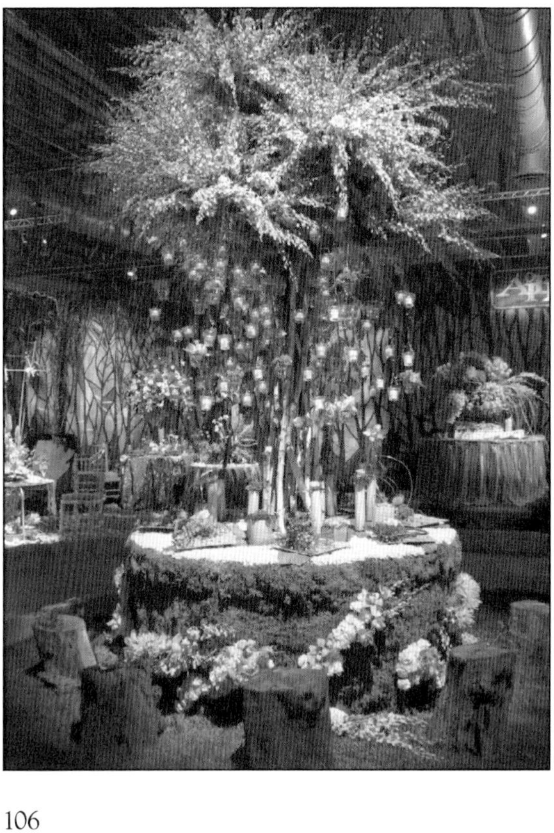

In 2006, the theme of the show was "Enchanted Spring . . . A Tribute to Mother Nature." The central exhibit featured a towering figure—25 feet high and 60 feet long—called *Natura* that was constructed from foam, flowers, trees, shrubs, and grass. The sculpture was surrounded by elaborate floral creations by Life 3, an international team of renowned floral designers.

The American Institute of Floral Designers (AIFD) brings their cutting-edge designers to the show to create floral magic. Combining the newest trends in floral design with wonderful theatricality, they have delighted and challenged Flower Show visitors with their exhibits for many years. AIFD created "Enchanted Evening" for the 2006 show.

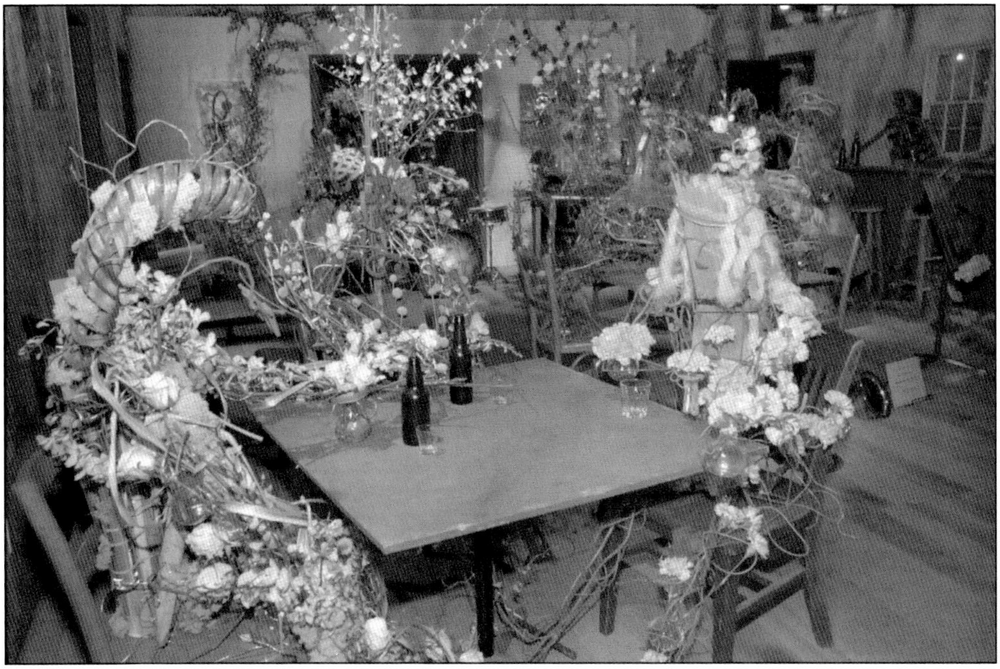

For the 2008 show, "Jazz It Up!," which celebrated the gardens, music, and culture of New Orleans, Bill Schaffer and Kris Kratt, of Schaffer Designs in Philadelphia, created a Rue Bourbon nightclub inhabited by topiary-framed figures, including a trio in mid-performance, a world-weary bartender, after-hours workers, and young lovers.

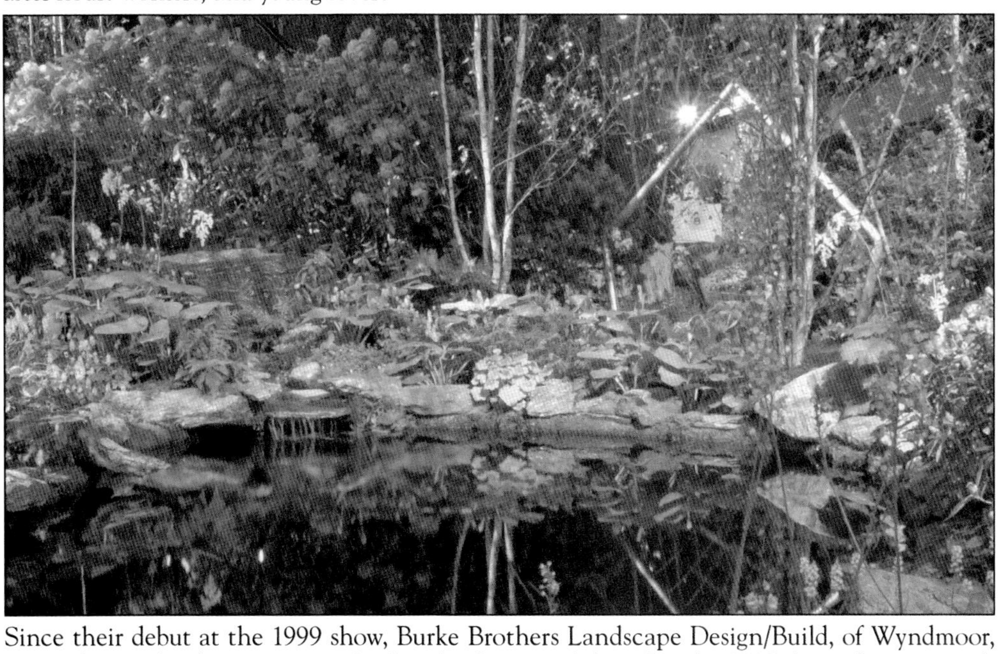

Since their debut at the 1999 show, Burke Brothers Landscape Design/Build, of Wyndmoor, Pennsylvania, has been creating dazzling landscape exhibits. For the 2007 show, the company's exhibit featured two traditional Irish pastimes—golf and gardening. A lush, green, tree-enclosed fairway was surrounded by boulders, a water feature, and tall grasses—a look typical at many Irish golf courses.

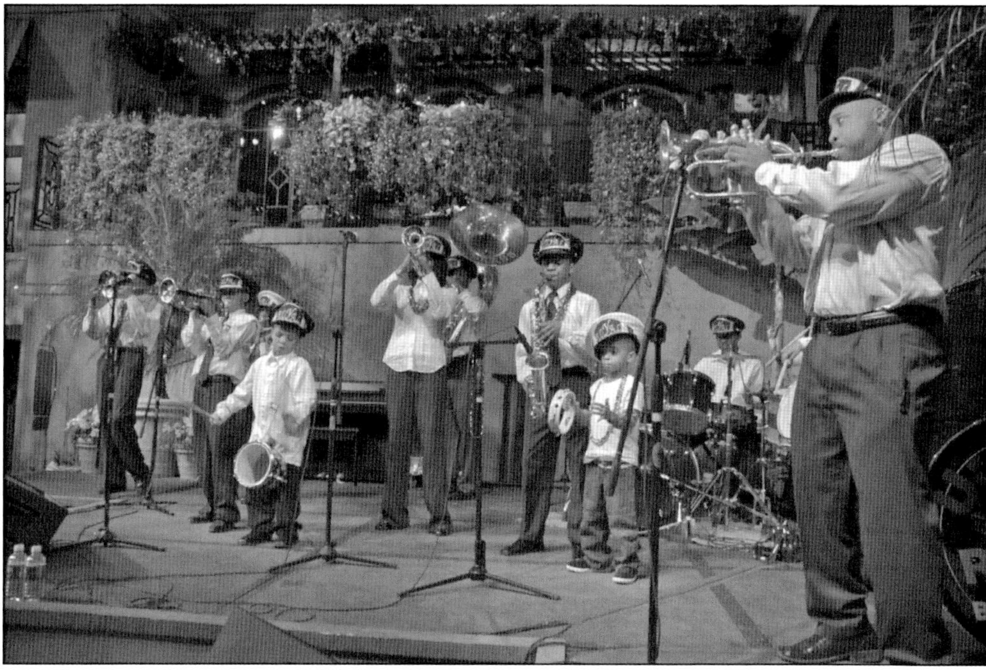

The theme for the 2008 Philadelphia Flower Show was "Jazz It Up!," focusing on New Orleans. Coming three years after Hurricane Katrina, the show provided an opportunity to help promote New Orleans tourism, and PHS invited the city's tourism board to exhibit in the Marketplace. Live entertainment on the Bourbon Street stage featured Big Sam's Funky Nation, from New Orleans, and the Camden City Brass Band (pictured).

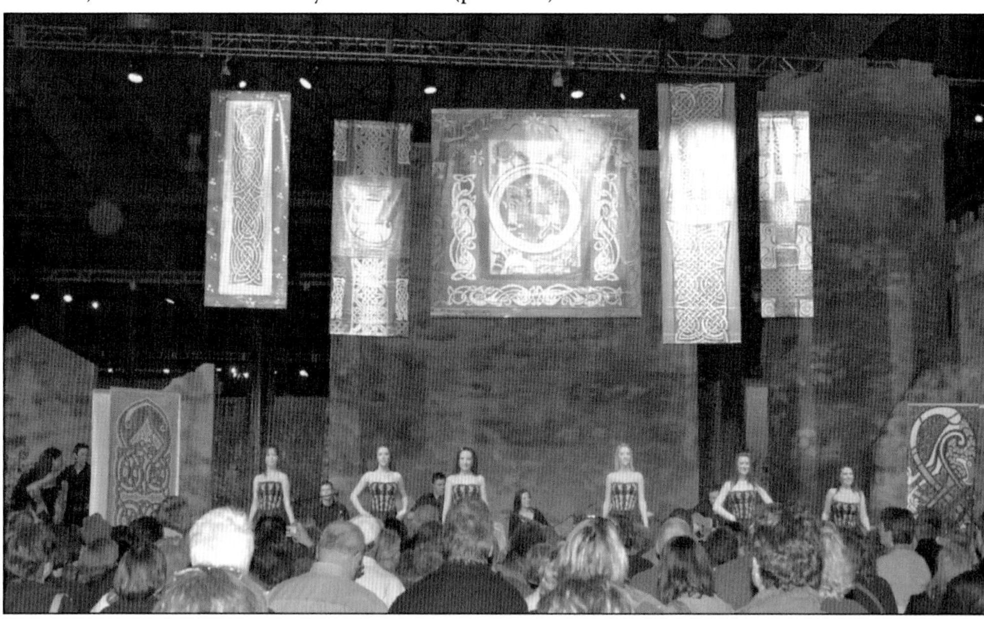

The 2007 Philadelphia Flower Show presented the theme "Legends of Ireland." A large castle, knot gardens, and enchanted woods greeted visitors. On the stage of the castle, an Irish troupe called Ragus performed traditional Irish music and dance to the delight of huge crowds at every performance. The Irish theme was extremely popular.

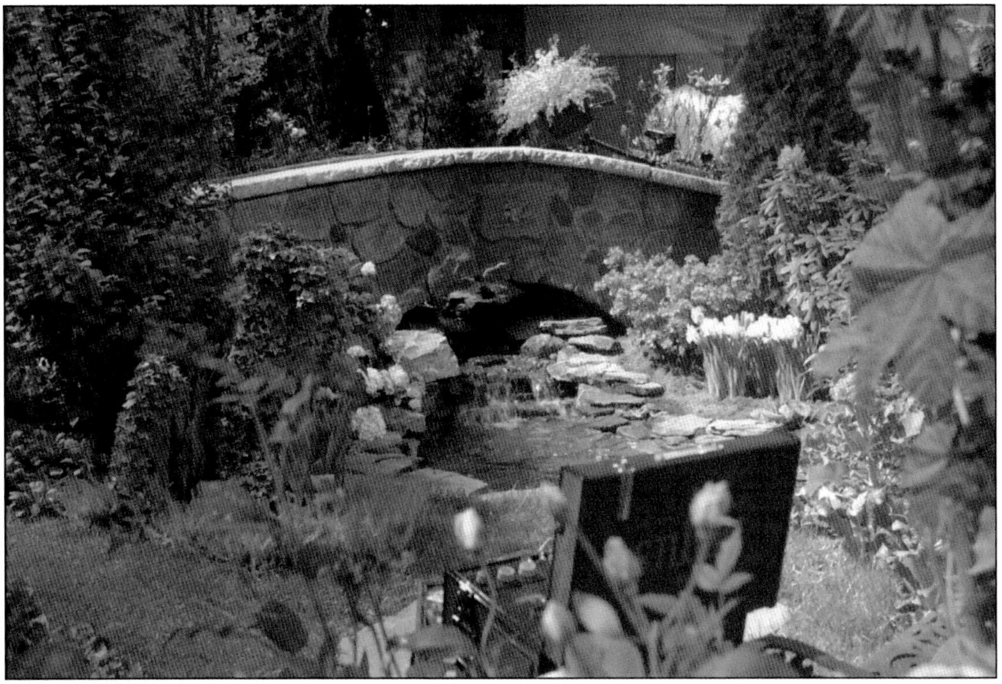

After nearly three decades as president of the PHS, Jane G. Pepper retired in 2010 and was honored with an exhibit at that year's show. The garden, created by volunteers and show exhibitors, featured Pepper's many passions and gave a nod to her native Scotland.

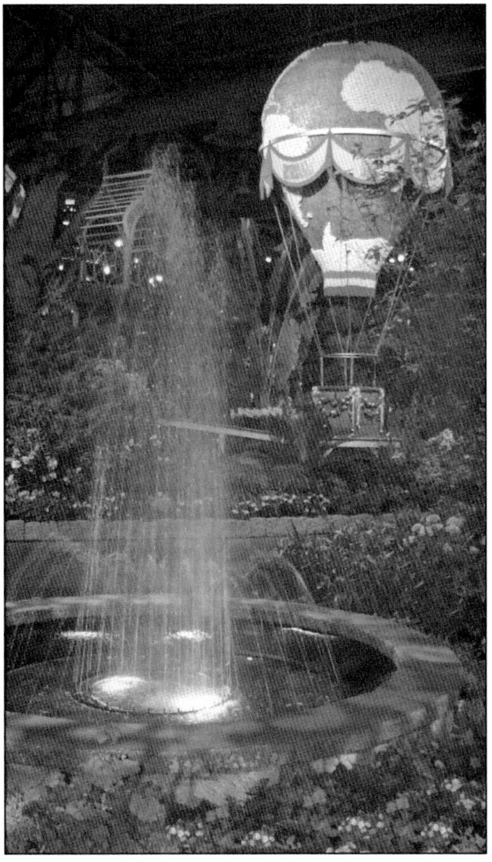

The 2010 Philadelphia Flower Show presented a global tour with the theme "Passport to the World." Showcasing the plants and garden design of Brazil, India, the Netherlands, New Zealand, Singapore, South Africa, and the United States, this show was truly international. A World Bazaar offered visitors a chance to buy products from the featured countries.

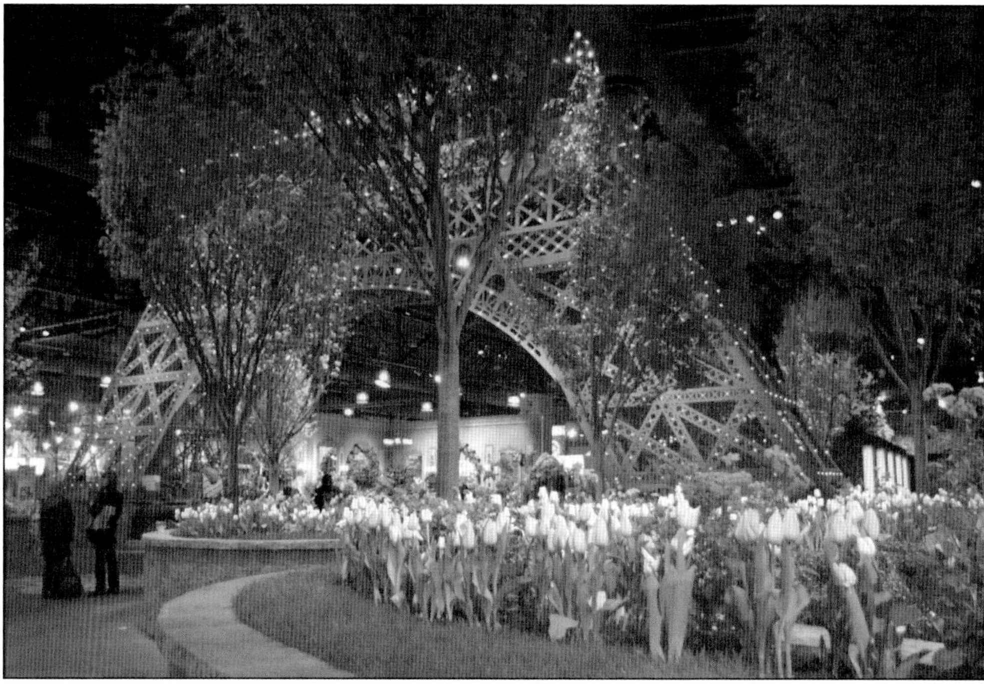

"Springtime in Paris," the theme for the 2011 Philadelphia Flower Show, took its inspiration from the Jardin des Tuileries. Formal plantings of blooming trees, shrubs, and thousands of tulips lined the undulating walkways leading to the largest structure ever created for a show exhibit: a replica of the Eiffel Tower. The tower proved a spectacular centerpiece, with light and music shows taking place every hour.

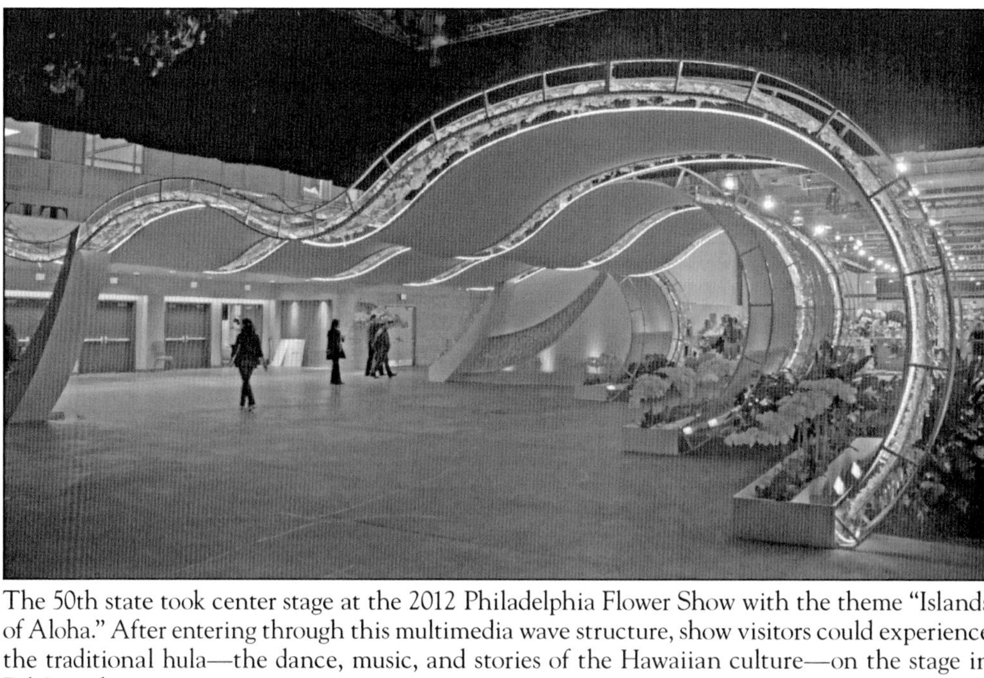

The 50th state took center stage at the 2012 Philadelphia Flower Show with the theme "Islands of Aloha." After entering through this multimedia wave structure, show visitors could experience the traditional hula—the dance, music, and stories of the Hawaiian culture—on the stage in Pele's garden.

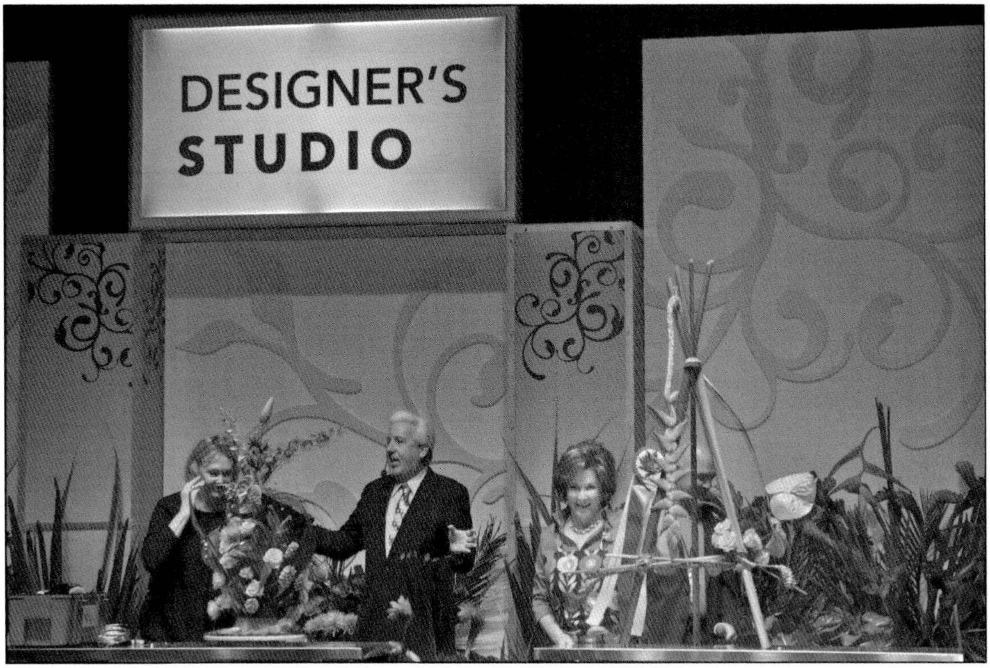

Inaugurated in 2012, the Designer's Studio offers outstanding floral design in an entertaining and exciting format. Several times a day at the show, designers from all over the world share their expertise through demonstrations and competitions. Tim Farrell hosted throughout show week, involving the audience and inviting them to vote on their favorite arrangement. The lively format has been a huge hit with Flower Show visitors.

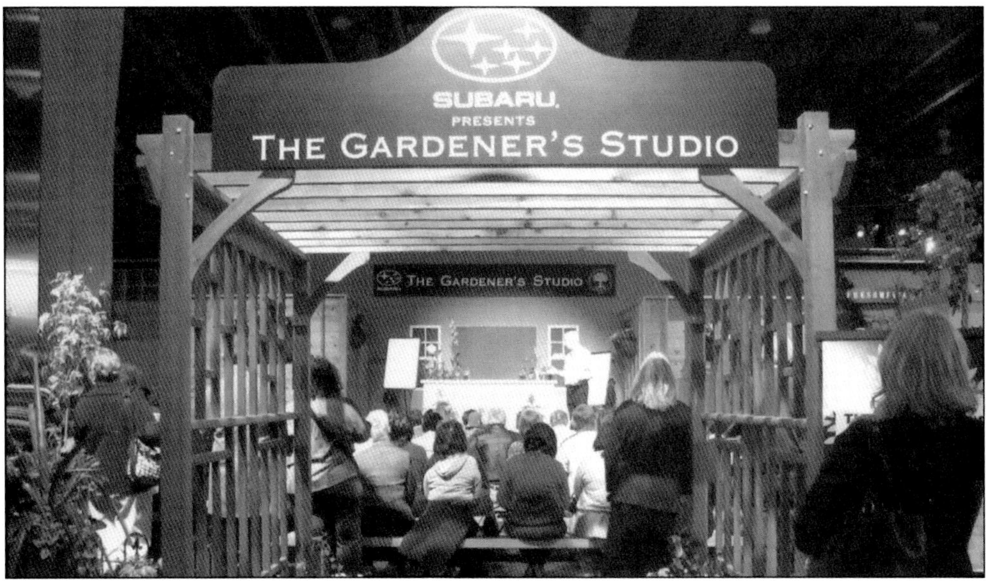

The Gardener's Studio, presented by Subaru, became a regular feature of the show beginning in 1998. Located in the center of the show floor, the Gardener's Studio allows more than 100 gardening and greening experts to share their passion with the public via hourly lectures and demonstrations. Topics include growing vegetables in containers, proper pruning techniques, forcing bulbs for the winter, and more.

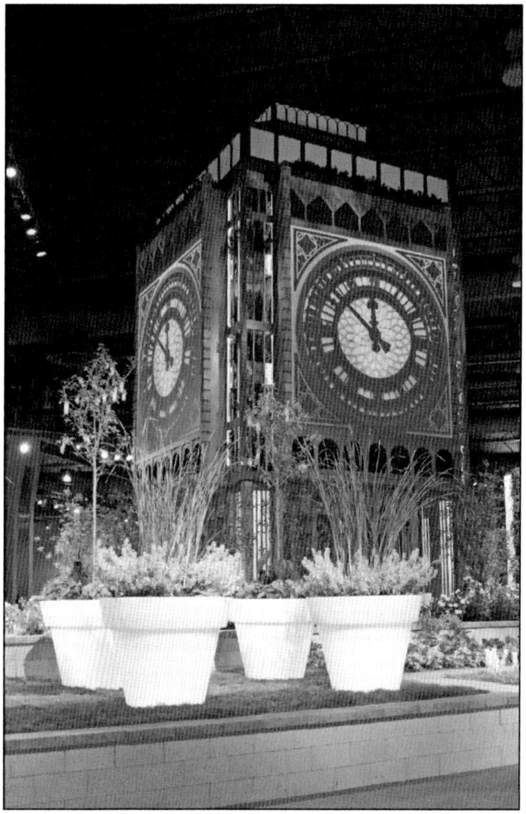

"Brilliant!" was the 2013 Philadelphia Flower Show theme, with an emphasis on everything British. After entering through the Royal Gates and walking down an allée of birch trees, visitors arrived at Big Ben Plaza. The clock came to life with a huge video production of music and animation on all four faces every hour.

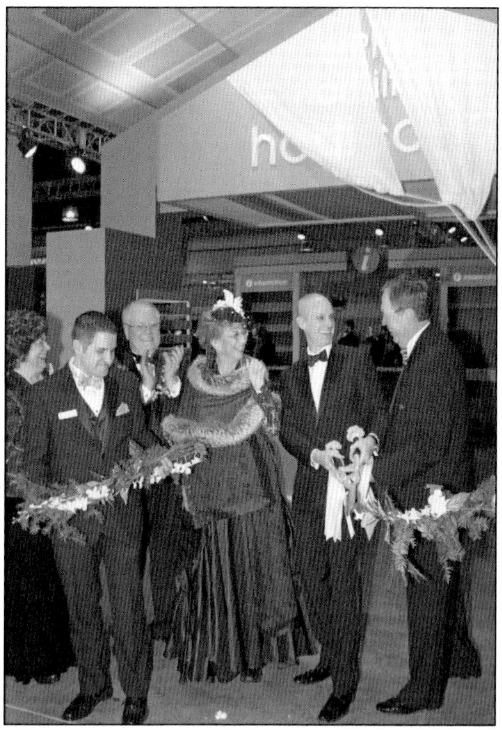

The 2013 Flower Show Preview Party opened with the dedication of the Hamilton Horticourt—a spectacular new showcase for horticultural entries. Cutting the ribbon are, from left to right, Francesca Northrup, Flower Show vice chair; PHS staff member Nick Pytel; Steven Besselieu, Flower Show chair; Dorrance H. Hamilton; Drew Becher, PHS president; and Howard Meyers, PHS Board chair. Hamilton, a longtime exhibitor, donated $1 million for the new Horticourt.

Cecily Clark won the Edith Wilder Scott Award, which is given to the best of the blues in the show's horticulture division, a record four times. Perhaps more remarkably, she exhibited in every show from 1945 until her last show in 2011. A mentor to countless neophytes, Clark generously shared her knowledge and enthusiasm for growing traffic-stopping entries at the show.

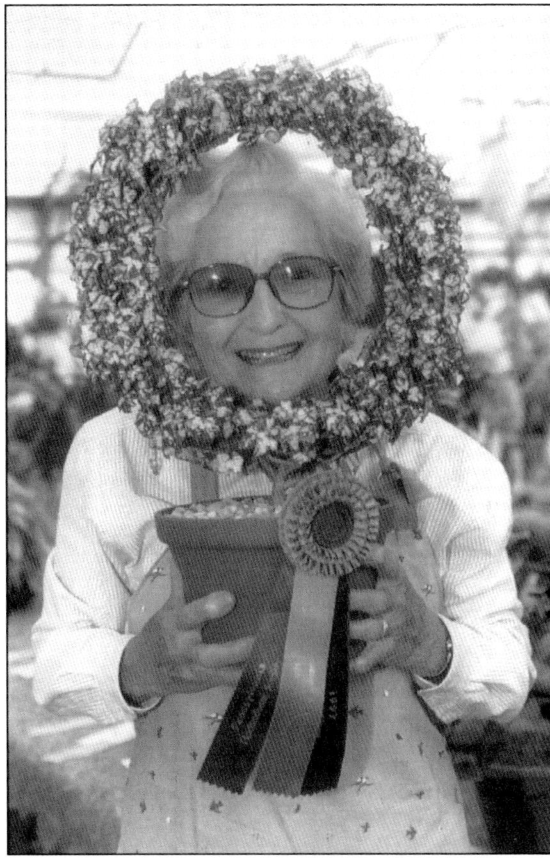

The team of Lynn Cook (left) and Troy Ray (right) continues the tradition of horticultural excellence by capturing the highest honor in the competitive classes—the PHS Grand Sweepstakes. The duo has won the sweepstakes from 2007 through 2013. Cook and Ray are pictured here with competitive classes chair Francesca Northrup at the 2009 awards luncheon.

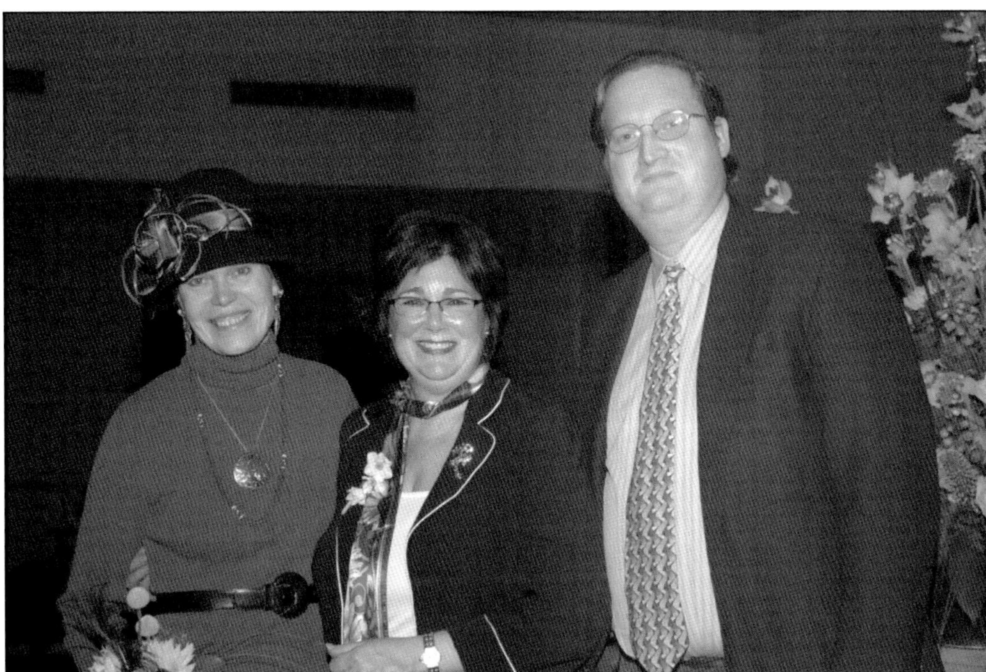

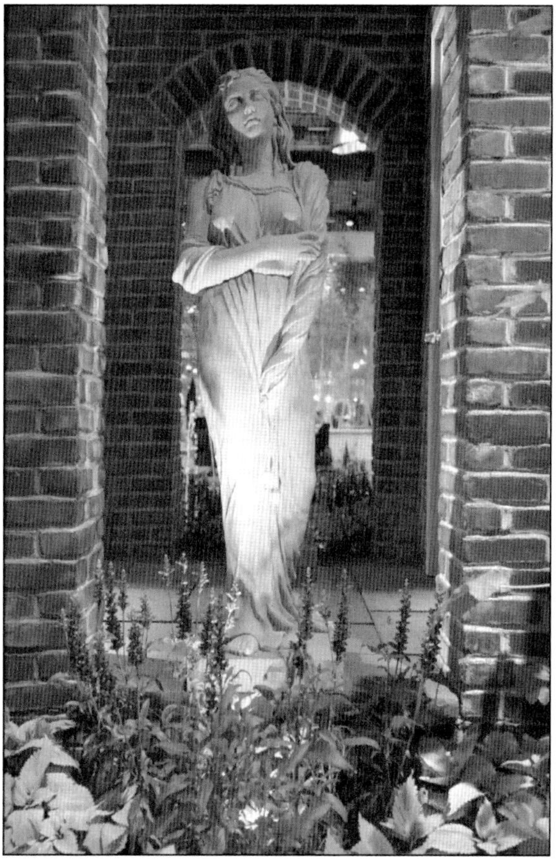

For the 2013 show, with its British theme, "Brilliant!," EP Henry created a display that juxtaposed two very British characteristics: cautious restraint and droll humor. Formal boxwood hedges and beds of flowering perennials set the tone for this proper English statue garden. But upon closer inspection, visitors were startled to discover that this figure watching over the garden was not a statue at all but a real woman.

Sam Lemheney, Flower Show designer and PHS chief of shows and events, shares a light moment with Barb King, of Valley Forge Flowers, during the setup of the 2011 Philadelphia Flower Show. Valley Forge Flowers helped create the central display that included fanciful carousel topiary animals made of wire, dried flowers, and other natural materials.

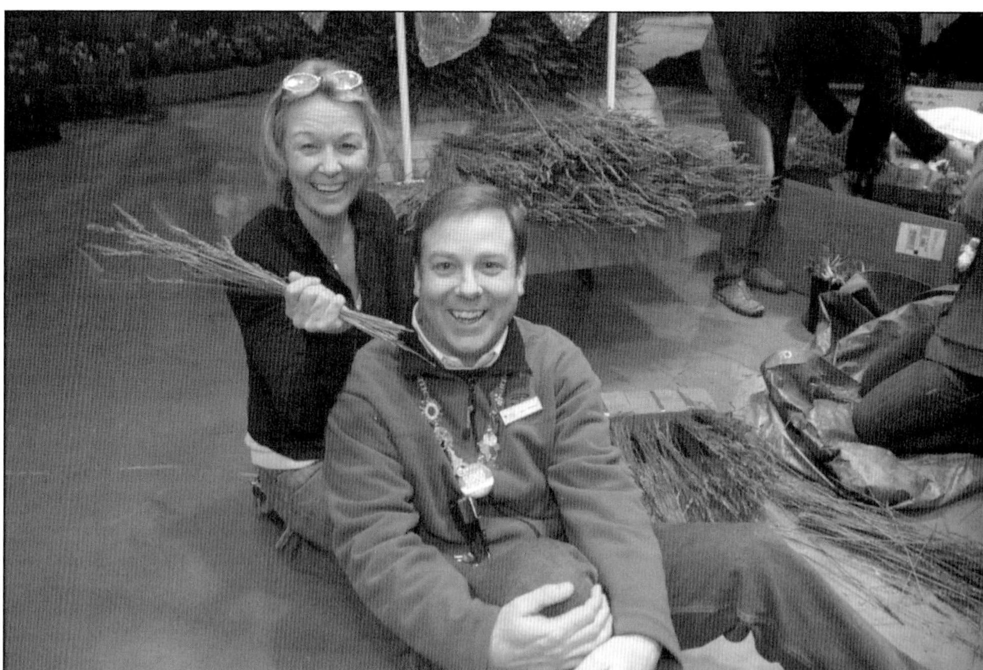

Five

Harvest Shows

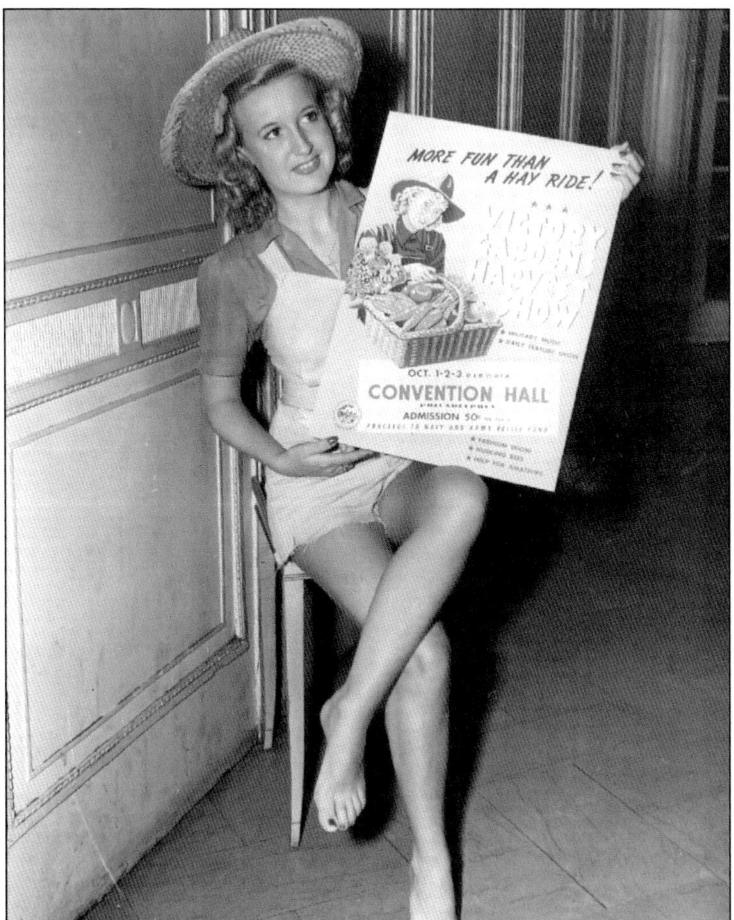

Victory Garden Harvest Shows, held during the World War II years, were part of a national movement to promote the vital role played by gardening and home food production in helping to win the war. It was both patriotic and practical to have a victory garden, since commercially produced food was sent overseas. PHS continued holding Harvest Shows after the war, first in Memorial Hall and later at the Horticulture Center, both in Fairmount Park.

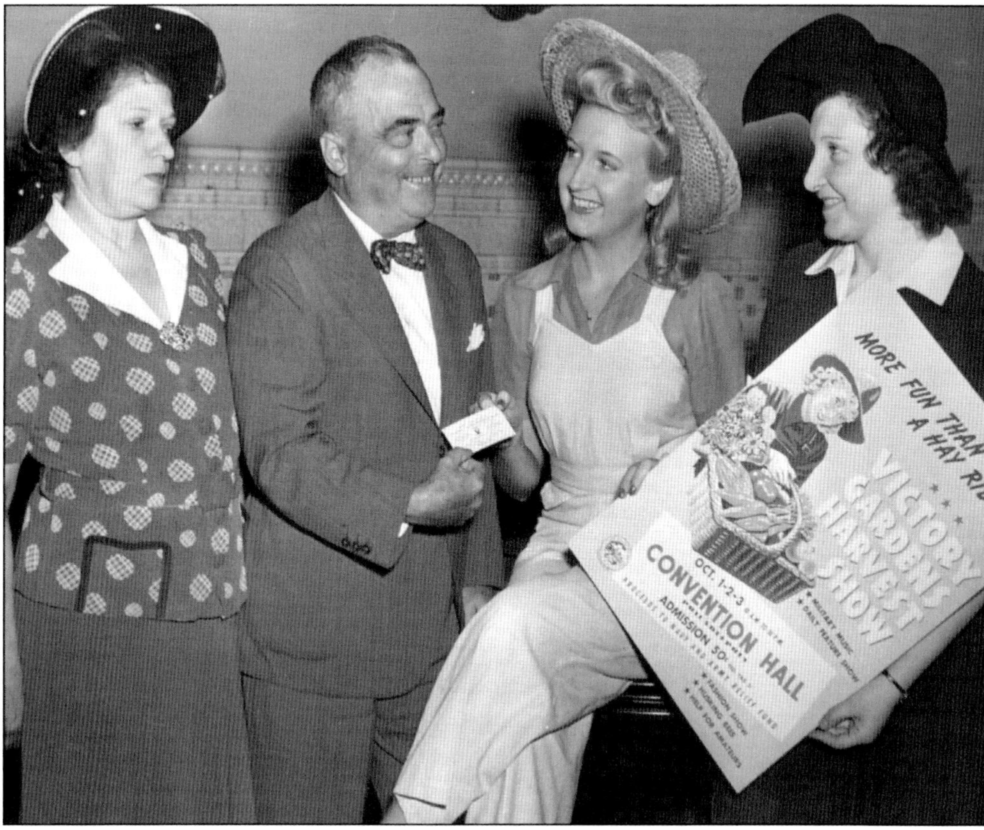

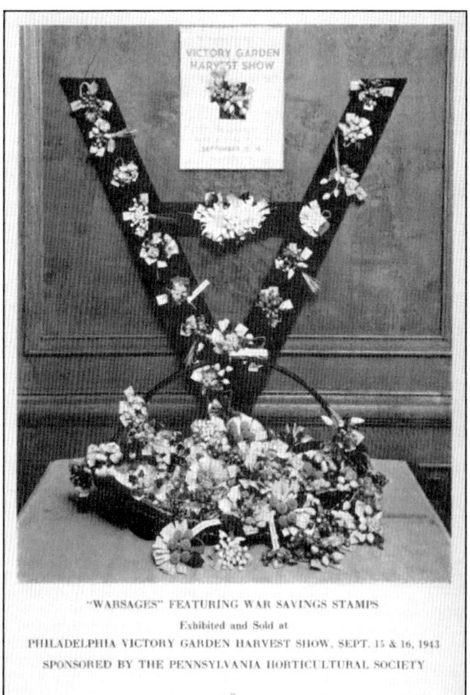

The 1942 Victory Garden Harvest Show, organized by PHS, was one of 20,000 events held nationwide that year to raise $3 million for the Army and Navy Relief Fund. Above, Philadelphia mayor Bernard Samuel (second from left) is shown purchasing the first ticket to the show from Miss Victory Garden, Loretta Hannings (second from right), as Army mother Reba Feldman (left) and Navy widow Jennie Sanders (right) look on.

"Warsages," corsages made of war savings stamps, were exhibited and sold at PHS's Philadelphia Victory Garden Harvest Show of 1943. War savings stamps were issued by the US Treasury Department to raise money to support the war effort and were offered in denominations ranging from 10¢ to $5. Florists across the country sold these patriotic "warsages."

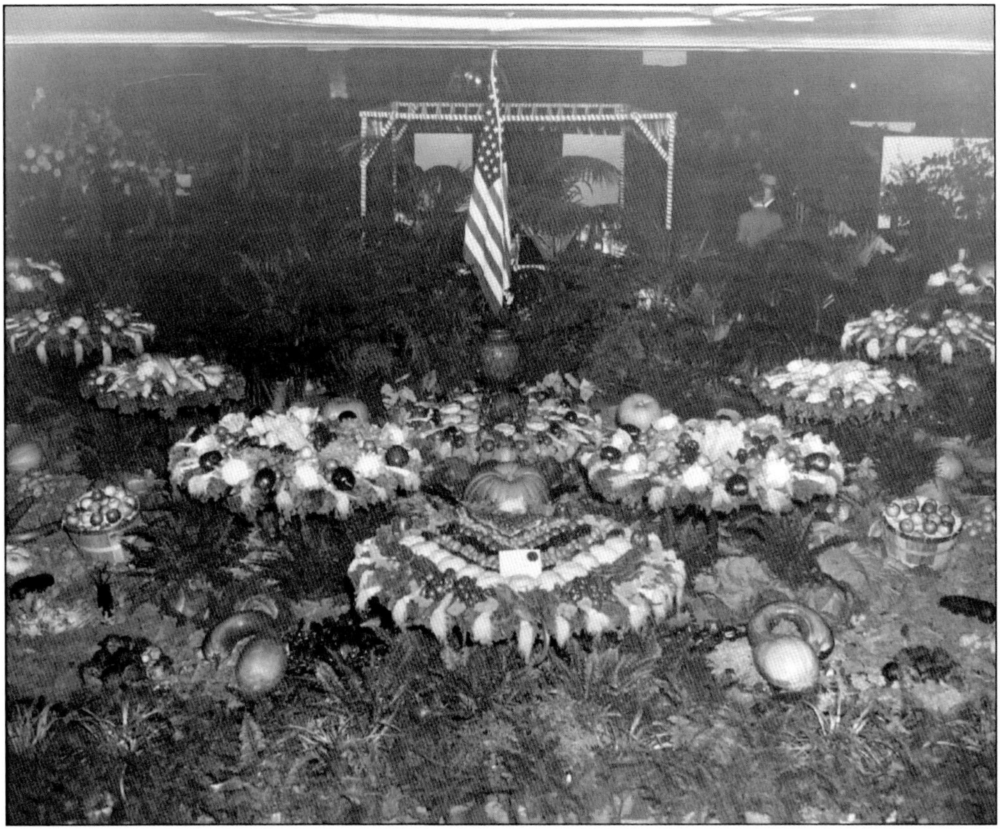

In this colorful 1942 Victory Garden Harvest Show exhibit, the National Association of Gardeners staged vegetable arrangements on tables that were set up to form a huge "V" for victory. They used kale for ground cover as well as large crookneck squash, gigantic pumpkins, tomatoes, beets, and yellow corn.

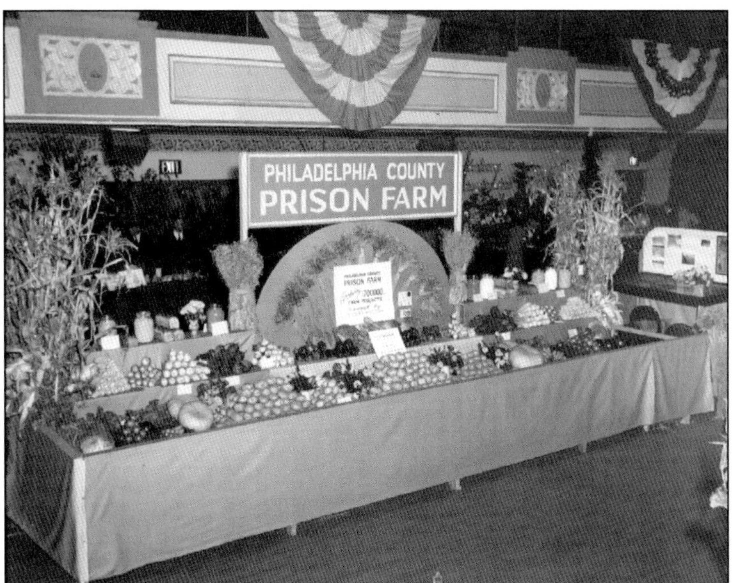

Part of the goal of the wartime Victory Garden Harvest Shows was to demonstrate how every member of society came together to support the war effort. This Philadelphia County Prison Farm exhibit proudly displayed a sampling of the 1.7 million pounds of farm products the prisoners grew to feed city and county institutions.

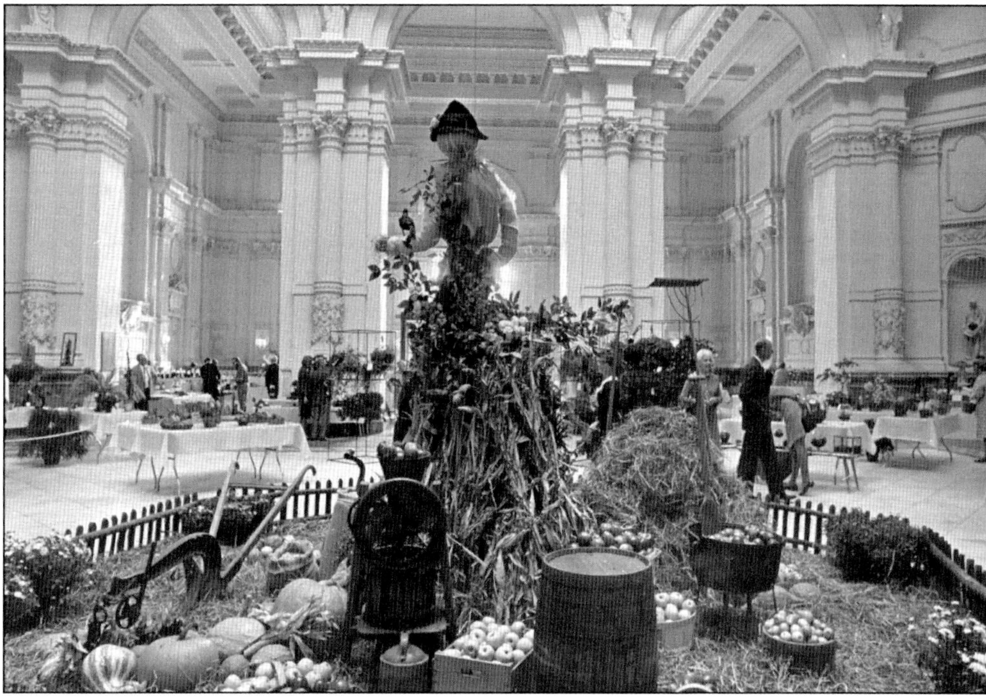

From 1969 to 1981, PHS produced Harvest Shows at Memorial Hall in Fairmount Park. These shows were opportunities for gardeners to display the fruits of their labor. Harvest Shows were smaller and more intimate than the spring flower shows, with a typical attendance of 6,000 visitors over three days. The shows included 300 to 800 individuals submitting up to 1,500 entries. In 1982, the Harvest Show moved from Memorial Hall to the Horticulture Center in Fairmount Park.

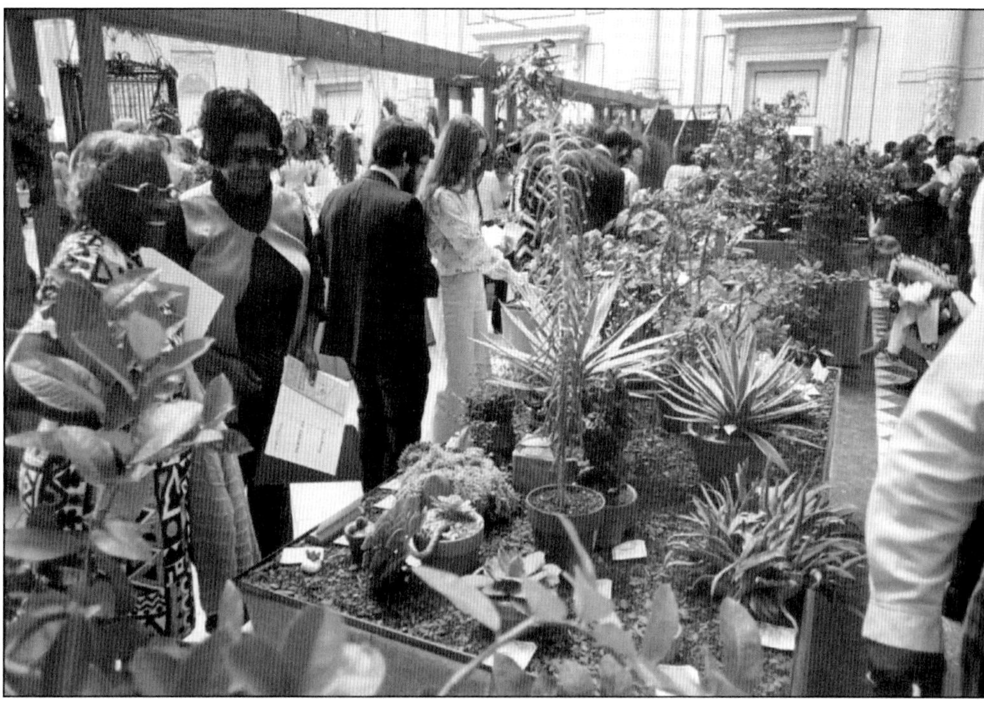

Lori Hayes, Fairmount Park horticultural educator, set this "nesting squash" in place at the 1987 Harvest Show and won a ribbon. She grew the gooseneck gourd in a community garden in the Hunting Park area of the city. Her success with that year's entry encouraged her to continue entering the Harvest Show.

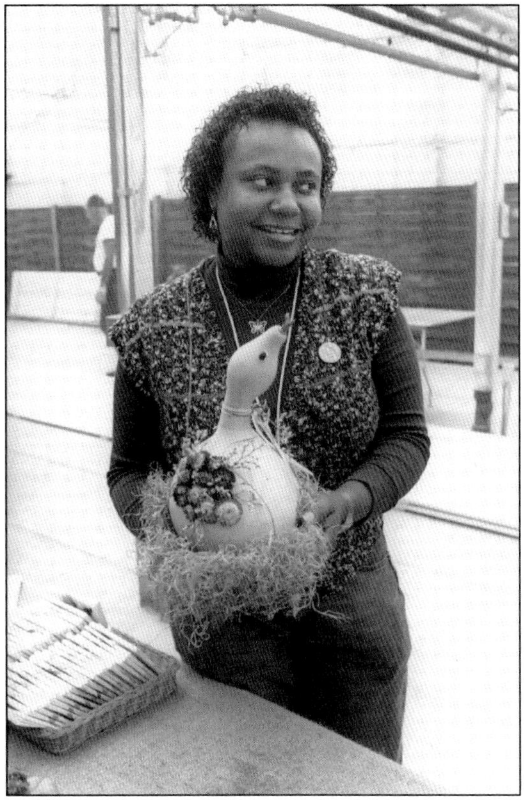

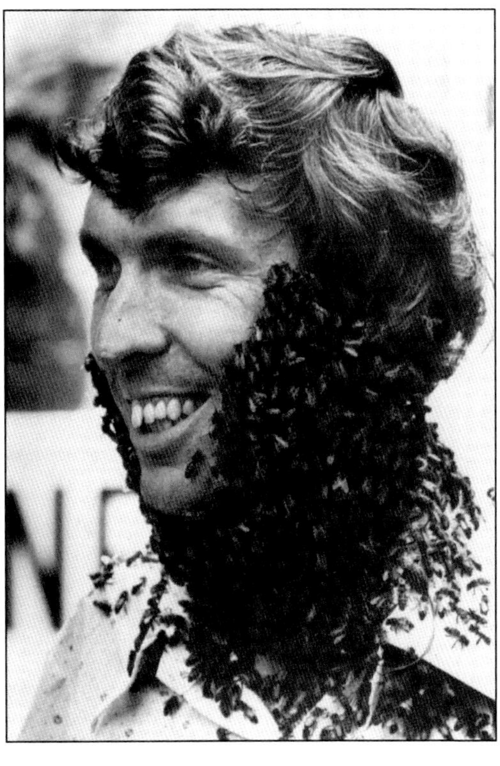

No Harvest Show was complete without the appearance of a beekeeper sporting a "bee beard" to demonstrate the close and safe relationship between humans and honeybees. How did he do this? The hive bees are attracted by the queen bee; she is in a small cage under the beekeeper's chin.

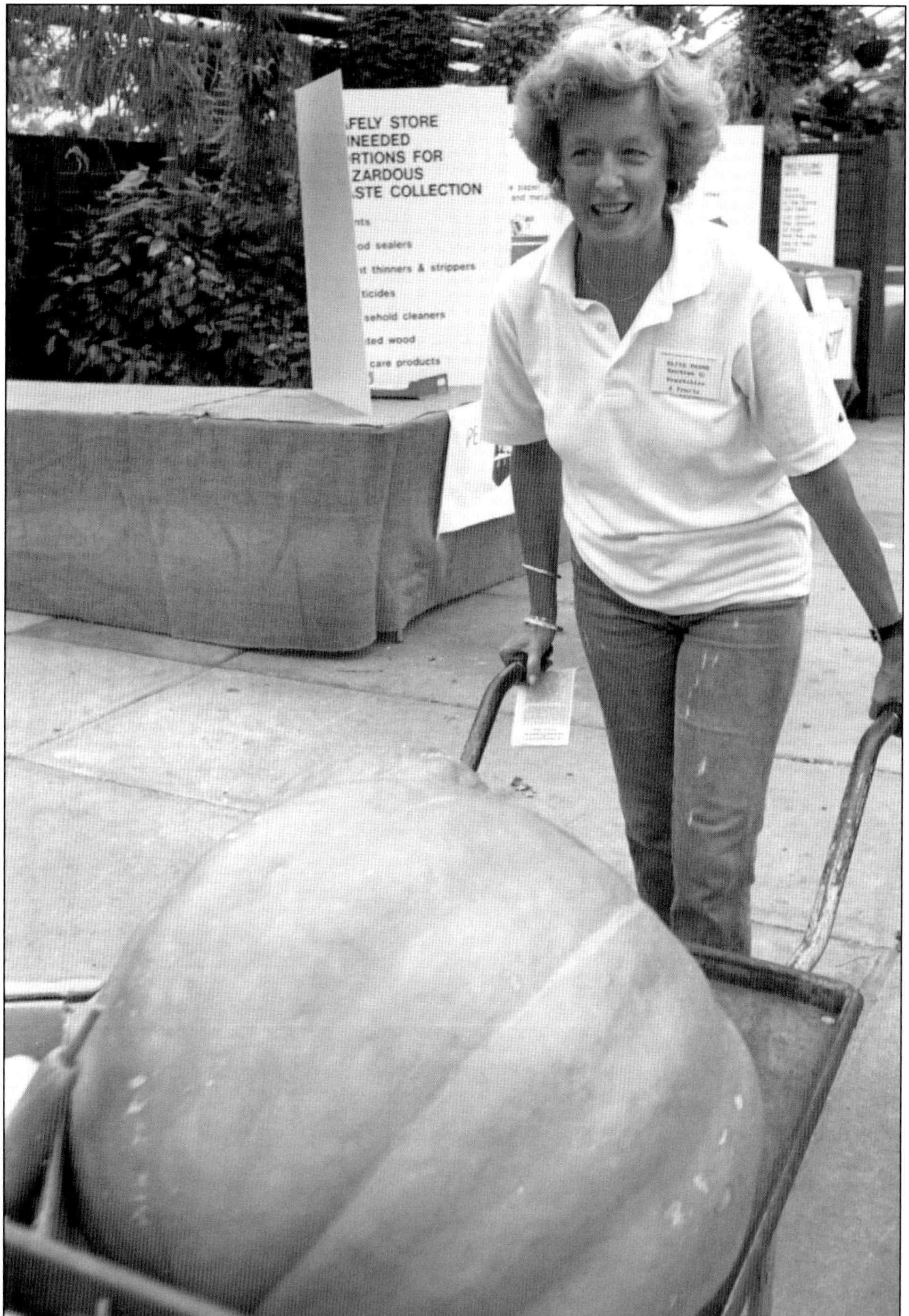

Elise Payne, Harvest Show cochair of vegetables and fruits and second runner-up in the Gardener's Sweepstakes, wheels her 300-pound pumpkin into the 1990 Harvest Show, where her entry won a blue ribbon. There were more than 300 individual and community entries in the 1990 show at the Horticulture Center in Fairmount Park.

Six

The Greening of Philadelphia

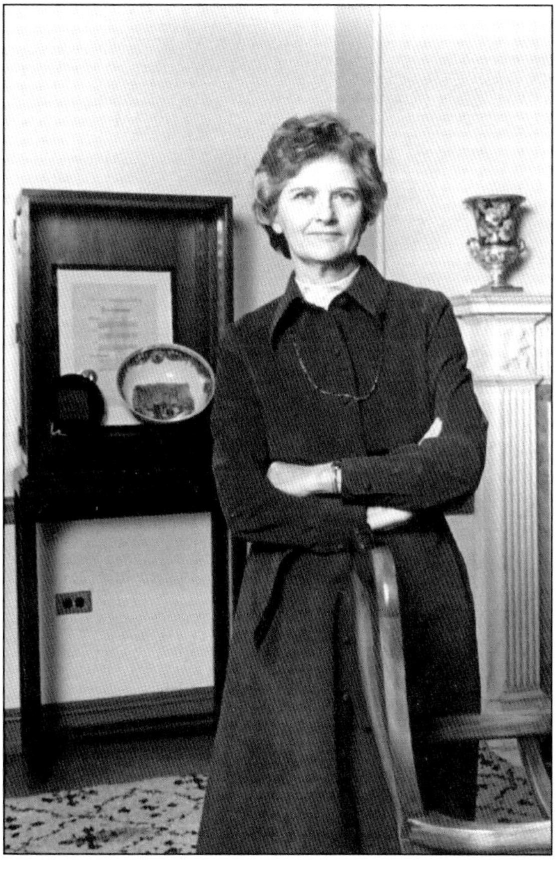

The Philadelphia Flower Show was reenergized under the leadership of Ernesta Ballard (shown here), whose vision has had a lasting impact on Philadelphia. By the late 1970s, PHS had begun using show revenues to turn abandoned vacant lots into thriving community gardens, to plant street trees in neighborhoods, and to improve the quality of life for residents through horticulture.

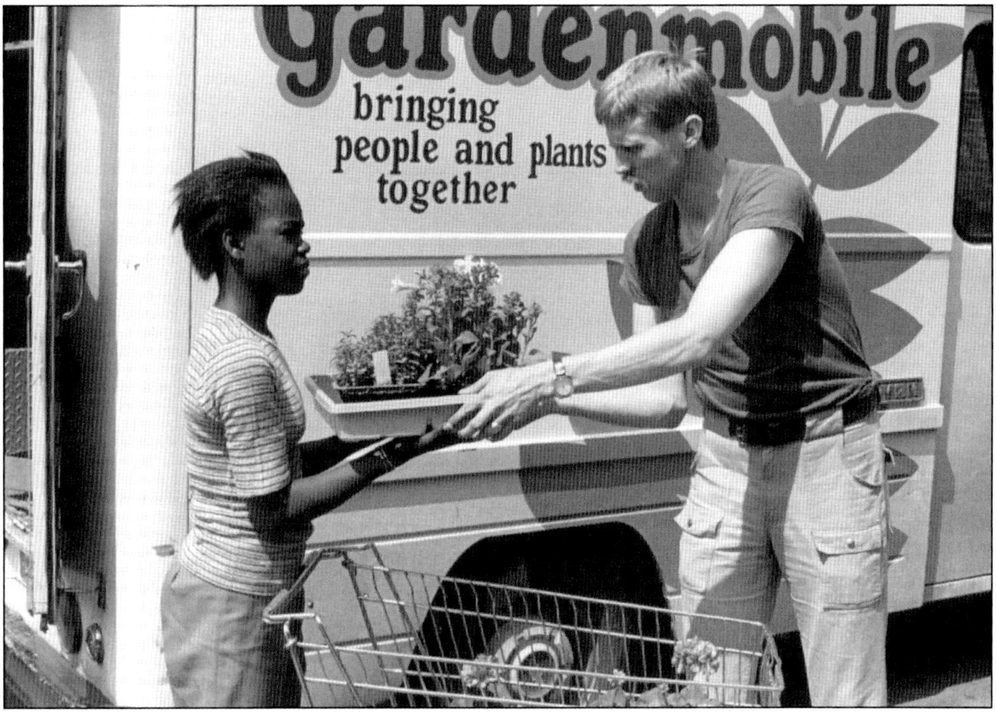

Here, an unidentified young gardener (left) receives plants from Blaine Bonham (right), PHS director of community gardening programs. By 1977, PHS had sponsored more than 120 community gardens in Philadelphia. Workshops and frequent visits from the staff in the Gardenmobile kept the gardens growing. Over time, Bonham and his staff built the urban greening program, known as Philadelphia Green, into the largest of its kind in the country.

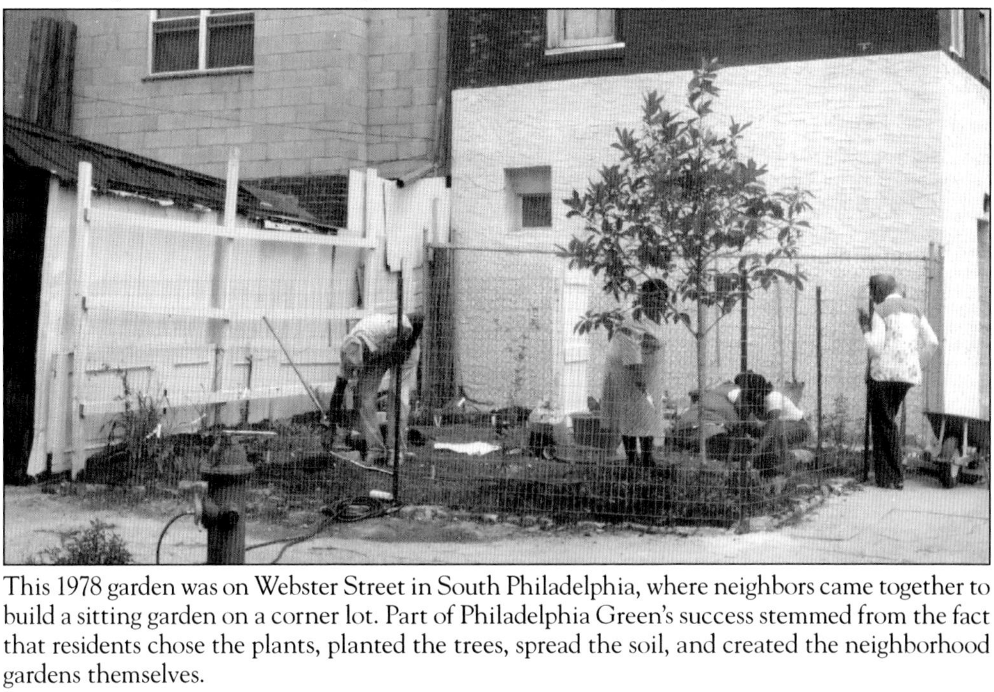

This 1978 garden was on Webster Street in South Philadelphia, where neighbors came together to build a sitting garden on a corner lot. Part of Philadelphia Green's success stemmed from the fact that residents chose the plants, planted the trees, spread the soil, and created the neighborhood gardens themselves.

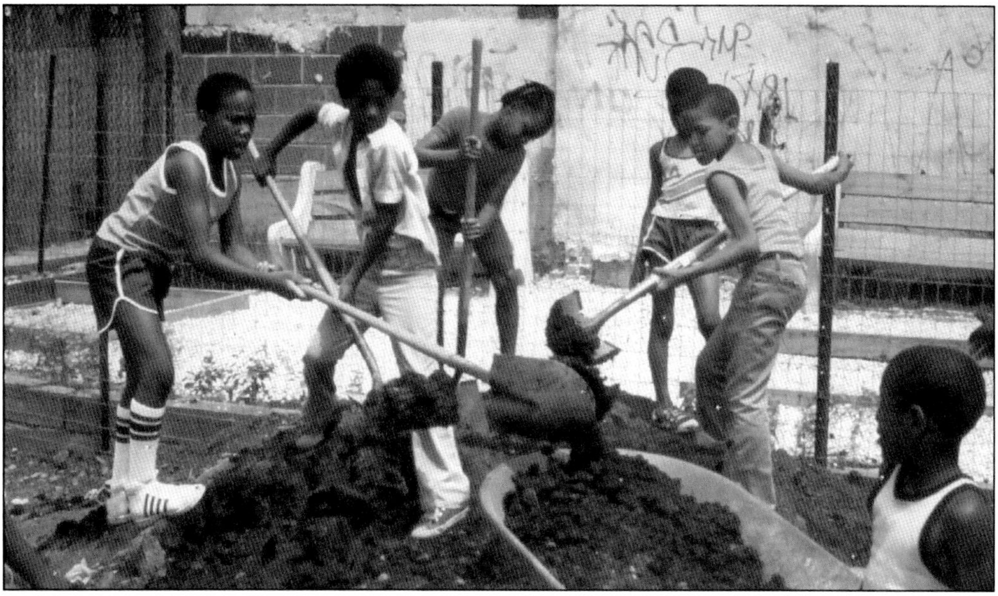

Building community gardens harnessed the energy of neighborhood youth. These North Philadelphia children are shoveling soil into the planting beds of their "sitting garden." Philadelphia Green provided these small gardens with trees, benches, gravel, shrubs, and flowers, creating important neighborhood gathering places.

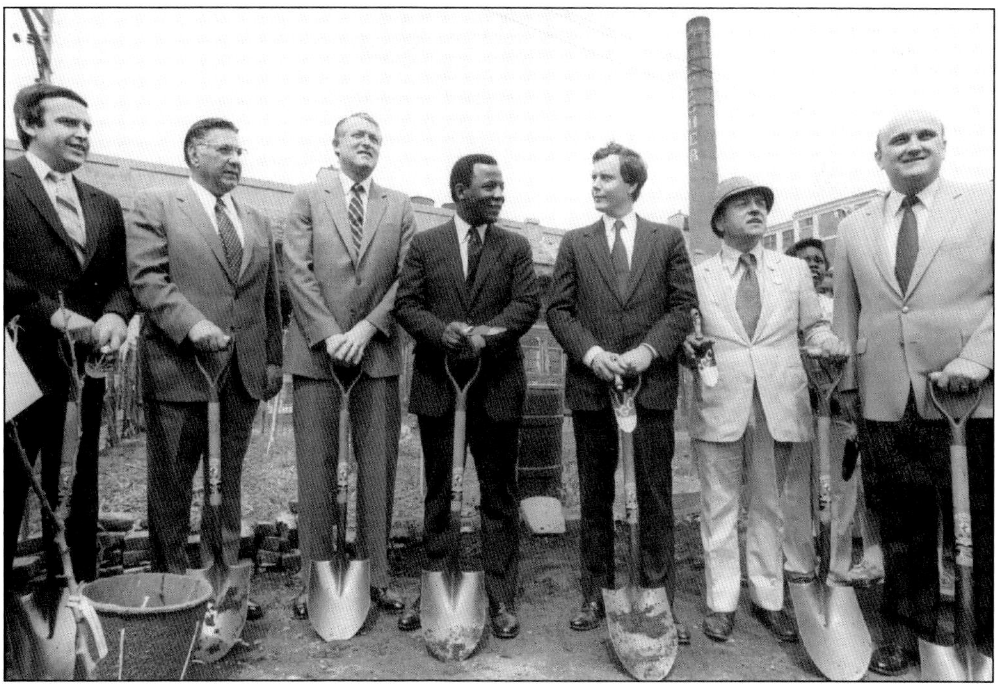

All seven candidates running for mayor of Philadelphia in the 1983 election were invited to the PHS City Gardens Contest kickoff event—and all showed up. The event was held at the Garden of Eatin', a community garden at South Twenty-fifth and Dickinson Streets. The candidates are, from left to right, John J. Egan Jr., Frank Rizzo, Thomas Gola, W. Wilson Goode, Thomas A. Leonard, Charles Dougherty, and Anthony Bateman. Goode won the election.

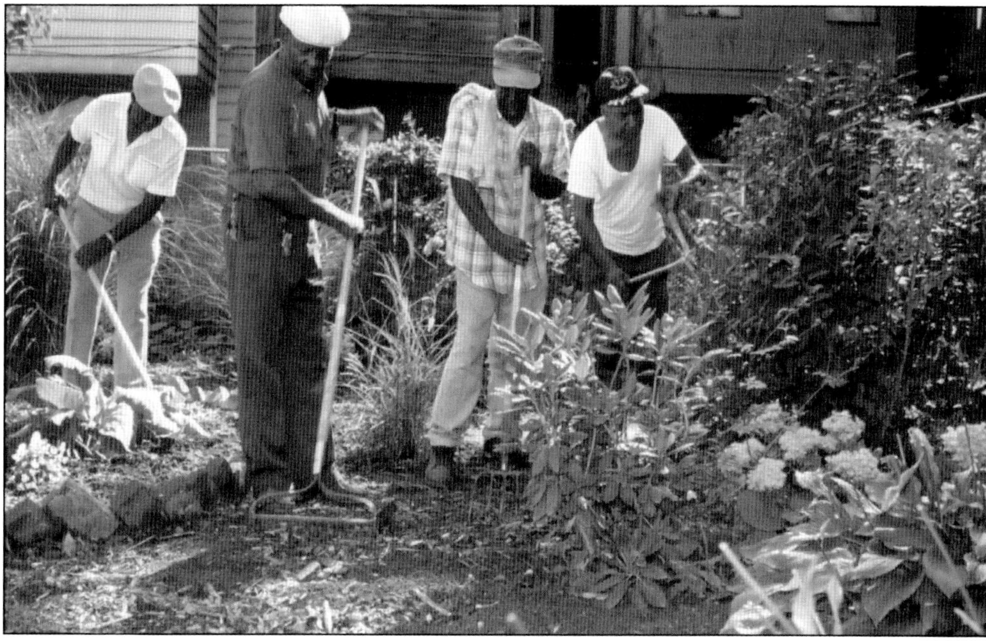

In this picture from the early 1990s, a group works in their garden in Strawberry Mansion, one of the PHS "Greene Countrie Towne" neighborhoods. To qualify for Green Countrie Towne status, residents of this 200-square-block North Philadelphia neighborhood completed 170 greening projects, installing gardens, street trees, and containers filled with flowers.

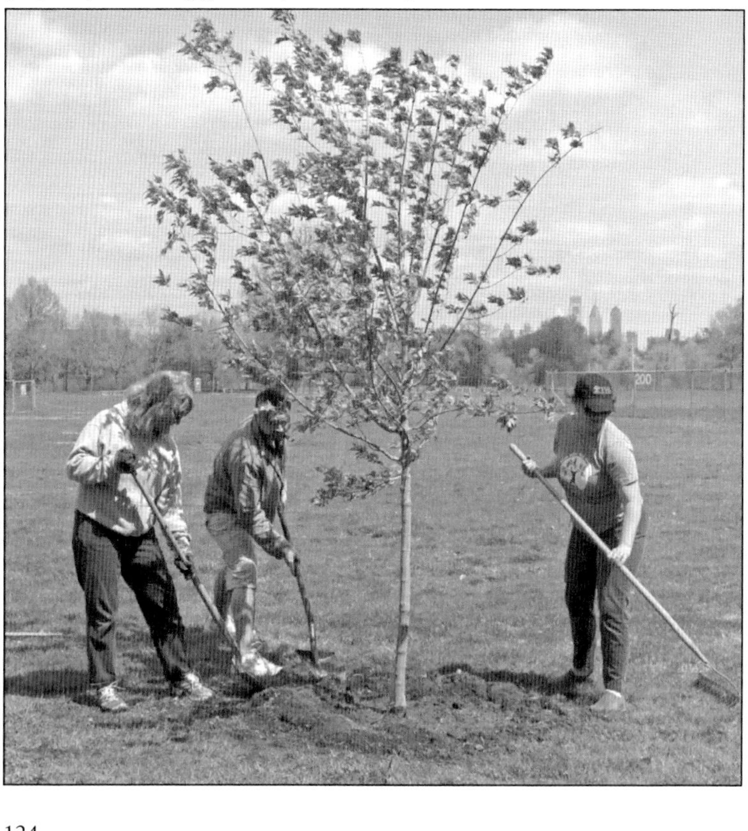

In 1993, PHS launched PHS Tree Tenders, which trains citizen volunteers to plant and care for neighborhood trees. It has trained more than 4,000 volunteers who have been responsible for the planting of 20,000 trees in the five-county Philadelphia region. The PHS Tree Tenders program has since been replicated in communities across the nation.

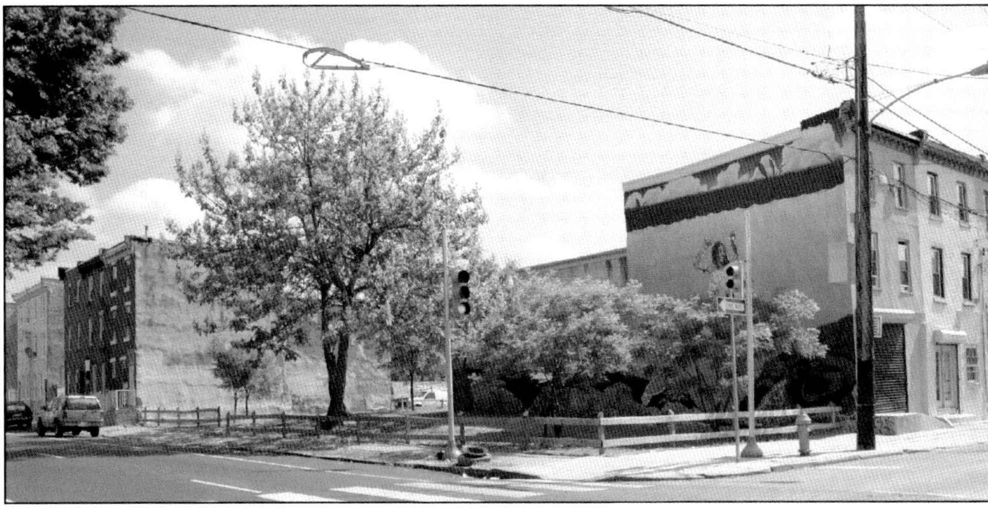

PHS Philadelphia LandCare is a nationally recognized model of landscape management that addresses the challenge of land vacancy that is plaguing many city neighborhoods. PHS works with community-based organizations and city agencies to transform vacant land into neighborhood assets. The program "cleans and greens" trash-filled lots—removing debris and weedy vegetation, grading the land, adding topsoil, and planting grass and trees to create a parklike setting. A signature post-and-rail fence defines the land as a cared-for property. Academic studies have found that the program contributes to public health and safety, raises property values, and stimulates new investment.

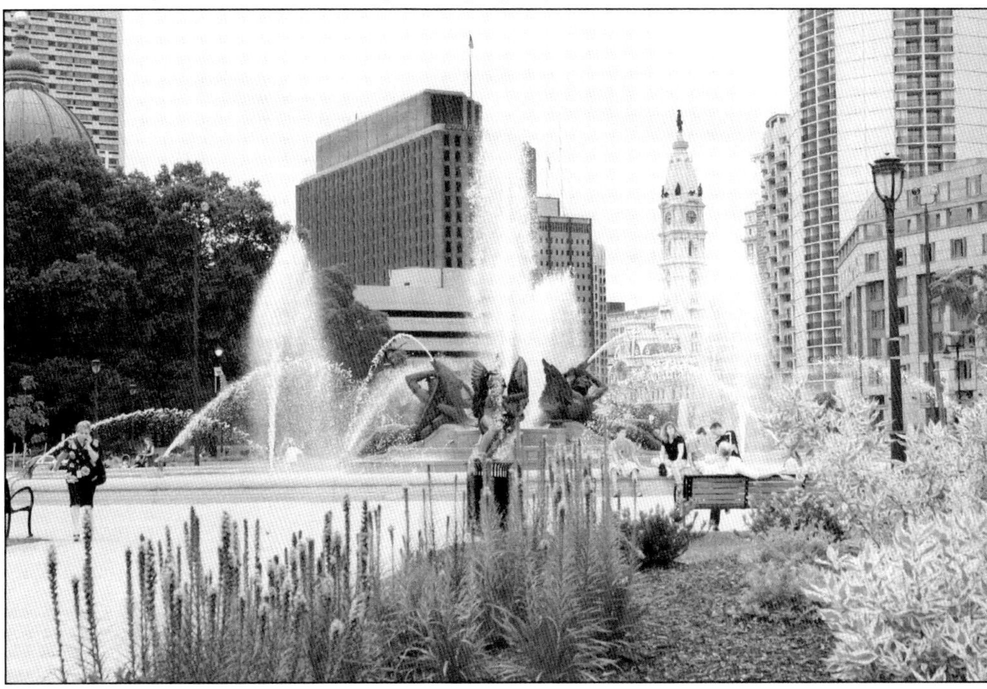

In recent years, PHS and its partners have renovated some of Philadelphia's most beloved public spaces, including prominent plazas and major gateways, many of which had suffered due to municipal budget constraints. In 2006, PHS led a full-scale renovation of the landscape surrounding the iconic Swann Memorial Fountain at Logan Square. PHS works in cooperation with Philadelphia Parks & Recreation to maintain the landscape.

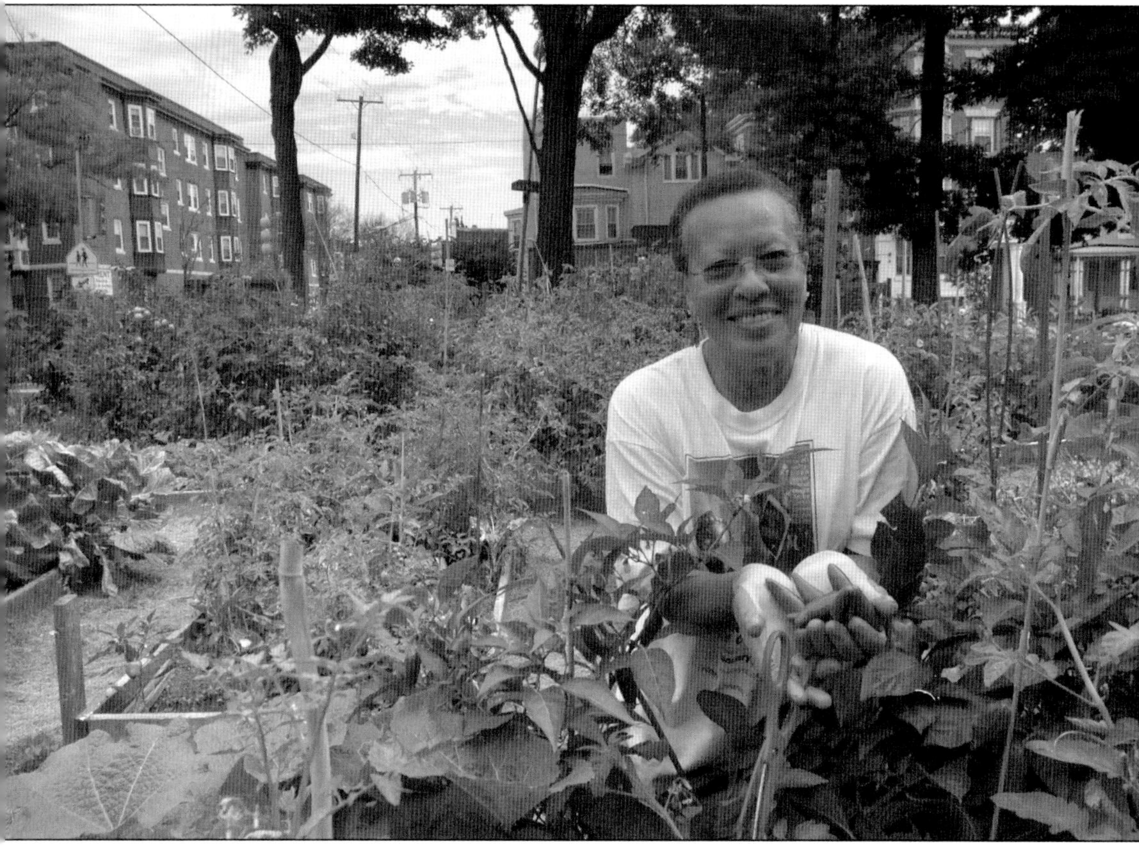

The PHS City Harvest program taps the skills and energy of urban gardeners to make fresh, nutritious produce more widely available. Through City Harvest, PHS and its partners have empowered urban gardeners like Pat Schogel (shown here), at the Hansberry Garden and Nature Center in Germantown, to share the fruits of their labor with families in need. Proceeds from the PHS Philadelphia Flower Show help support these vital efforts and plant the seeds for a greener, healthier future for all residents of the Philadelphia region.

About the Pennsylvania Horticultural Society

The Pennsylvania Horticultural Society is a nonprofit membership organization founded in 1827 and dedicated to building beauty and community through gardening, greening, and learning.

The first Philadelphia Flower Show was organized by the early 19th-century members of PHS, and over the course of its nearly 200-year history, the show has become the major fundraiser for PHS programs.

PHS offers educational programs and special events for gardeners of all levels and works with volunteers, organizations, agencies, and businesses to create and maintain vibrant green spaces.

The major initiatives of PHS:

*The PHS Public Landscapes program, working with partners such as Philadelphia Parks & Recreation, has restored and manages Philadelphia's most treasured public spaces—including Logan Square, the grounds of the Philadelphia Museum of Art, the Azalea Garden, Rodin Museum gardens, and the gateways to the city—and is working with neighborhoods to create beautiful landscapes in long-overlooked sections and corridors.

*The Philadelphia LandCare program, a partnership between PHS and the city, has greened more than 4,000 blighted urban lots, helping to transform some into community gardens, small parks, and gathering places and spurring economic redevelopment in the neighborhoods.

*In 2011, PHS launched Plant One Million, the largest multistate tree-planting campaign in the nation. The goal of the program is to restore the tree population of southeastern Pennsylvania, southern New Jersey, and the state of Delaware, thereby ensuring the region's environmental and economic well-being.

*PHS City Harvest is a program that creates green jobs and supports a network of community gardens that raise fresh produce for more than 1,200 families in need each week during the growing season. More than 106 tons of vegetables have been grown through City Harvest.

Through these programs and other efforts, PHS brings the spirit and inspiration of the Philadelphia Flower Show into communities throughout the year.

Proceeds from the PHS Philadelphia Flower Show and donations from foundations, corporations, government, and individuals support PHS programs. For information or to support PHS, please visit PHSonline.org.

Consistent with our mission to preserve history on a local level, this book was printed in South Carolina on American-made paper and manufactured entirely in the United States. Products carrying the accredited Forest Stewardship Council (FSC) label are printed on 100 percent FSC-certified paper.

MADE IN THE USA